W9-BXZ-333

Common Knowledge Abo

中国文化常识

（中英对照）

国务院侨务办公室
The Overseas Chinese Affairs Office of
the State Council

国家汉语国际推广领导小组办公室
The Office of Chinese Language
Council International

高等教育出版社
Higher Education Press

前　言

　　《中国文化常识》、《中国历史常识》和《中国地理常识》是由中华人民共和国国务院侨务办公室组织北京华文学院、南京师范大学和安徽师范大学编写的一套汉语教学辅助读物，供海外华裔青少年通过课堂学习或自学的方式了解中国文化、历史、地理常识，同时供家长辅导孩子学习使用，在海外反响很好。

　　近年来，随着中国经济社会的迅速发展和国际影响的不断扩大，海外学习汉语的人数，尤其是非华裔汉语学习者人数大幅度增加。为了进一步适应广大海外汉语学习者了解中国文化的需求，促进中外文化交流，中华人民共和国国务院侨务办公室授权中国国家汉语国际推广领导小组办公室对《中国文化常识》、《中国历史常识》和《中国地理常识》进行改编。

　　《中国文化常识》、《中国历史常识》和《中国地理常识》改编本是一套面向世界各国汉语学习者的普及型、口语化的文化辅助读物，适用于海外对中国文化和汉语感兴趣的各类人员。在中华人民共和国国务院侨务办公室编写的中英文对照版基础上，此次改编增加了中文与德、法、日、韩、俄、泰、西班牙、阿拉伯语的对照版本。

　　中国国家汉语国际推广领导小组办公室委托高等教育出版社对《中国文化常识》、《中国历史常识》和《中国地理常识》进行改编，高等教育出版社对原书的部分内容进行了增删，修订了部分数据，重新遴选和修改了插图，并翻译出版英、德、泰语版本；外语教学与研究出版社翻译出版法、日、韩语版本；华语教学出版社翻译出版俄、西班牙、阿拉伯语版本。此次改编力求在原书强调科学性、思想性和实用性的基础上做进一步创新。希望本系列读物成为您了解中国的窗口，成为您通向汉语世界的桥梁。

　　此次改编得到了海内外诸多专家、学者和教师的关心与支持，他们提出了许多中肯的建议，在此向他们表示诚挚的谢意。

　　由于时间所限，书中不免会有疏漏和不当之处，希望使用者和专家学者不吝赐正，以供今后修订时改正。

中国国家汉语国际推广领导小组办公室

2006 年 11 月

Preface

Common Knowledge About Chinese Culture, Common Knowledge About Chinese History and Common Knowledge About Chinese Geography are a series of readers initiated by the Overseas Chinese Affairs Office of the State Council of the People's Republic of China. The readers were jointly developed by Beijing Chinese Language College, Nanjing Normal University and Anhui Normal University. Serving as teaching aids for learners of Chinese, these readers make the general knowledge of Chinese culture, history and geography accessible to the young generation of overseas Chinese by means of either classroom delivery or self-study. These books are also for parents to help their children with the study. The previous versions of these readers were well received.

In recent years, with the rapid economic and social development in China and the rising of her international status, the world witnesses a phenomenal increase in learners of the Chinese language outside China, especially from non-Chinese ethnic groups. To meet the demand from overseas Chinese learners to better their knowledge about Chinese culture, and to foster cultural exchanges between China and the world, a revision of the above-mentioned readers has been decided by the Overseas Chinese Affairs Office of the State Council of the People's Republic of China. They assigned the Office of Chinese Language Council International to work out the new edition of Common Knowledge About Chinese Culture, Common Knowledge About Chinese History and Common Knowledge About Chinese Geography.

The revised version of Common Knowledge About Chinese Culture, Common Knowledge About Chinese History and Common Knowledge About Chinese Geography is intended to be a popular edition of learning aid for Chinese culture in a conversational style. These readers make Chinese culture, history and geography more accessible to all people. Based on the original Chinese-English version edited by the Overseas Chinese Affairs Office of the State Council of the People's Republic of China, the newly-revised version has kept its bilingual format, only broadening the foreign language coverage to German, French, Japanese, Korean, Russian, Thai, Spanish and Arabic.

The Office of Chinese Language Council International delegates the revision of Common Knowledge About Chinese Culture, Common Knowledge About Chinese History and Common Knowledge About Chinese Geography to Higher Education Press, who adds and subtracts parts of the original Chinese version with amendments to some data and illustrations. The bilingual versions of Chinese-English, Chinese-German and Chinese-Thai are developed by Higher Education Press. The versions of Chinese-French, Chinese-Japanese and Chinese-Korean are developed by Foreign Language Teaching and Research Press. The Chinese-Russian, Chinese-Spanish and Chinese-Arabic versions are done by Sinolingua. All revisions are meant to be innovative while maintaining the original focus of being accurate, instructive and practical. It is our sincere hope that this series of readers become windows for you to know more about China, and bridges leading you to the world of Chinese.

We would especially like to express our sincere appreciation to many experts, scholars and Chinese teachers both at home and abroad for their pertinent suggestions.

Developed under a tight schedule, the new editions might be blotted with oversights and inappropriateness. We sincerely welcome readers, especially those better versed in the relevant fields to contribute ideas for the correction and future revision of these books.

The Office of Chinese Language Council International
November, 2006

目 录
Contents

中国传统思想
Traditional Chinese Ideology

中国传统美德
Traditional Virtues of China

中国古代文学
Ancient Chinese Literature

中国古代科技
Science and Technology of Ancient China

中国传统艺术
Traditional Chinese Art

中国文物
Chinese Cultural Relics

中国古代建筑
Ancient Chinese Architecture

中国工艺美术
Chinese Arts and Crafts

中国民俗
Chinese Folk Customs

中国人的生活
Life of the Chinese People

中国传统思想

Traditional Chinese Ideology

概 述

Introduction

　　中国人注重人与自然的和谐，在中国传统思想中，"天人合一"是一个著名的话题。中国传统思想更注重个人修养的提升，更关注"修身养性"；更为重视智慧的体悟而对逻辑推理不是特别在意。

　　可以说，中国有一套完整的影响了中国几千年的思想体系，而这套体系最重要的组成部分就是孔子、孟子开创的儒家思想和老子、庄子开创的道家思想以及佛学思想。其中，对中国影响最大、最深远的是儒家思想。

Introduction

Compared with Westerners, the Chinese people paid more attention to the harmonious relation between human beings and nature; "Nature and Man are one." is a familiar statement in traditional Chinese ideology. Much emphasis is laid upon the moral cultivation and temper refinement as well as the spiritual enlightenment on the part of the individual rather than upon the logic reasoning.

For thousands of years, China, so to speak, has been under the influence of a holistic system of thoughts, which is largely composed of Confucianism initiated by Confucius and Mencius, Taoism initiated by Laozi and Zhuangzi, as well as Buddhism with Chinese characteristics, among which Confucianism played a fundamental role in shaping the traditional Chinese ideology.

1. 老子
   Laozi
2. 庄子
   Zhuangzi
3. 汉字"禅"
   The character of *chan* (Chan)
4. 木刻佛像版画
   Wood engraving of Buddhist images

孔子

Confucius

孔子（公元前551—公元前479），名丘，字仲尼，鲁国人。中国春秋末期伟大的思想家和教育家，儒家学派的创始人。

孔子的远祖是宋国的贵族，殷王室的后裔。在孔子很小的时候，他的父亲就去世了，以后孔子的家境逐渐衰落。虽然孔子年轻的时候很贫困，但是他立志学习，他曾经说过："三人行，必有我师焉。"后来，他开始授徒讲学，他一共教授了3 000多个学生，其中不乏贫困家庭的孩子，改变了以往只有贵族子女才有资格上学的传统。孔子晚年还编订上古书籍，保存了很多古代的文献，我们现在看到的《诗经》、《尚书》、《周易》等等都经过他的编订。

孔子的很多思想即使在今

天看来也很有价值。比如，孔子丰富了"仁"的内涵，他认为要做到"仁"，就要关爱别人，"己所不欲，勿施于人"；他还认为，"君子和而不同"，也就是说，在处理人际关系上要承认人与人之间的差异，不要用单一的标准来衡量对方，这样才能够达到社会的和谐与稳定；他在教育上还主张用启发的方法促使学生独立思考，在学习书本知识的同时还要有自己独立的见解等等。

孔子的言行被他的弟子们收集在《论语》一书中，孔子的思想也被后人吸收和发扬光大，成为中国传统思想的最主要的组成部分，并逐渐传播到周边国家，形成了影响范围很广的儒家文化圈。

孔子是属于中国的，他在中国家喻户晓，绝大多数中国人的思想都或多或少地受到他的学说的影响；孔子也是属于世界的，联合国教科文组织曾将他列为世界十大文化名人之一。

1	2
	3
	4

1、3. 孔子
Confucius
2. 孔子纪念币
Coins commemorizing Confucius
4. 孔庙供奉的孔子
Confucius enshrined in the Confucian Temple

Confucius

Confucius (551 BC — 479 BC), whose personal name was Qiu and styled Zhongni, was born in the Lu State. Confucius was a great thinker and educator in the late Spring and Autumn Period. He was also the founder of Confucianism.

Confucius was a descendant of a noble family in the Song State, who descended from royals of the Yin Dynasty. When he was still a child, his father died, and his family went to a decline as a result, but he studied very hard. He once said, "From any three people walking, I will find something to learn for sure." Later, Confucius began to travel about and instruct disciples. In his life, Confucius had instructed more than 3 000 disciples, some were from poor families. In this way, Confucius had gradually changed the tradition that nobody but nobilities had the right to receive education. In his later years, Confucius compiled and preserved many literary works of ancient times, including *The Book of Songs*, *The Book of Documents* and *The Book of Changes*.

Even in modern times, many of Confucius' ideas are quite valuable. For instance, Confucius established and developed a moral and ethical system called *ren* (benevolence). To achieve "*ren*", he believed that one should show benevolence to others, and therefore "Do as you would like to be done by others". Confucius also believed that "Gentlemen are harmonious but different" which reveals that difference between people should be recognized in dealing with human relationship, thereby it is inappropriate to judge with a single standard, and thus the harmony and stabilization of a society will be accomplished. In terms of education, Confucius maintained that teachers should enlighten students to think independently, and that students should formulate their own opinions when acquiring knowledge from textbooks.

The sayings and behaviors of Confucius' were compiled in *The Analects of Confucius* by his disciples. Confucius' ideology has been absorbed and carried forward by later generations, composing the essential part of Chinese traditional ideology. It was also spread into the border regions and areas, building up a circle of culture of Confucianism exerting profound influence on the whole East Asian countries.

Confucius belongs to China. He is a household name in China,

and most of the Chinese people have been influenced by Confucius in one way or another. Confucius also belongs to the world, UNESCO (United Nations Educational, Scientific, and Cultural Organization) has labeled him one of the "Ten Cultural Celebrities".

1	3
2	

1、2. 孔子
Confucius

3. 山东曲阜孔庙中门
The Middle Gate of the Confucian Temple in Qufu, Shandong Province

"四书五经"与儒家思想

"Four Books and Five Classics" and Confucianism

"四书"在先秦时期就存在了，但是当时还没有"四书"这一说法，其中除了记录孔子言行的《论语》之外，还有《孟子》、《大学》和《中庸》。《孟子》是记述儒家学派另一位代表人物孟轲的政治思想的书。而《大学》与《中庸》本来是《礼记》里的两篇文章，主要是讲如何做学问和如何修身的，到南宋时，著名学者朱熹把它们分别独立出来加以注解，和《论语》、《孟子》一起，作为学习儒家经典的初级入门教材，叫做《四书章句集注》，也简称"四书"。"五经"是指《易经》、《尚书》、《诗经》、《礼记》和《春秋》五部典籍。

明清时期，科举考试都是根据"四书五经"里面的文句出题，考生对字句的解释必须依照朱熹的《四书章句集注》等。于是，"四书五经"成为知识分子最重要的教科书，而"四书五经"中的儒家思想也主要通过这样的方式成为当时人们为人处世的准则。"四书五经"中蕴涵的思想也深深地影响着现在的人们。

"Four Books and Five Classics" and Confucianism

"Four Books"(*Si Shu*) came into existence before the Qin Dynasty, although they were not called "Four Books" at that time. *The Analects of Confucius* (*Lun Yu*), one of the Four Books, is a collection of words and deeds of Confucius. The other three are *Mencius* (*Mengzi*), *The Great Learning* (*Da Xue*) and *The Doctrine of the Mean* (*Zhong Yong*). Mencius recorded the political thought of Master Meng Ke (Mengzi) who was another prominent figure of Confucianism. *The Great Learning* and *The Doctrine of the Mean* are two chapters from the corpus of *The Records of Rites* (*Li Ji*) originally. They are the collections of treatises on the rules of propriety and ceremonial usages. Zhu Xi, the well-known scholar of the Southern Song Dynasties, offered elaborate comments on the two books. Together with *The Analects of Confucius* and *Mencius*, they

were called *The Collected Notes on Passages in the Four Books*, commonly known as "Four Books". They were regarded as the elementary textbooks for Confucianism study. Five Classics refer to five ancient classics: *The Book of Changes* (*Yi Jing*), *The Book of Documents* (*Shang Shu*), *The Book of Poetry* (*Shi Jing*), *The Records of Rites* (*Li Ji*) and *The Spring and Autumn Annals* (*Chun Qiu*).

In the dynasties of Ming and Qing, the sentences from "Four Books and Five Classics" were the basis for the Imperial Examinations. Examinees had to explain them according to *The Collected Notes on Passage in the Four Books*. Therefore, "Four Books and Five Classics" became the most important textbooks for scholars of the time. Then

the Confucian thought of "Four Books and Five Classics" became the guideline of behavior. Furthermore, as the most important ancient corpus of China, it still has great influence on the current generation.

1. "四书"
   Four Books
2. 《易经》：八卦图
   Book of Changes: Eight Trigrams
3. 卦占吉凶
   The divination of good or ill luck with Eight Trigrams

老庄与 道 家思想

Laozi, Zhuangzi and Taoism

中国道家思想的创始人是春秋末年的老子。老子，姓李，名耳，曾经做过周代管理政府藏书的史官。老子的著作《道德经》虽然只有5 000多字，但是对后来的中国人却产生了非常深远的影响。老子用"道"来说明宇宙万物的产生和演变，他告诉人们在思想和行为上也要遵循"道"的特点和规律，顺应自然，要以柔克刚，因为表面脆弱的东西往往本质坚强。

后来的庄子继承和发展了老子的思想。庄子，名周，曾经做过宋国"蒙"这个地方的漆园吏。庄子在他的著作《庄子》中，继承和发展了老子的"道法自然"的观点，主张将外在的万物与自我等同起来，将生与死等同起来，庄子追求的是精神世界的超越和逍遥。因为老子和庄子的思想有很多相似性，所以后人习惯以"老庄"并称。

Laozi, Zhuangzi and Taoism

The founder of Taoism was Laozi, whose family name was Li and given name was Er. He lived in the later years of the Spring and Autumn Period, and worked as an archivist in the Imperial Library of the Zhou's court. His masterpiece *Tao Te Ching* (*The Book of the Way and Its Virtue*), although with only about 5 000 characters, had a significant impact upon the thoughts of later generations. Laozi applied "*Tao*" to elucidating the origin and evolvement of the universe. Moreover, Laozi maintained that the characters and law of "*Tao*" could be applied to guide people's thinking and behavior, which should be in conformance with the nature.

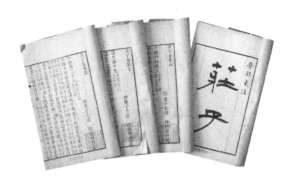

Laozi believed that what appears soft and weak can actually defeat what is hard and strong, inasmuch as what looks fragile is hard in nature.

Proficient in the philosophy of Laozi, Zhuangzi was an inheritor and promoter of Taoism. Zhuangzi, whose given name was Zhou, once worked as an official in charge of painting work at the town of Meng in the Song State. In the book bearing his name, Zhuangzi succeeded to and developed Laozi's viewpoint that "*Tao* is defined by nature", and claimed that everything exterior can be equated with self, and life and death are equal. What Zhuangzi had been pursuing is a spiritual realm of absolute freedom. Since there are so many similarities between Laozi and Zhuangzi in terms of thinking, descendants usually mention them comparably.

```
        | 2
   1    |____
        | 3
```

1. 老子
   Laozi
2. 《庄子》
   Zhuangzi
3. 庄子讲学
   Zhuangzi gives lectures.

佛学思想

Buddhism

　　早在汉代，产生于印度的佛教就已经传入中国，佛教在中国的发展过程中不断中国化，成为深刻地影响着中国人的宗教思想体系——佛学思想。

　　隋唐时期是佛教中国化的重要时期。这一时期，随着国家的统一、经济的发展和文化交流的日益频繁，佛学获得了空前的发展。唐代统治者实行儒、佛、道并行的政策。佛学在与中国传统文化融合的过程中，吸收了儒家和道家的思想，形成了一些中国化的佛学宗派。禅宗是其中最有生命力的一派。佛学的思辨哲学弥补了传统思想直观朴素的不足，丰富了中国文化。

Buddhism

As early as in the Han Dynasty, Buddhism, originated from ancient India, had been introduced to China. During its development in China, Buddhism had to constantly adapt itself to the actual conditions in China so as to become one of the most important religions in China and to deeply influence upon thoughts and living habits of the majority of Chinese.

The Sui and Tang dynasties are the important periods for the localization of Buddhism in China. In this period, with the unity of country, the development of the economy and the more and more frequent exchange of culture, the study of Buddhism reached an unprecedented height. In the Tang Dynasty, the state put forward the policy that Confucianism, Taoism and Buddhism would coexist. In the process of amalgamation of Buddhism and Chinese traditional culture, Buddhism had absorbed the thought of Confucianism and Taoism and therefore some Chinese schools emerged, amongst which Zen is considered to be full of vitality. The speculative philosophy of Buddhism made up the shortage of directness and simplicity of the traditional ideology, and enriched Chinese culture.

	2
1	
	3

1. 《碛砂大藏经》扉画
   The head page of a Buddhist scripture
2. 如来佛像
   The Buddha statue
3. 合掌手
   Palms-clasping hand

中国传统美德

Traditional Virtues of China

概 述

Introduction

千百年来，中华民族创造了光辉灿烂的历史和文化，同时也形成了自己的道德观念。其中的精华部分，对社会的发展和进步起到了积极的促进作用，这就是我们所说的传统美德。

这些传统美德是中华民族宝贵的精神财富，直到今天，仍然具有积极的意义。它的价值已被全世界越来越多的人所认同，并在人类文明进程中发挥着重大的作用。

Introduction

Over thousands of years of history, the Chinese have created a brilliant history and culture, and at the same time have formed their own moral code that has played an important role in social development and progress. This is what we call traditional virtues, which still have great significance today and whose value to the development of human civilization is now widely recognized.

```
1
—————  3
2
```

1. 梅花图
   A painting of plum
2. 赏梅图
   A painting of ancient women admiring the plum
3. "岁寒三友" 图
   A painting of "Three Friends in Cold Weather"

孝敬父母

中国人将奉亲养老视为义不容辞的责任。中国人相信，只有那些在家里无微不至地关爱、体贴自己的父母的人，才能够在与其他人交往的过程中做到诚实、守信，感恩图报。中国古代流传着许多关于孝顺的故事，"亲尝汤药"、"怀橘遗（wèi）亲"等就是其中的代表。

"亲尝汤药"说的是以仁孝而闻名天下的汉文帝刘恒，在他的母亲卧病3年期间，常常整夜不睡，母亲所服的汤药，都是他亲口尝过之后才放心让母亲服用。他在位的24年，重德治，兴礼仪，注意发展农业，使西汉社会稳定，人丁兴旺，经济得到恢复和发展，他与汉景帝的统治时期被誉为"文景之治"。

"怀橘遗亲"说的是三国时期的陆绩在6岁时，跟随父亲陆康到九江拜见袁术，袁术拿出橘子招待，陆绩往怀里藏了两个橘子。临行时，橘子滚落地上，袁术笑道："陆郎来我家做客，走的时候还要怀藏主人的橘子吗？"陆绩回答说："我的母亲喜欢吃橘子，我想拿回去送给母亲尝尝。"袁术见他小小年纪就懂得孝顺母亲，十分惊奇。

这些故事中虽然有很多想象的成分，但其推崇的孝敬父母的美德被中国人学习继承下来。

Filial Virtue

Respecting and taking care of the aged parents is regarded as an obligatory duty in China. Chinese people believe that only those who are concerned with and practise filial devotion to their parents would be honest, faithful, and be grateful to others and seek ways to return their kindness. There are many stories which show the filial respect in ancient China. "Taste Liquid Medicine for Mother" and "Stealing Oranges to Take Home for His Mother", are the most famous two of them.

The story of "Taste Liquid Medicine for Mother" tells us the filial virtue of Han Wendi (Emperor Wen of the Western Han Dynasty). His mother had been sick for three years. He often stayed up by her bedside and nursed her day and night. He tasted the liquid medicine first before giving to her. (Chinese people take herbal medicine prescribed by Chinese doctors. Herbs are boiled with water to make a liquid medicine. Before giving such medicine to his mother, Han

Wendi first tasted it to ensure it was not too hot or too bitter.) Han Wendi was on throne for 24 years. He governed the country with morals, advocated rites and etiquette, and paid great attention to agricultural development. As a result, the Western Han became a stable and prosperous society. The economy was resumed and developed. This period is known as the "Peace and Prosperity During the Reign of Emperors Wen and Jing" in history.

"Stealing Oranges to Take Home for His Mother" is a story of the Three-Kingdom period. A young boy named Lu Ji of only six years old traveled with his father Lu Kang to visit Yuan Shu in Jiujiang. Yuan Shu served them with oranges. Lu Ji secretly put two oranges in the sleeve of his robe. When he was leaving, unexpectedly, the two oranges came rolling out and fell to the ground. Yuan Shu saw the oranges and laughed, "Little Brother, you're my guest today. How come you steal your host's oranges?" Lu Ji

replied, "Pardon me, my mother likes oranges very much. Today I enjoyed these ripe, sweet oranges, and I could not help taking a few of them back for Mother." Yuan Shu was impressed by the six-year-old's concern for his mother.

Though there are some parts of imagination in these stories, Chinese people are deeply influenced and transformed by these models of filial virtue.

1 | 2

1. 亲尝汤药
   Taste Liquid Medicine for Mother
2. 宋代书法："孝"字
   Calligraphy in the Song Dynasty: *xiao*
   (filial piety)

尊老爱幼

To Respect the Aged and Love the Young

尊敬老人、爱护儿童是中国人的优良传统。几千年来，人们一直把尊老爱幼作为一种社会责任和行为规范。战国时期的孟子就曾说过：要像尊敬自己的老人一样尊敬别人的老人，要像爱护自己的孩子一样爱护别人的孩子。在中国，违背了这种道德的人，不光会受到舆论的批评，严重的还要受到法律的惩处。

早在汉朝时，政府就曾多次发布命令，提倡、奖励孝敬老人的行为。当时政府发给70岁以上的老人一种拐杖，用这种拐杖的老人，在社会上可以得到特殊的优待和照顾。清朝康熙、乾隆年间都举行过大型的尊老敬老活动，皇帝亲自在宫里宴请65岁以上的老人，每次人数都多达千人。

中国人对后代的关怀爱护是爱中有教，慈中有严，包含着强烈的道德责任感。古人留下的《诫子书》、《家训》等大量有关教育子女的著作，是中华民族一笔宝贵的道德教育财富。

尊老爱幼的传统在当代得到了继承和发扬。现在，中国的老人和儿童有自己的节日"敬老节"和"儿童节"；政府还专门制定了保护妇女儿童的法律；法律中也明文规定了公民必须履行赡养父母、抚养子女的义务。

尊老爱幼这种传统的美德保证了家庭的和睦和社会的稳定，也为中华民族繁衍发展提供了坚实的社会基础。

To Respect the Aged and Love the Young

Respecting the aged and loving the young is a traditional Chinese virtue. For thousands of years, people have always considered it a social responsibility and behavioral norm. Mencius in the Warring States Period (475 BC—221 BC) said that one should respect the elderly relatives of other people as one's own, and take good care of others' children as one's own. In China, those who ignore these moral tenets will not only be criticized by public opinions, but also be punished by law.

In as early as the Han Dynasty, the government issued orders frequently advocating and encouraging and rewarding behavior related to treating the senior with filial respect. At that time, the government distributed a kind of walking stick to those over 70, and those with the stick could get special treatment and care. In the Qing Dynasty (1644 —1911), when Emperor Kangxi and Emperor Qianlong reigned, they held large-scale activities to show respect for the senior; each time, the emperor held a banquet in person for more than 1 000 seniors aged 65 and over in his palace.

Chinese people treat their offspring with love and education, with kindness and strictness, embodying a strong sense of moral responsibility. A number of books on educating children left by ancient people, such as *Advice to My Son* and *Parental Instruction*, are precious tracts on moral education.

The tradition of respecting the old and loving the young has been carried forward in modern

times. At present, the aged and the young in China have their own holidays: Elders' Day and Children's Day. The government has promulgated specific laws to protect women and children; and the law also stipulates in explicit terms that Chinese citizens have the obligation to support parents and rear children.

It is the pleasant virtue of respecting the aged and loving the young that ensured the harmony of the family and stabilization of society. It also provided firm social base for the development of the Chinese nation.

"岁寒三友"

Three Friends in Cold Weather

青松、翠竹和冬梅这三种植物历来被中国人所喜爱，原因就在于它们即使在寒冷的冬天也显示出生机勃勃的活力，像三位志同道合的朋友一样迎接春天的来临，所以它们被人们誉为"岁寒三友"，象征着中国人所敬慕和追求的高尚情操。

在中国，"岁寒三友"的图案很常见，不管是在器皿、衣料，还是在建筑上都留下了它们的影子。仁人志士向往它们傲霜斗雪、铮铮铁骨的高尚品格，而老百姓则看重它们常青不老、经冬不凋的旺盛的生命力。

松树是一种生命力极强的常青树，即使天寒地冻，它也依然葱茏茂盛。所以人们赋予它意志刚强、坚贞不屈的品格。在中国民间，人们更喜欢它的常青不老，将它作为长寿的代表。

每当寒露降临，很多植物便会逐渐枯萎，而竹子却能凌霜而不凋，坚强地屹立在风雪之中。竹节中空、挺拔，所以被人们赋予坚贞和虚心的品格，有着"君子"的美誉。在中国的民间传统中有用放爆竹来除旧迎新、除邪恶报平安的习俗，所以竹子在中国也被作为平安吉祥的象征。

梅花是中国的传统名花，它清香幽雅、冰肌玉骨，梅花以它的高洁、坚强、谦虚的品格，激励着人们洁身自好、不断奋发向上，所以中国历代文人志士喜欢梅花、歌颂梅花的极多。梅花还常常被民间作为传春报喜的吉祥象征。有关梅花的传说故事、梅的美好寓意在中国流传深远，应用很广。

除了松、竹、梅这"岁寒三友"之外，中国还有很多植物，如菊花、兰花和莲花等，也被人们寄寓了美好的品格，成为中国人所追求的人格操守的象征。

Three Friends in Cold Weather

Pine, bamboo and plum have always been regarded by Chinese people as the most beloved plants because they all thrive through the cold winter days, just like friends who cherish the same ideas welcoming the advent of the spring together. For this very reason, they are called "Three Friends in Cold Weather", symbolizing the noble characters esteemed and pursued by Chinese people.

In China, the figure of "Three Friends in Cold Weather" is very common, which can be seen on containers, clothes and infrastructures. People with lofty ideals respect them for their pride and honor, while the common ones for their ever-lasting energy.

Pines are ever-green trees with strong vitality. They flourish even in cold winter, for this very reason they are honored with a character of strong will. However, they are more generally regarded as the symbol of longevity among the masses.

When the day of Cold Dew arrives, many plants are withered, while bamboo survives and flourishes as usual in the cold wind. Because bamboo has hollow joints and is upstanding, it is gifted with characters of inflexibility and modesty and is honored as a "gentleman". While Chinese have the folk custom of firing the bamboo cracker to break away from the old and evil, bamboo is also regarded as the symbol for security and auspice, as shown in the traditional decorative paintings.

The plum is one kind of the famous flowers of China. They are appreciated for their nobleness, purity and modesty which encourage people to improve themselves. Therefore they have always been cherished and extolled by Chinese poets in the past. Plums are also characterized as the advent of good news. Stories about plum and its meaning have been widespread for a long time.

There are still some other plants, such as chrysanthemum, orchid and lotus that are given a noble character mostly aspired after by people.

| 1 | 2 |

1. 坚韧傲寒的梅花
   The lofty plum
2. 墨竹扇面
   Fan painting: ink bamboos

诚实守信

Integrity and Credit

诚实，就是忠诚正直，言行一致，表里如一。守信，就是遵守诺言、不虚伪欺诈。"言必信，行必果"、"一言既出，驷马难追"这些流传了千百年的古话，都形象地表达了中华民族诚实守信的品质。在中国几千年的文明史中，人们不但对诚实守信的美德大加赞赏，而且努力地身体力行。

孔子早在2 000多年前就教育他的弟子要诚实。他认为，在学习中知道的就说知道，不知道的就说不知道，这才是对待学习的正确态度。

曾子也是个非常诚实守信的人。有一次，曾子的妻子要去赶集，孩子哭闹着也要去。妻子哄孩子说，你不要去了，我回来杀猪给你吃。她赶集回来后，看见曾子真要杀猪，连忙上前阻止。曾子说："你欺骗了孩子，孩子就会不信任你。"说完，就把猪杀了。曾子不欺骗孩子，也培养了孩子讲信用的品德。

秦朝末年有个叫季布的人，一向重诺言，讲信用。人们都说"得黄金百斤，不如得季布一诺"。这就是成语"一诺千金"的由来。后来，季布遇到了灾祸，正是靠了朋友的帮助，才幸免于难。可见，一个人如果言而有信，自然会得到大家的尊敬和爱护。

旧时中国店铺的门口，一般都写有"货真价实，童叟无欺"八个大字。这说明，中国自古在商品买卖中，就提倡公平交易、诚实待客、不欺诈、不作假的行业道德。

Integrity and Credit

Integrity means righteousness, word being true to action, keeping one's word and never cheating others. "To be always true in word and resolute in deed", "What is said cannot be unsaid", these are the old sayings that lasted for generations, which depicted a good picture of Chinese people with integrity and keeping their word. For thousands of years, these qualities have been honored and practiced diligently by people.

About 2 000 years ago, Confucius taught his disciples that "When you know a thing, to hold that you know it; and when you do not know a thing, to allow that you do not know it. This is the right attitude toward study."

Zengzi was also a person who was upright and always abided by his word. One day, Zeng's wife was about to go to the market, her little son was making a tearful scene insisting to go with her. In order to calm him down, she coaxed him into not going with her with a prize of slaughtering a pig for him to eat when she returns. When she got back from the market, she saw Zengzi was on his way to slaughter a pig and tried to stop him. Zengzi said, "Once you deceived him, he would not believe in you any more." Therefore, the pig was killed. By never lying to his son, Zengzi taught his son with his action to keep faith.

In the late Qin Dynasty, there was a man called Ji Bu, who was always true to his word. It is said that "Ji Bu's promise is more valuable than tons of gold", which is the origin of the famous saying "One promise equals to one ton of gold". Later on, Ji Bu got in trouble, he escaped it thanks to his friends' help. It is obvious that when someone keeps to his word, he will be rewarded with respect and honor.

In the past, there was always a sign at the entrance of the store, saying "genuine goods at a fair price, equally honest with aged and child customers", which shows that during trade transactions in old China, it is honorable to be honest in business.

```
      |  2
  1   |
      |  3
```

1. 老字号茶庄
   An old and famous teahouse
2. 山西平遥古城里的曾子塑像
   The statue of Zengzi in the ancient city of Pingyao, Shanxi Province
3. 曾子家谱中的曾子像
   The portrait of Zengzi in Zengzi's family tree genealogy

尊师重教

To Respect Teachers and Value Education

重视教育，尊敬师长，在中国有悠久的传统。自古以来，中华民族都把教育放在十分重要的地位。早在2 600多年前，管仲就说过，考虑一年的事情，要种好庄稼；筹划十年的目标，要种好树木；规划百年大事，就要培养人才。在中国第一部教育学专著《学记》中也提出了"教学为先"的思想，认为国家的首要任务就是教育。3 000年前的周代，国家按行政区划，设立了不同规模、不同层次的学校，由官员兼任教师。到了春秋时期，孔子在他的家乡开办了私学，并提出人无论贵贱还是贫富，都有受教育的权利。

由于教育得到重视，在中国，读书人有较高的社会地位，有知识、有文化的人非常受人尊重。自古以来，无论贵族还是百姓，无论富人还是穷人，都千方百计地让孩子上学读书，掌握知识。

对教育的重视，决定了教师的地位。中国民间有许多尊师的说法，如：尊师不论贵贱贫富；一日为师，终身为父等。自古以来，从百姓到皇帝都十分敬重教师。在北京的孔庙里，有清代多位皇帝为孔子题写的牌匾，表达了帝王们对这位古代伟大教育家的景仰。

在中国，对老师的尊重，表现在社会生活的方方面面。人们称老师为"恩师"、"先生"，在日常生活中以师为先，以师为尊。现在，中国还把每年的9月10日定为"教师节"，以表达对教师职业的尊重。

To Respect Teachers
and
Value Education

It has been a long-standing tradition to value education and respect teachers in China. From ancient times, education has been paid much attention to by the Chinese people. About 2 600 years ago, Guan Zhong the Wise said that "When a schedule of one year is covered, we should think about crops. While making up a ten years' plan, we should take care of trees. However when it is extended to one hundred years, persons of talent are everything." In China, the first monograph about education *Record of Learning* has brought up the idea of "education is the top priority". Back in the Zhou Dynasty 3 000 years ago, the government set up schools of different scopes and levels on the basis of various administrative divisions. In the Spring and Autumn Period, Confucius even ran private schools in his hometown with a slogan that everyone rich or poor, had the right to receive education.

Since education is so highly

respected in China, men of knowledge would have a higher social status and be esteemed by other people. There is an old saying that to be a scholar is to be the top of society, which shows the important position of education in the mind of people.

Respect for education has determined the status of teacher. There are a lot of sayings that show respect towards teachers, for example, "A teacher for a day is a father for a lifetime". For a long time, the position of teacher was honored by both the masses and the emperors. In the temple

of Confucius in Beijing, many emperors in the Qing Dynasty had written inscriptions to show their appreciation to Master Confucius.

In China, the honor shown to teachers is displayed in every aspect of social life. The teacher is always called sir or mentor. Nowadays, September the tenth is designated to be the Teachers' Day.

1 | 2

1. 孔庙
   The Confucian Temple
2. 孔墓
   The Confucian Tomb

中国古代文学

Ancient Chinese Literature

概 述

Introduction

文学是中国文化中最有活力、最灿烂辉煌的一部分。在历史发展的长河里，中国古代文学蕴涵了中华文化的基本精神，体现了中国人的美学追求，承载了中华民族的理想信念，表现出自己独特的个性和风采。从远古神话到唐诗宋词、明清小说……各种文学形式，高潮迭起，连绵数千年，涌现出许多古今闻名的文学家和不朽的文学作品。

Introduction

Literature is the most dynamic and splendid part of Chinese culture. Throughout the long history, Chinese ancient literature has embodied the underlying spirits of Chinese culture, reflected the Chinese people's pursuit for esthetics and faith for ideal society, and moreover, demonstrated the distinctive Chinese character. For centuries, a succession of diversified literary forms, for instance, mythologies in primeval times, poems and *Ci* in the Tang and Song dynasties, novels in the Ming and Qing dynasties, etc., have come into being. Many great litterateurs are still remembered today and their masterpieces have gained perpetual fame.

1	
2	3

1. 《红楼梦》人物：林黛玉
   Lin Daiyu: a character in *A Dream of Red Mansions*
2. 《红楼梦》人物：贾宝玉
   Jia Baoyu: a character in *A Dream of Red Mansions*
3. 《三国演义》故事：诸葛亮舌战群儒
   Zhuge Liang Arguing Against Scholars: a story from *Romance of Three Kingdoms*

远古 神话

Ancient Mythology

中国的远古神话，是原始社会的人们面对周围这个充满未知的世界，以丰富神奇的想象所构筑的一个遥远又神秘的世界。

中国远古神话是原始先民的集体创作，它们经历了口头流传的漫长岁月，直到文字发明以后，才被记载下来，内容多是反映远古社会丰富多彩的历史内容。其中有：解释世界起源的"盘古开天地"、"女娲造人"、"女娲补天"等；反映人类与自然做斗争的"后羿射日"、"夸父追日"、"精卫填海"等；歌颂献身精神的"神农尝药"、"鲧禹治水"等等。

"女娲补天"讲的是：在远古时候，天空突然崩塌，出现了一个大洞，大地上洪水泛滥，猛兽横行，人类面临巨大

反映了远古先民对身边自然现象的认识和征服自然的愿望，体现了中华民族祖先不怕困难、英勇顽强与自然灾害做斗争的伟大精神。

充满着原始浪漫主义色彩的远古神话对中国文学的发展影响很大，可以说是中国文学的源头，后世的许多著名作家都从古代神话中吸取营养，创作出了优美、动人的文学篇章。

的灾难。这时，人类的母亲女娲挺身而出，炼出五彩石修补天空，天地重新恢复了平静，人们又过上了幸福的生活。

"鲧禹治水"讲述了鲧、禹父子两代治理洪水、拯救人类的故事。远古时候，大地被洪水淹没，大神鲧偷了天帝的宝贝"息壤"——一种能自己生长的土，去堵塞洪水，然而用这种堵截的方法治理洪水没有成功，事后被天帝处死。三年后，禹从鲧的肚子里跳出，继承父亲的事业，继续治水，他采用了疏导的方式，在他治理洪水的八年之中，三过家门而不入，终于疏通了河道，平息了水患，使洪水流进了大海。

这些美丽动人的神话，

1 | 2
　| 3
　| 4

1. 《山海经》：应龙
   Ying Long from *The Book of Mountains and Seas*
2. 汉画像石：女娲
   N ü Wa, the stone relief in the Han Dynasty
3、4. 汉画像石：神人
   The Immortal, the stone relief in the Han Dynasty

Ancient Mythology

Chinese ancient mythology, a remote and mystic world, was created with the wildest imagination by people in primitive ages, when faced with the unknown.

Chinese ancient mythologies were created collectively by people of the primitive society, and underwent the far-flung years of oral circulation until the Chinese characters were invented to provide a more permanent way of recording. The content of most mythologies reflected the rich and colorful life style of ancient society, including: *Pan Gu Separates the Sky from the Earth, Nü Wa Makes Men, Nü Wa Mends the Sky*, etc., which interpret how the world came into being; *Hou Yi Shoots Down Suns, Kua Fu Chases the Sun, Jing Wei the Bird Determines to Fill Up the Sea* reflecting mankind's incessant struggle against the nature; *Shennong Shi Tastes Medicine, Gun and Yu Harness Water* written in praise of their selfless devotion, and so on.

Nü Wa Mends the Sky tells a story that at the earliest time, half of the sky suddenly collapsed and a huge hole appeared. Floods ravaged the land and beasts ran amok, so that the human race was in great danger. When, a woman named Nü Wa came out to mend the sky with five-colored rocks that the world regained peace and people lived a happy life like before.

Gun and Yu Harness Water narrates a story about Gun and his son Yu who harnessed floods and saved mankind. Long, long ago, the land was flooded. An immortal called Gun stole from Heavenly Emperor one of his treasures, "*xirang*", a kind of earth that could grow by itself to stop floods. However, he failed and later was put to death by Heavenly Emperor. Three years later, Yu jumped out of Gun's belly and succeeded his father's cause and continued to harness the waters. He showed such devotion to his work that legends said that he had never stepped into his home for 8 years in succession, even three times when he passed by his house. The floods were finally subdued.

Such fascinating mythologies not only reflect ancient people's understanding of nature and their wish to harness nature, but also represent their dauntless, hard-bitten spirit in the struggle against natural disasters.

The ancient mythical stories, endowed with a deep sense of romanticism, had a great impact upon the development of Chinese literature. They were widely regarded as the origin of Chinese literature, where writers of later generations continuously looked for their subjects, drew their inspiration, found their resources.

<table>
<tr><td>1</td><td>2</td></tr>
</table>

1. 精卫填海
   Jingwei the Bird Determines to Fill Up the Sea
2. 龙凤仕女图
   A scroll of Dragon, Phoenix and Royal Maid

《诗经》

The Book of Songs

　　《诗经》是中国第一部诗歌总集。它收录了从西周初年到春秋中叶大约500年间的诗歌作品，共计有305首。相传，周代的采诗官经常到民间收集诗歌，当时，也有官员们向天子献诗的制度。这些诗歌经过乐官的整理编订后，形成了这部诗歌总集。据说《诗经》中的诗，当时都是能演唱的歌词。

　　《诗经》最初叫《诗》或《诗三百》，后来，孔子把《诗三百》作为教科书传授给弟子。汉代以后又被称为《诗经》。

　　《诗经》内容丰富，很多作品都真实地描写了当时的社会风貌，其中表现青年男女爱情、婚姻生活的特别多。除此

以外，有的诗歌描写了下层人民的劳动生活；有的反映了人民反抗压迫，追求自由幸福的愿望；有的控诉了战争造成的苦难。在形式上以四字句为主，语言清新，音韵和谐，风格朴素，琅琅上口。

如：

……

彼采萧兮，

一日不见，

如三秋兮。

……

这首名叫《采葛（gé）》的诗，表达了一位男子思念情人的焦急心情。诗的大意是：她去采集香草了，一天没见，好像隔了三年那么长。成语"一日不见，如隔三秋"就是由此而来的。

《诗经》不仅是研究周代社会的一面镜子，也是中国诗史的光辉起点，是中国诗歌的源头。它所取得的思想和艺术成就，对后世诗歌的发展产生了巨大而深远的影响。

1. 《诗经》
The Book of Songs
2、3. 采薇图局部
Part of Rosebush Picking

2
1
3

The *Book of* Songs

*T*he *Book of Songs* is the first collection of poems in China. It recorded a total of 305 poems created over a period of 500 years or so, from the early Western Zhou Dynasty (11th century BC—771 BC) to the middle of the Spring and Autumn Period. It was said that specific officials were appointed with a sole role of collecting poems among the mass. There was also a rule requiring officials to compose poems and present them to the emperor at that time. The anthology came into being after further compilation. According to the story, all the poems in *The Book of Songs* were lyrics of the ancient days.

At the very beginning, *The Book of Songs* was known as *Poems* or *Three Hundred Poems*. The great thinker Confucius used it as a textbook to teach his disciples. It was named as *The Book of Songs* after the Han Dynasty.

The Book of Songs is rich in contents. Many of its works depicted the genuine landscape picture of society at that time. Among

them, many stories were devoted to love and marriage between young people. Besides, some poems portrayed the hard life of social underclass, some reflected the general public's resistance to oppression, and aspiration for freedom and happiness. Others denounced the war and the sufferings caused by it. The poems in *The Book of Songs* mainly consist of four-character verses. They are original in wording, harmonious in rhythm, concise in style, and pleasant to read. For instance,

There she is gathering vine
A day without seeing her
Is like three autumns.

...

This poem entitled *Gathering Vine* expresses a young man's pinning for his love. The tenor is that she has gone to gather vine and was unseen for one day which is like three years for that young man. The popular idiom "One day without seeing is like three autumns" originated from this poem.

The Book of Songs was not only a valuable resource for studying ancient Zhou society, but also the root of Chinese poetry. It has a great impact upon the development of poetry in later times, in terms of both its ideological and artistic achievements.

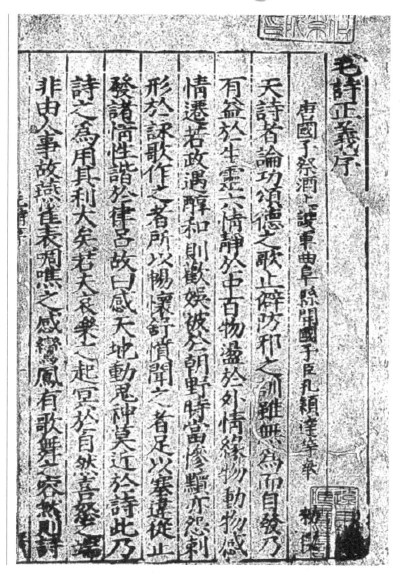

1. 《诗经》地理图
   The geographic map of *The Book of Songs*
2. 《诗经》
   The Book of Songs

楚辞

Chu Ci

　　"楚辞"是在《诗经》之后出现的一种新诗体，公元前4世纪前后诞生在位于中国南方的楚国。"楚辞"在形成过程中，受到了楚地民歌、音乐及民间文学的影响，带有浓厚的楚国地方色彩。

　　屈原是"楚辞"最主要的代表作家，楚国人，是中国历史上最受尊敬的伟大爱国诗人之一。他眼看国家日益衰弱，忧心如焚，写了大量抒发忧愤之情的诗作，后因被人陷害，长期流浪，最后投汨罗江而死。每年端午节，中国人都要以包粽子①、举行龙舟赛等活动纪念他。他的主要作品有《离骚》、《天问》②、

《九歌》③等。

《离骚》是一首宏伟壮丽的政治抒情诗。全诗共370多句，2 400多字。诗人运用浪漫主义的手法，讲述了自己的身世、品德和遭遇，倾诉了他对楚国命运的关心和坚持理想的决心。他在诗中驾起玉龙，乘上彩车，在月神、风神和太阳神的护卫下，神游天上，追求理想，最后不得不离开他深爱的楚国。屈原的爱国热情和不屈精神，感动了世世代代的读者，陶冶了一代又一代人的思想情操。

继屈原之后，宋玉、唐勒也写过优美的"楚辞"作品，楚辞最终成为一个时期诗歌的代表性体裁，后人称之为"骚体诗"。

"楚辞"大量运用神话传说，词章华美，文风瑰丽，想象奇特，情感奔放，突破了《诗经》的四言格式，扩大了诗句的含量，提高了诗歌的表现力，展现了一种独特的浪漫主义色彩，为中国文学的发展开辟了一条新路。

1	
2	3

1. 《九歌》：山鬼
   Ghost of hills from *Nine Songs*
2. 《楚辞集注》
   The Annotated Anthology of Chu Chi
3. 屈原故里
   Qu Yuan's hometown

Chu Ci

Chu Ci, also known as *Poetry of the State of Chu*, was a new style of poetry emerged after *The Book of Songs*. It was created in the Chu State in South China in the 4th century BC. In the course of its formation, it was influenced by folk songs, music and the folk literature of the Chu State, and as a result, it was characterized by a strong local flavor.

Qu Yuan was the central figure of *Chu Ci*. Born in the Chu State, Qu Yuan was regarded as one of the greatest patriotic poets who are held in the highest esteem in Chinese history. Witnessing the corruption of his colleagues and the inability of his king, Qu Yuan was rather worried, so he wrote a great number of poems expressing his resentment. Afterwards, defamed by other villains, Qu Yuan was exiled to lead a vagrant life for a long time and finally drowned himself in the Miluo River. On the Dragon Boat Festival every year, Chinese people will wrap glutinous rice dumplings and hold dragon boat race to commemorate him. His main works include *On Encountering Trouble* (*Li Sao*), *Heavenly Questions* (*Tian Wen*), *Nine Songs* (*Jiu Ge*), etc.

On Encountering Trouble (*Li Sao*) is a colossal political lyric made up of over 370 lines with 2 400 characters. Drawing on the technique of romanticism, the poet recounted his life, his beliefs and misfortunes, expressed his concern over the fate of the Chu State and his determination to maintain his lofty aspirations. In this poem, riding on a rainbow chariot driven by dragons as white as jade, guarded by the god of wind, god of sun, and god of moon,

in a certain period, which was called the "Poetry of Sorrow".

The profusion of myths and fantasies, the unusual twists of imagination, the vigorous surge of feelings and exotic use of verses in *Chu Ci* was a complete breakthrough compared with the "Four-Character-Trim-Verse" style in *The Book of Songs*, thus enlarging the content of every line of poem and enhancing the expressiveness, thereby demonstrating a unique romanticism that has never faded and pioneered a new road for the development of Chinese culture.

he soared to heaven in search of his ideals. Finally he was forced to leave his most beloved Chu State. Qu Yuan's patriotism and unyielding spirit has moved and encouraged many readers down through the generations, edifying their sentiment.

After Qu Yuan, Song Yu and Tang Le also wrote exquisite works in *Chu Ci* style, making *Chu Ci* a typical genre of poetry

▶ 注解 Notes

① 粽子是一种将糯米包裹在竹叶或苇叶中，用水煮熟的食品。
Glutinous rice dumpling is made of glutinous rice wrapped in bamboo or reed leaves.
② 《天问》用诗歌的形式，一口气提出了170多个关于"天"的问题。
Heavenly Questions is a long poem with more than 170 questions concerning heaven put forward in one breath.
③ 《九歌》是屈原根据楚国民间神话故事，采用民间祭歌的形式写成的一组抒情诗，包括《东皇太一》、《云中君》、《湘君》、《湘夫人》等。
Nine Songs are based on folk legends of the Chu State. Drawing on the form of obit songs, Qu Yuan composed a group of lyrics, including *East Emperor Tai Yi*, *The Person in the Clouds*, *The Person from Hunan*, *The Madam from Hunan*, etc.

| 2 |
|1| |
| 3 |

1. 湘夫人像
   A portrait of Madam Xiang
2. 屈原
   Qu Yuan
3. 《楚辞》
   Chu Ci

汉乐府

Yuefu Songs of the Han Dynasty

"乐府"原指汉代的一种音乐机构，它的职责是收集、采撷文人诗和民间歌谣，并配上乐曲。后来，由乐府收集、编制的诗也被称为乐府。汉乐府中的精华是汉乐府民歌①。

这首《江南》就是汉乐府民歌里的代表作。

江南可采莲，莲叶何田田。鱼戏莲叶间。鱼戏莲叶东，鱼戏莲叶西，鱼戏莲叶南，鱼戏莲叶北。

这首民歌表现了江南百姓人家水上采莲的生动情景和劳动时的愉快心情。诗的大意是：江南大湖里的莲蓬到了可以采摘的季节，湖里长满了莲花荷叶，小鱼儿在莲叶间自由地游来游去……全诗质朴无华、琅琅上口，洋溢着浓郁的生活气息。

汉乐府民歌的体裁大多是叙事诗，这些诗真实地表达了人民的喜怒哀乐。有的反映了劳动人民的穷困生活；有的揭露了战争给人民带来的痛苦；有的表现了反对封建婚姻、追求美好爱情的愿望；有的揭露了贵族的腐朽生活和社会的黑暗。

《孔雀东南飞》是汉乐府中最有名的诗篇，也是中国历史上第一部长篇叙事诗，它生动地叙述了一个封建家庭的爱情悲剧故事：

孔雀东南飞，五里一徘徊。十三能织素，十四学裁衣，十五弹箜篌②（kōng hóu），十六诵诗书……

聪明、美丽、善良的女子刘兰芝和自己喜爱的男子焦仲卿结婚后，互敬互爱，感情深厚。但是，焦仲卿的母亲却狠毒地拆散了这对夫妻。刘兰芝、焦仲卿双双自杀殉情，变成了一对永不分离的鸳鸯，"仰头相向鸣，夜夜达五更"，鸳鸯这种鸟从此也成为坚贞爱情的象征。这首长诗，通过刘兰芝、焦仲卿的悲剧，控诉了封建礼教、家长统治的罪恶，表达了青年男女追求婚姻自由的愿望和决心。

汉乐府民歌具有浓厚的生活气息，真实反映社会现实的精神和伟大的艺术成就，对后世诗歌的发展产生了直接和深远的影响。

▶ 注解 Notes

① 采集于民间的诗歌。
Folk ballad refers to the poems / songs collected from the folks.

② "箜篌"是中国古代的一种弹拨乐器，它有弦数组，不仅能演奏旋律，也能奏出和弦。唐代时，箜篌先后传入日本、朝鲜等邻国，在14世纪后逐渐失传。
Konghou (like the harp) was an ancient plucked instrument consisting of several groups of strings. Not only the rhythm, but also chord it can play. The harp was introduced to Japan, Korea and other neighboring countries in the Tang Dynasty, but was lost gradually in the fourteenth century.

Yuefu Songs

of the Han Dynasty

采莲图
Lotus-Picking

Yuefu originally referred to the "music bureau" in the Han Dynasty, a reference to the government organization originally in charge of collecting or writing the literati's poems, folk ballads, which were set to music. Later, poems and folk ballads collected and compiled by *Yuefu* were given this generic name. Folk ballads are the essential part of the *Yuefu* songs of the Han Dynasty.

The following folk ballad entitled *Jiangnan* (south of the Yangtze River) is one elaborate work of *Yuefu* songs of the Han Dynasty.

Time to gather lotus in the Yangtze Valley, / As lotus leaves are fair and lusty. / Fish frolic amidst the lotus leaves. / Fish frolic to the east of the lotus leaves, / Fish frolic to the west of the lotus leaves, / Fish frolic to the south of the lotus leaves, / Fish frolic to the north of the lotus leaves.

This folk ballad depicted the vivid scene of lotus-gathering in Jiangnan, where local people were in joyous mood while they were working. The tenor of this ballad was as follows: It was the right time to gather lotus in the huge lakes of Jiangnan. There teemed with lotus leaves in the lake, where small fishes were swimming freely… The simple, unadorned and vivid atmosphere permeates the whole folk ballad from beginning to end.

Most of the *Yuefu* songs of the Han Dynasty are narrative poems, which truthfully uncovered the sentiment of people at that time. Some poems mirrored the poverty-stricken life of laboring people; some exposed the misery caused by wars; some manifested the opposition to feudal marriage customs and the pursuit for true love; and some revealed the decadent life of aristocrats and the darkness of the society.

The best-known poem in *Yuefu* songs of the Han Dynasty is *Peacocks Flying Southeast*, which is also the first long narrative poem in Chinese history. It gives a vivid account of a tragedy of two lovers in a feudal family.

Southeast the lovelorn peacock flies. Alack, / At every five li she falters and looks back! / At thirteen years Lanzhi learned how to weave; / At fourteen years she could embroider, sew; / At fifteen music on her harp she made; / At sixteen knew the classics, prose and verse…

Liu Lanzhi, a smart, pretty and kind-hearted girl, got married to Jiao Zhongqing, her beloved man. They loved each other deeply, but Jiao's mother was so cruel that she forced them to separate. As a result, both Jiao and Liu committed suicide for the sake of love, and turned into a pair of lovebirds. "*They cross their bills and sing to one another. / Their soft endearments all night long till dawn.*" Hence the lovebirds became the symbol of true love. The tragedy condemned the feudal ethics and evil clan rule, and expressed the wish and determination of the young who were in pursuit for the free marriage.

With rich flavors of life, *Yuefu* songs of the Han Dynasty are in the pursuit of faithful reflection of social reality and have accomplished artistic achievements, which have had a direct and far-reaching impact on the development of poetry in later generations.

南北朝民歌

Folk Songs of the Northern and Southern Dynasties

从东晋灭亡到隋朝统一的100多年间，是中国历史上南北对峙的南北朝时期。

南北朝民歌是汉乐府民歌之后出现的又一批民歌。

南朝民歌大多是情歌，反映了人们真挚纯洁的爱情生活，而且多数是从女子的口中唱出，更显得清丽缠绵。《西洲曲》是南朝民歌中的代表作。

……采莲南塘秋，莲花过人头。低头弄莲子，莲子清如水。……海水梦悠悠，君愁我亦愁……南风知我意，吹梦到西洲。

这几句的意思是：情人未归，女主人公去采莲以消遣自己无聊的心绪，……一水之隔，两地都是一样的愁绪，最后女子无奈地请求风儿把自己的梦带到西洲。

南朝民歌多为五言四句，

木兰从军图
The Maid Mulan Serving in the Army

清新自然，诗中喜欢用双关语①，与江南优美的自然环境和富裕的经济条件也有着直接的关系。保留到今天的南朝民歌大约有500首。

北朝民歌大部分是少数民族人民创作的。这些民歌从多方面反映了北方各民族的社会生活面貌。由于北朝战争频繁，因此，民歌中反映战争的作品比较多。长篇叙事诗《木兰辞》是北朝民歌中最杰出的作品。

《木兰辞》塑造了一个女扮男装、代父从军、勇敢聪慧

而又品格高尚的巾帼英雄花木兰的形象，这在重男轻女的封建社会，具有特殊的意义。这首诗深受人民喜爱，木兰从军的故事还被搬上了银幕、舞台，一直流传到今天。

北朝民歌除去战争题材，多写北方风物和人们游牧、流浪的生活场景，表现北方人的豪迈，和南朝民歌形成了鲜明的对比。《敕（chì）勒歌》、《折杨柳歌辞》也是北朝民歌中的精品。

南北朝民歌对后来唐朝的诗人有很大的影响。

Folk Songs of the Northern and Southern Dynasties

The period of more than one hundred years from the decline of the Eastern Jin (317—420) to the foundation of the Sui Dynasty (581—618) was in the confrontation between two powers, one in the north and the other in the south. This period is known in Chinese history as the Northern and Southern Dynasties (420—589).

Folk songs of the Northern and Southern Dynasties were created orally by people in the wake of *Yuefu* songs.

Folk songs of the Southern Dynasties are mostly love songs which reflect the sincere and pure love life of people. Most of them were sung by women with refreshing and touching appeal. *Ode to Xizhou* can be regarded as the representative work of them.

When they gather lotus at Nantang in autumn, / The lotus blooms are higher than their heads; They stoop to pick lotus seeds, / Seeds as translucent as water... / The waters is beyond the scope of eyesight, You are lovesick, me either... / The south wind knows my mood; It blows my dream to Xizhou.

The connotation of those lines is as follows: The heroin's lover hadn't come back home, so she went to gather lotus to divert herself from loneliness and boredom. At a distance from the lake, both of them were lovesick apart. Finally, she begged the wind to bring her dream to Xizhou where her lover was staying.

Most of folk songs of the Southern Dynasties belong to the 4-line poems with 5 characters in each line, whose language is refreshing and natural, which possibly has a direct relation with the beautiful environment and rich condition of the south. Moreover, pun was often used in folk songs. Currently, there remain about 500 such songs.

Folk songs of the Northern Dynasties were mostly created by ethnic groups and reflected the society and their lives from every profile. As the Northern Dynasties were often at wars, the content of most folk songs had connection with wars. The long narrative poem *Mulan Ci* is the best-known work of that period.

Mulan Ci figures the heroine Mulan who was brave, smart and high-minded. In the poem, disguised as a man, Hua Mulan joined the army on behalf of her father to fight against the enemies. As for a feudal society in which women were universally regarded to be inferior to men, this poem had its special significance. The story about Hua Mulan's enlistment has maintained its great popularity among people and has been adapted for the screen and the stage so that it can come down till today.

Besides the theme concerning warfare, most folk songs of the Northern Dynasties describe scenery of the north and the people's life of nomadism thus manifesting straightforward complexion of Northerners which has a clear contrast with those of the Southern Dynasties. *Chile Song* and *Song of the Breaking of the Willow* are the elaborate works of folk songs of the Northern Dynasties.

Folk songs of the Northern and Southern Dynasties had great influences on poets of the Tang Dynasty (618—907).

> ▶ 注解　Note

① 用词造句时，表面上是一个意思，暗中则隐藏另一个意思，常利用同音字构成，如：莲—可怜，丝—思念，梨—分离等。
Pun is the use of a word in such a way as to suggest two of its meanings: one is the ostensible meaning, the other is the concealed. Such a rhetoric is formed by means of homophone, for example, *lian* (lotus) — wretchedness, *si* (thread) — miss, *li* (pear) — separate, etc.

唐诗

Tang Poetry

唐代文化是中国文化的一个高峰。尤其是古典诗歌到唐代发展到全盛时期。在唐代300余年的历史中，产生的流传于后世的诗歌就有48 900多首。

如此丰富的作品也使2 300多位诗人在历史上留下了他们自己的名字。

唐诗在创作方法上，现实主义与浪漫主义并举；在形式上有五言、七言绝句和律诗，还创造了优美整齐的近体诗。

唐代最著名的诗人是李白和杜甫，他们都是具有世界声誉的诗人，后人将他们合称为"李杜"。

李白被人们称为"诗仙"，是一位热情奔放、才华横溢的诗人。他的诗歌豪迈奔放，想象奇特，热情地歌颂了祖国的壮丽河山。李白的诗保存到现在的有990多首，其中《将进酒》、《蜀道难》、《望庐山瀑布》等名诗，世代被人们传颂。

杜甫被后人尊为"诗圣"。他年轻时游历过许多名胜古迹，后来生活曲折、经历坎坷，逐渐了解了人民的苦难。他在诗歌中深刻地反映了人民生活的疾苦。杜甫的诗保留到今天的有1 400多首，其中著名的有《春望》、《兵车行》以及"三吏"①、"三

别"②等。

唐代的著名诗人还有王维、白居易、李贺、李商隐、杜牧等。

直到今天，唐诗还为人们所喜闻乐见。许多诗篇连儿童都能背诵，如：《静夜思》③、《春夜喜雨》④等。"欲穷千里目，更上一层楼"⑤、"黄河之水天上来"⑥等唐诗名句，经常被人们引用。唐诗的普及读本《唐诗三百首》，更是受到了中外读者的欢迎。在今天的中国，还流行"熟读唐诗三百首，不会写诗也会吟"的口头禅，可见中国人对唐诗的热爱。

描写古诗意境的扇面
Fan painting depicting the artistic conception of ancient poems

静夜思

李白

床前明月光，
疑是地上霜。
举头望明月，
低头思故乡。

绝句

杜甫

两个黄鹂鸣翠柳，
一行白鹭上青天。
窗含西岭千秋雪，
门泊东吴万里船。

Tang Poetry

Thoughts in the Silent Night
Li Bai

Beside my bed a pool of light
Is it hoarfrost on the ground?
I lift my eyes and see the moon,
I bend my head and think of home.

A 4-Line Poem with 7 Characters in Each Line
Du Fu

From vivid green willows comes the
call of two orioles;
A file of white water birds rises into
the clear blue heavens;
As if held in the mouth of my window
are the mountains ranges with their
snows of many autumns;
Anchored by our gate are the long dis-
tance boats of Wu.

The Tang Dynasty witnessed a peak in Chinese culture. Especially for ancient poetry, it had its flowering in the Tang Dynasty. In more than 300 years of history of the Tang Dynasty, some 48 900 poems were handed down and remain widely known today.

So many works also made more than 2 300 poets famous in history.

As far as the writing technique is concerned, the Tang poetry combined realism and romanticism. In form, poetry of the Tang Dynasty contained four-line and eight-line verse with five or seven characters in each line. Moreover, "modern style" poetry, which is regular and polished, also appeared in the Tang Dynasty.

The best-known poets of the Tang Dynasty were Li Bai and Du Fu, who are very prestigious in the whole world. Therefore, people of later generations have

praised both of them as "Li Du" collaboratively.

Being widely praised as the "Immortal of Poems", Li Bai was a poet who abounded with passion and talent. With lofty sentiments and a powerful imagination, he created many poems in praise of magnificent mountains and mighty rivers of the motherland. Over 900 poems of Li Bai have been preserved, of which the most famous are *Invitation to Wine*, *The Sichuan Road*, and *Watching the Waterfall at Lushan*, intonated by people for generations.

Du Fu is revered as "Sage of the Poems" by the posterity. When he was young, Du Fu visited many scenic spots and places of historical interest. But his later life was full of frustrations, which enabled him to gradually have a clear idea of the people's sufferings. In his poems, Du Fu boldly exposed the corruption of the feudal society and profoundly portrayed people's miserable lives. More than 1 400 of his poems have been preserved till today, and the best-known ones are *Spring Outlook*, *Ballad of the Army Carts*, *The Conscripting Officer at Shihao*, *The Conscripting Officer at Tongguan*, *The Conscripting Officer at Xin'an*, *Farewell to My Husband*, *Farewell to My Old Wife* and *Farewell of a Lonely Soul*.

The noted poets in the Tang Dynasty also include Wang Wei, Bai Juyi, Li He, Li Shangyin and Du Mu, etc.

Even today, Chinese people are still very fond of the Tang poetry, many of which can be recited even by children, for example, *Thoughts in the Silent Night* written by Li Bai, *Welcome Rain One Spring Night* written by Du Fu, etc. Famous verses like "*We widen our view three hundred miles by ascending one flight of stairs*", "*Do you not see the Yellow River come from the sky*" are often quoted by most people. The book *Three Hundred Tang Poems* is a bestseller at home and abroad. Currently in China, the tag "If you have recited 300 poems of the Tang Dynasty, you will be able to intonate them even though you cannot produce them" has been popular. Thus, it can be seen how Chinese people are fond of the Tang poetry.

▶ 注解 Notes

① 《石壕吏》、《新安吏》、《潼关吏》三首诗的合称。
The Three Conscripting Officers include *The Conscripting Officer at Shihao*, *The Conscripting Officer at Tongguan* and *The Conscripting Officer at Xin'an*.

② 《无家别》、《新婚别》、《垂老别》三首诗的合称。
The Three Farewells include *Farewell to My Husband*, *Farewell to My Old Wife* and *Farewell of a Lonely Soul*.

③ 作者李白。诗中描写了思念家乡的心情。
The author is Li Bai, who expressed his yearn for hometown.

④ 作者杜甫。诗中描写了春夜下雨的景象。
The author is Du Fu, who described the scenery of rain in one spring evening.

⑤ 出自王之涣的《登鹳雀楼》。
From *To Mount Guanque Building* written by Wang Zhihuan.

⑥ 出自李白的《将进酒》。
From *Invitation to Wine* written by Li Bai.

1　　2

1

1. 李白醉酒图
   Li Bai is drunk.
2. 莲塘纳凉图:写杜甫五律之一
   Enjoying the Cool by the Lotus Pond: painting based on one of Du Fu's poems

宋词

Song *Ci* Poetry

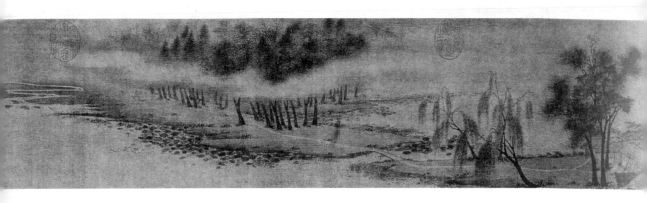

词，是古典诗歌的一种。词的名称很多，因为它可以配乐歌唱，所以也叫曲子词；因为它的句子长短不齐，也被称为长短句。这些名称说明了词与音乐的密切关系及其与传统诗歌的不同形式。词有很多种调名，叫做词牌，如西江月、满江红、如梦令等。

词作为一种新体诗歌，宋代时发展到了鼎盛时期。"宋词"与"唐诗"一样，在中国文学史上占有相当重要的地位。

宋词在发展过程中，产生了苏轼、李清照、辛弃疾、陆游等众多杰出的词人。

苏轼的词具有热情豪放、清新流畅的特点。他的词作内容十分广泛，有的抒发了报国的壮志；有的描写了农村的景象；有的写出了离愁别恨……

李清照是宋代杰出的女词人。她的词作清新精巧，满怀真情，有的表达了她对爱情的理解和追求；有的描写了春花秋月的变化对人的影响；有的表现了国破家亡带来的人生苦难……像"知否，知否？应是绿肥红瘦"①、"此情无计可消除，才下眉头，却上心头"②等优美动人的词句，表现了李清照出众的才华。

辛弃疾是宋代词人中词作最多的作家。他的词大都洋溢着豪迈的英雄气概，如"醉里挑灯看剑，梦回吹角连营"③、"青山遮不住，毕竟东流去"④等千古流传的词句，不仅描写了豪壮的军旅生活，也抒发了他坚持抗金的决心和激昂的爱国之情。辛弃疾的词大大地拓展了宋词的思想内容和艺术风格。

直到今天，宋词仍然受到人民大众的喜爱，《宋词三百首》是许多家庭必备的读物，很多有名的词作还被重新谱曲，广为传唱。

水调歌头

苏 轼

明月几时有？把酒问青天。不知天上宫阙，今夕是何年。我欲乘风归去，又恐琼楼玉宇，高处不胜寒。起舞弄清影，何似在人间！

转朱阁，低绮户，照无眠。不应有恨，何事长向别时圆？人有悲欢离合，月有阴晴圆缺，此事古难全。但愿人长久，千里共婵娟。

1 | 2

1、2. 古代山水画描绘词中意境
Ancient landscapes paintings depicting the artistic conception of *Ci poems*

▶ 注解　Notes

① 出自李清照的《如梦令》，该词新颖生动地描写了春天的景物。
From *Dreamlike Song* written by Li Qingzhao. The poem vividly described spring scenery.

② 出自李清照的《一剪梅》，该词写尽了别离思念的心情。
From *A Twig of Plum Blossoms* written by Li Qingzhao. It expressed her yearning for her absent husband.

③ 出自辛弃疾的《破阵子》，该词回忆了昔日抗击金兵、立功报国的英雄气概和战斗经历，同时也表达了壮志难酬的悲愤。
From *Dance of the Cavalry* written by Xin Qiji, who recalled the experience of oppugning Jin troops with a heroical mettle to make contributions and finally dedicate himself to the service of his motherland, and meanwhile also expressed his grief and indignation due to the unconsummated lofty ideals.

④ 出自辛弃疾的《菩萨蛮》，该词回忆了金兵入侵给人民造成的苦难，表达了不能去前线参加战斗的痛苦心情。
From *Song of the Country Norm* written by Xin Qiji, which recalled how people suffered from the war and how he was regretful for he was not able to fight at the front.

Song *Ci* Poetry

Ci poetry is one type of the ancient poetry. *Ci* poetry has several names, and it is also known as musical *Ci* poetry because it can be sung to the music. As the length of verses in a *Ci* poem differs, it is also called "Long and Short Verses". The reason why there are more than one name concerning *Ci* poetry lies in the close relationship between *Ci* poetry and music and its difference from traditional poetry in terms of characteristic of form. *Ci* poetry has various names of cadence which we called "tune" such as *The Moon over the West River*, *The River All Red* and *Dreamlike Song*, etc.

As a new type of poetry, *Ci* reached its zenith in the Song Dynasty (960—1279). Like Tang poetry, the Song *Ci* poetry holds a very important position in the history of Chinese literature.

In the course of its development, many outstanding *Ci* poets, such as Su Shi, Li Qingzhao, Xin Qiji and Lu You emerged.

Su Shi's *Ci* poems are characteristic of passion, refreshment and mellifluence. The contents of his poems are rich in terms of subject: some expressed his patriotism, some described scenes of country, some depicted grievance when lovers had to part.

Li Qingzhao is an outstanding *Ci* poetess. Her works are exquisite, refined and full of true feelings. She expressed her understanding and pursuit of true love, described the impact of the changing seasons on human's sentiment, and reflected the misery of the people suffering from the decline of their country and the disasters befalling families. Many of her moving verses such as *"Can't you see? / Can't you see? / The green leaves are fresh but the red flowers are fading!"* *"This feeling is unable to be removed. / It was shown on my knitted eyebrows a moment ago but has now come to pain my heart."* show her poetic gifts.

Xin Qiji is the most prolific among the *Ci* poets of the Song Dynasty. His works teemed with heroism. His verses such as "*Half drunk I lit the lamp to look at my sword / After dreams of the bugles in our army camps.*" "*Green mountains are no bar / To the river flowing on to the sea.*" have been circulating for generations. They not only reflected grand army life but also indicated his determination to resist the Jin troops and his deep love for his own country. Xin's *Ci* poems greatly broadened the themes and enriched the artistic style of the Song *Ci* poetry.

Till today, Song *Ci* poems are still favored by the masses. The book *Three Hundred Song Ci Poems* can be regarded as a must for many families, and a great number of renowned *Ci* poems have been set to new tunes for extensive singing.

```
        2
1   |
        3
```

1. 李清照
   Li Qingzhao
2. 苏轼
   Su Shi
3. 辛弃疾
   Xin Qiji

Prelude to Water Melody
(*Shuidiao Getou*)
Su Shi

When will the moon be full and bright?
Raising my wineglass, I ask the blue sky.
I know not what year it is tonight,
In the far-away heaven palace.
I wish to return home with fair wind,
For fear I cannot bear the freezing cold,
So high in the marble towers and jade houses.
I dance with my lonely shadow wild,
As if I were not in the human world.

The moon rounds the red cabinet,
Peeps through the silk-pad windows,
And shines upon the sleepless man.
The moon should not suffer the hatred,
Why is it always full when people part?
People may have sorrows or joys,
And the moon may be dim or bright,
This cannot be perfect since ancient time.
I wish that we all would have a long life,
Sharing the beautiful moon even miles apart.

元杂剧

Yuan *Zaju* (Opera of the Yuan Dynasty)

中国的戏曲在经历了漫长的发展过程之后，到元代（1206—1368）形成了"元杂剧"。元杂剧把音乐、歌舞、表演、念白①融于一体，是比较成熟的戏剧形式。

元杂剧的兴盛，使元代成为中国戏曲史上的黄金时代，当时有姓名记载的杂剧作家就有200多位，有记载可查的杂剧剧本有700多种。元杂剧从多方面反映了当时的社会现实，表达了人民大众反抗压迫、追求美好生活的愿望。

关汉卿是元代成就最高、影响最大的剧作家，他一生写了60多部杂剧，现存的还有18部。关汉卿的杂剧大多表现了下层妇女的苦难和斗争，歌颂了她们的机智和勇敢。他的代表作《窦娥冤》是元杂剧中最著名的悲剧。剧中描写了善良的女子窦娥，遭到坏人陷害，

被官府关进监狱，最终含冤被杀的故事。在刑场上，她许下了血溅素练、六月飞雪、大旱三年的誓愿，果然应验。作品以强烈的悲剧效果表达了作家对社会的不满，对弱者的同情，是元杂剧中现实主义与浪漫主义相结合的优秀作品。关汉卿的创作对后世戏曲的发展产生了巨大的影响，他不仅是中国伟大的戏剧家，也是世界文化名人。

王实甫也是元代著名的戏剧家，他一生写了14种剧本。他所创作的《西厢记》，是中国古典戏剧的杰作。剧本描写了崔莺莺和张生的爱情故事，歌颂了他们追求自由婚姻、反抗封建礼教的精神，表达了"愿普天下有情人都成眷属"的美好愿望。剧中人物崔莺莺、张生和红娘在中国几乎家喻户晓。

除此以外，元代著名的杂剧作家还有马致远、白朴、郑光祖、纪君祥等。元杂剧中的许多剧目一直到今天仍在戏剧舞台上上演，有的还被拍成了电影和电视剧，影响十分广泛。18世纪，元杂剧《赵氏孤儿》曾流传到欧洲，被改编成《中国孤儿》，受到了世界的瞩目。

1. 《西厢记》插图
   An illustration in *The West Chamber*
2. 京剧:《西厢记》
   The West Chamber (Beijing Opera)
3. 舞剧:《西厢记》
   The West Chamber (dance drama)
4. 《西厢记》人物: 崔莺莺
   Cui Yingying: a character in *The West Chamber*

1	3
2	4

Yuan *Zaju*
(Opera of the Yuan Dynasty)

It was after long years of development that the Chinese local opera, Yuan *zaju,* came into being during the Yuan Dynasty (1206—1368). It is a relatively matured form of opera appropriately integrating music, singing, dancing, performing and speaking.

The rise of Yuan *zaju* made the Yuan Dynasty the golden age of Chinese opera. Within less than one hundred years, according to records, there were more than 200 recorded playwrights and more than 700 *zaju* scripts. Yuan *zaju* provided image of the social reality of that time from every aspect and expressed the people's wish of resisting the oppression and pursuit of happy life.

Guan Hanqing was the greatest and most prolific playwright of the Yuan Dynasty. He created over 60 plays, of which 18 still exist. Most of them reflected on the misery and struggles of women at the bottom of society and highly praised their wisdom and courage. His representative work *The Grievance of Dou'e* (also translated as *Snow in Midsummer*) is the best-known of the *zaju* tragedies. It tells of a kind-hearted young woman named Dou'e, who was falsely accused and thrown into prison by the local authorities, and was finally sentenced to death. On the execution ground, she predicted that blood would be splashing and that it would snow in June with great drought lasting for three years. As expected, all of them came true. With

an intense tragical impression throughout the play, the author expressed his indignation and sympathy for the weak in society. Guan's plays had great influence on the development of drama of later generations. He is not only the greatest drama composer in China, but also one of the cultural celebrities of the world.

Wang Shifu was another renowned playwright of that period. Throughout his whole life, Wang had written altogether 14 plays, of which *The West Chamber* was considered as the masterpiece in the history of Chinese drama. This play, through the love story of Cui Yingying and Zhang Sheng, highly praised their courage in the pursuit of a free marriage and in the opposition to feudal ethics, conveying that "All those in love shall be wedded." The main characters such as Cui Yingying, Zhang Sheng and Hong Niang are widely known in China.

Besides that, other well-known playwrights include Ma Zhiyuan, Bai Pu, Zheng Guangzu and Ji Junxiang, etc. Like the Tang poetry and Song *Ci* poetry, Yuan *zaju* also holds a very high position in the history of Chinese literature. Many plays of Yuan *zaju*

are still performed on the stage nowadays, and some have been made into films and TV plays, which have exerted a broad influence. In the 18th century, *The Orphan of the Zhao Family* was introduced to Europe and then converted into a play entitled *The Orphan of China*, catching the global attention.

▶ 注解 Note

① 念白是戏剧中的对话和独白。
Speaking refers to the spoken parts of drama, like dialogue, monologue and so on.

1. 京剧:《窦娥冤》
   The Grievance of Dou'e (Beijing Opera)
2、3.《西厢记》
   The West Chamber

明清 小说

Fiction of the Ming and Qing Dynasties

明清时期，中国古典小说的创作取得了辉煌的成就，杰出的代表作品有四大文学名著《三国演义》、《水浒传》、《西游记》、《红楼梦》，还有鬼狐小说《聊斋志异》等。如今，这些享有世界声誉的作品，已被改编成影视剧，受到中外观众的喜爱。

《三国演义》是中国第一部完整的长篇历史小说。作者罗贯中是元末明初人。他根据历史记载和民间流传的三国故事创作了这部小说。《三国演义》主要描写了魏、蜀、吴三国之间在军事上、政治上的种种斗争，反映了当时动乱的社会现实。书中塑造了许多不同性格的人物，如神机妙算的诸葛亮、奸诈多疑的曹操、忠勇的关羽、鲁莽的张飞等，给人留下了深刻的印象。

《水浒传》是一部描写农

打虎"、"鲁智深倒拔垂杨柳"等故事，至今令人百读不厌。

《西游记》是一部著名的神话长篇小说。明代人吴承恩根据唐僧②取经的故事和传说，创作了这部小说。小说描写了孙悟空、猪八戒、沙和尚保护唐僧去西天取经的故事。他们一路上降妖伏魔，经历了81难，终于取回了真经。书中最吸引读者的形象是孙悟空，他机智勇敢，本领高强，敢于反抗天神和妖魔，深受人们喜爱。这部小说充满了奇特的幻想，表现出丰富的艺术想象力，在中国影响极大。

《红楼梦》是中国古典小说中最优秀的作品。作者是清代文学家曹雪芹。这部小说通过贵族青年贾宝玉和林黛玉的恋爱悲剧，叙述了一个封建贵族家庭由盛到衰的历史。书中塑造了400多个栩栩如生的人物，如王熙凤、薛宝钗、晴雯等。整部小说情节生动，语言优美，是中国古典小说创作的最高峰，在世界文学史上也占有重要的地位。

《聊斋志异》是一部中外闻名的文言③短篇小说集。作者是清代人蒲松龄。《聊斋志异》中的故事生动奇特，大都与鬼怪、花仙、狐仙有关，比如《香玉》描写了书生和牡丹花妖的恋爱。《聊斋志异》中的故事歌颂了美好的品德，表现了青年男女追求恋爱自由的愿望，揭露了封建制度的黑暗、不公，控诉了贪官污吏的罪恶，寄托了作者的理想和希望。这部小说深受人们喜爱，是中国文言短篇小说的高峰之作。

民起义的长篇小说。作者施耐庵是元末明初人。他根据民间流传的北宋末年宋江起义的故事，写成了这部小说。全书主要描写了宋江领导的梁山①农民起义从兴起到失败的过程，揭露了"官逼民反"的社会现实。书中成功地塑造了108位梁山好汉的英雄形象，歌颂了他们的斗争精神。其中"武松

1	2
	3

1. 《三国演义》故事：赵子龙大战文丑
   A Fierce Battle Between Zhao Zilong and Wen Chou from *Romance of Three Kingdoms*
2. 《红楼梦》人物：林黛玉
   Lin Daiyu: a character in *A Dream of Red Mansions*
3. 《红楼梦》人物蜡像
   The waxwork of characters in *A Dream of Red Mansions*

Fiction
of the Ming and Qing Dynasties

The Ming (1368—1644) and Qing (1644—1911) dynasties witnessed great achievements in the creation of fiction. The representative works are *Romance of Three Kingdoms, Outlaws of the Marsh, Journey to the West, A Dream of Red Mansions* and the ghost fiction *Strange Tales of Liaozhai*. Those works enjoy a high reputation throughout the world. What's more, they have been adapted for the screen and the stage, winning the favor of global audience.

Romance of Three Kingdoms is the

first complete historical novel in China. The author Luo Guanzhong lived in the late Yuan and early Ming dynasties. This novel was written on the basis of historical records and the stories about the three kingdoms that circulated among the people. It focused on the military and political rivalry between the kingdoms of Wei, Shu and Wu, reflecting the upheavals of the time. In the novel, the author successfully created a number of impressive characters with different characteristics, such as Zhuge Liang, a superb strategist, cunning and suspicious Cao Cao, loyal and brave Guan Yu, reckless Zhang Fei, etc.

Outlaws of the Marsh is a novel about a peasant rebellion. The author Shi Nai'an also lived in the late Yuan and early Ming dynasties. Based on popular stories about a peasant rebellion led by Song Jiang in the later years of the Song Dynasty, Shi wrote this

novel. It describes the rise and fall of the peasant rebellion in the area of Liangshan, uncovering the social reality of a rebellion of civilians forced by persecution of officials. The novel successfully depicts 108 Liangshan heroes and heroines and lauds their dauntless acts. Episodes like *Wu Song Strikes a Tiger* and *Lu Zhishen Pulls Out a Willow Tree* remain vivid till now.

Journey to the West is a renowned mythical novel. The author Wu Cheng'en of the Ming Dynasty wrote this novel in accordance with stories about Tang Seng (Xuanzang), a monk of the Tang Dynasty who traveled to India in the face of many difficulties in order to learn the Buddhist scriptures. The author created a cast of figures like Monkey, Pig and Sandy who escorted and protected their master, the Tang Monk on the way to the West. They subdued all kinds of demons during the journey and survived 81 calamities to eventually bring back the scriptures. As the most attractive figure in the novel, Monkey was clever and brave as well as possessed the great power. He showed no fear in the face of heavenly gods or sinister monsters, which made him in high favor with most readers. The novel is full of fantasies that indicate the author's abundant imagination. It has always had a tremendous impact on the Chinese people.

A Dream of Red Mansions can be regarded as the best Chinese classic novel. The author was Cao Xueqin, one of great litterateurs of the Qing Dynasty. Through a tragedy of romance between Jia Baoyu of a noble clan and Lin Daiyu, the novel gives an account of the history of a feudal clan from its heyday to its final collapse. There are more than 400 characters vividly depicted in the novel, like Wang Xifeng, Xue Baochai and Qing Wen, etc. With its fascinating scenario and superb language, *A Dream of Red Mansions* has reached the zenith of the Chinese classic novels, and holds an important position in the history of world literature.

Strange Tales of Liaozhai is an internationally renowned collection of short stories written in the classical Chinese. The author Pu Songling lived in the Qing Dynasty. Stories in this book are vivid and strange, mostly concerned with the spirit world where ghosts, immortals of flower or immortals of fox coexist with human beings. For instance, "Xiang Yu", is an account of a love story between a scholar and a peony immortal. Through stories in this novel, the author praised fine moral ethics, expressed the wishes of young men and women to have a marriage of their own free will, uncovered the darkness and unfairness of the feudal society, denounced evil of corrupt officials and expressed his own ideals and hopes. This story collection is widely read and it can be regarded as the classic novel written in the classical Chinese.

1. 《西游记》故事：二郎收八戒
   Er Lang Subdues Pig from *Journey to the West*
2. 《西游记》故事：大圣偷丹
   Monkey Steals the Elixir from *Journey to the West*

▶ 注解 Notes

① 梁山在中国山东省境内，是《水浒传》中农民起义军聚义山寨的所在地。
Located in Shandong Province, the area of Liangshan is the place where the peasant rebels depicted in *Outlaws of the Marsh* originally banded together.

② 唐僧指中国唐代著名的僧人玄奘，他曾用17年的时间去印度取佛经。
Tang Seng refers to the famous Tang monk named Xuanzang, who had spent 17 years in India to study the Buddhist scriptures.

③ 文言指1919年"五四运动"以前通用的以古汉语为基础的书面语。
The classical Chinese is the literary language developed through classical patterns, and used exclusively in writing before the May 4th Movement of 1919.

四大民间传说

Four Great Folklores

　　中国四大民间传说故事，是指在中国民间以口头、文字等形式流传最为广泛、影响最大的四个传说故事。它们和其他民间传说故事构成了中国民间文学的一个重要组成部分。这四个传说全部是爱情故事，也从一个侧面反映了人们对真挚感情的认可。

孟姜女

　　秦朝时候，有个善良美丽的女子叫孟姜女，她与范喜良一见钟情，在征得了父母的同意后，准备结为夫妻。当时秦始皇为了修筑长城，到处抓人做劳工，在两人成亲的当天，硬把范喜良抓走，派到千里之外的长城去做工。孟姜女悲愤交加，日夜思念丈夫。随着天气越来越寒冷，孟姜女精心做好了寒衣，千里迢迢到长城去寻找自己的丈夫。

孟姜女经历了风霜雨雪、千辛万苦，终于来到长城。可她看到的却是冷冰冰的万里长城，没有丈夫的踪影。最后经过查问，才知道范喜良已经被折磨致死，尸体被埋到了长城脚下。听到这个噩耗，孟姜女不由在长城边大哭起来，泪飞如雨，整整三天三夜，感天动地，将长城哭倒了八百里，砖瓦中露出来的正是范喜良的尸首，她终于见到了自己日思夜想的丈夫。

白娘子与许仙

清明时分，杭州西湖花红柳绿，湖光山色，非常美丽。两个修炼多年的蛇妖白素贞和小青到此游玩。春雨蒙蒙，两人趁借伞之际，认识了年轻书生许仙。白素贞和许仙情投意合，互倾爱慕之情。不久，两人结为夫妻，开了一间药店，治病救人，日子过得非常和美。

不料金山寺的法海和尚看到他们人妖结合在一起，要拆散他们。他首先将白娘子是蛇妖的身份偷偷告诉许仙，并设计让白娘子显出原形，后又将许仙关在金山寺里。白娘子和小青来到金山寺，苦苦哀求，但是法海拒不放人。白素贞无奈掀起滔滔大浪，水淹金山寺，和法海斗法。因有孕在身，白娘子最后被法海打败，收进金钵，压在了西湖边的雷峰塔下。一对恩爱的夫妻就这样被拆散了。

此后，小青逃离金山寺，潜心练功，最终打败了法海，将他逼进了螃蟹腹中，救出了塔下的白娘子。白娘子和许仙从此团圆。

白蛇传的故事塑造了一个美丽、善良、坚强的“蛇仙”形象，歌颂了美好的爱情。

1 | 2
 | 3

1. 川剧：《白蛇传》
White Snake Biography (Sichuan Opera)
2. 位于杭州西湖湖畔的雷峰塔
The Leifeng Pagoda beside the West Lake, Hangzhou
3. 雷峰塔上的《白蛇传》木雕：水漫金山
The Flooding of Jinshan Temple: the wood sculpture of *White Snake Biography* on the Leifeng Pagoda

Four Great Folklores

Chinese four great folklores refer to the four folklores which have come down with the greatest influences upon the Chinese in verbal and literal forms. Together with other folklores, Chinese four great folklores compose the essential parts of Chinese folk culture. All the four great folklores are concerned with love stories, which reflect people's recognition of true love from different profiles.

Mengjiangnü

In the Qin Dynasty, there was a virtuous and beautiful girl whose name was Mengjiangnü. She and Fan Xiliang fell in love at first sight, and prepared to get married after asking for their parents' consent. At that time, for the construction of the Great Wall, the First Emperor of the Qin Dynasty drafted people to serve as labors. On the day when Mengjiangnü and Fan were getting married, Fan was caught and forced to go to build the Great Wall, which was thousands of *li* away from Fan's home. Mengjiangnü was full of grief and indignation, missing her husband day and night. The weather became colder and colder, Mengjiangnü made fine cotton-padded clothes, and went to the Great Wall to look for her husband.

Going through misery and hardships, Mengjiangnü finally arrived at the Great Wall. To her disappointment, what Mengjiangnü found was not her living husband but the icy Great Wall of which the beginning and ending could not be seen. Finally, she was told that her husband had died and his body was buried underneath the Great Wall. Hearing this sad news, Mengjiangnü could not help but cry beside the Great Wall and continued to cry for three days and nights. As a result, the Great Wall collapsed for eight hundred *li*, some bones of the dead appeared and they were just Fan Xiliang's. Thus, Mengjiangnü finally saw her husband.

Lady White and Xu Xian

On Tomb-Sweeping Day, on the banks of the West Lake, there were red flowers and green willow everywhere, and there was the reflection of green hills on the surface of the West Lake. The whole scene was very beautiful. Two snake spirits, Bai Suzhen and Xiaoqing, came here to play. On a rainy day, taking the chance of borrowing an umbrella, they became

spirit with beauty, goodness and adamancy, paying a tribute to true love.

acquainted with the young intellectual Xu Xian. Lady White and Xu Xian fell in love with each other. Soon after they got married, and opened a drugstore to save people who were in need. In a word, they led a happy life.

Unexpectedly, Monk Fahai from Jinshan Temple witnessed Xu Xian living with the snake spirit and attempted to break them up. First, he told Xu Xian that Lady White was a snake spirit by stealth. Furthermore, Monk Fahai used machinations to make Lady White lose her superior magic skills and become a large white snake. Later, Monk Fahai enjailed Xu Xian in Jinshan Temple. Lady White and Xiaoqing came to beseech Monk Fahai for release of Xu Xian, but their

request was refused by Fahai. In order to save her husband, Lady White summoned up a surging flood to Jinshan Temple. But finally she failed in the fight due to the pregnancy and was suppressed by Fahai under the Leifeng Pagoda beside the West Lake. So this loving couple was broken up.

Afterwards, Xiaoqing fled from Jinshan Temple and involved herself with practice of her magic skills. Finally, Xiaoqing defeated the Monk Fahai, forced him to retreat into the stomach of a crab and helped Lady White out of the bottom of Leifeng Pagoda. From then on, Lady White was reunited with Xu Xian.

The story concerning Lady White figured an image of a snake

1 | 2

1. 孟姜女
Mengjiangnü
2. 京剧:《白蛇传》
White Snake Biography (Beijing Opera)

牛郎织女

传说古代有一个勤劳、善良的放牛郎，日子过得十分清贫。有一天，在老牛的帮助下，牛郎结识了从天上思凡下界的仙女——织女。织女爱上了这个真诚可爱的放牛郎，两人结为夫妻。他们有了一男一女两个孩子，一家人过得非常幸福。

不料织女下凡的事激怒了天神，王母①命令织女返回天宫。织女尽管万般不舍，也不得不离开牛郎和自己的孩子，腾云而去。牛郎舍不得妻子，带上两个年幼的孩子，在老牛的帮助下，追赶而去。王母无法阻拦他们，就使出法术，在他们中间隔出了一道宽宽的银河。

从此，牛郎和织女只能站在银河的两端，遥遥相望。但是，牛郎织女之间的感情，不会因为一条银河而被阻隔，每年农历七月初七，会有成千上万只喜鹊飞来，在银河上架起一座长长的鹊桥，让牛郎织女一家团聚，共叙相思。七月初七，也成了现在许多情人约会、互赠礼物、表达爱慕的日子，可以说是东方的情人节。据说这一天，你如果坐在葡萄架下，静静地听，还会听到他们一家在鹊桥上亲热地说着悄悄话。

梁山伯与祝英台

从前有一位聪明、美丽的女子，名叫祝英台。女孩子在古时候是不许进学堂的，祝英台为了读书，说服家人，和丫环女扮男装，去杭州的学堂读书求学。

在学堂里，祝英台遇见了书生梁山伯，他学问出众，为人憨厚，两人结拜为兄弟，结下了深厚的感情。

三载过去，学年期满，祝

英台拜别老师，返回家乡。此时祝英台已经深深爱上了梁山伯，梁山伯虽不知实情，但对她也是十分敬慕。两人十八相送，依依不舍。祝英台假托为妹做媒，嘱咐山伯早去迎娶。梁山伯后来前往祝家拜访，不料祝英台的父亲已将英台许婚给有钱的马太守的儿子马文才。梁祝两人在楼台相会，见姻缘无望，不胜悲愤。梁山伯归家后，万念俱灰，一病不起，没多久就病故了。

祝英台无力反抗现实，被迫与马公子成亲，马家迎娶的当日，祝英台让花轿绕道至梁山伯坟前祭奠。霎时风雷大作，坟墓裂开，祝英台微笑着纵身跃入，马上风消云散，雨过天晴，百花开放，梁山伯与祝英台化作了两只蝴蝶，在花丛中翩翩飞舞，双宿双飞。

梁祝的故事诠释了古代年轻男女追求真爱的勇气，反映了人们对包办婚姻的痛恨和对自由幸福生活的渴望。

1	2
	3

1. 牛郎织女折扇：母子图
Mother and Son: the folding fan depicting *The Cowherd and the Girl Weaver*
2、3. 越剧：《梁祝》
Liang Shanbo and Zhu Yingtai (Yue Opera)

The Cowherd and the Girl Weaver

According to the legend, there was a laborious and virtuous cow-herd in old times. He led a poor life. One day, with the help of an old cow, the Cowherd got to know the Girl Weaver, who had descended from the Heaven to the secular world. The Girl Weaver fell in love with the Cowherd, who was so sincere and cute, and they got married. Later, they had a son and a daughter, leading a happy life.

When the Queen Mother of Heaven learned it, she was outraged so she asked the Girl Weaver to return to the Heaven. Although the Girl Weaver was so reluctant to leave her husband and children, she had to return to the Heaven. As for the Cow-herd, he was even more reluctant to part with his wife. For this reason, with the help of the old cow, he went to the Heaven with his children to look for his wife.

The Queen Mother of Heaven had no way to discourage them from reunion, therefore she had no choice but to draw a wide river (the Milky Way) in heaven between the Girl Weaver and the Cowherd.

From then on, the Cowherd and the Girl Weaver had to look into the distance at each other on different banks of the Milky Way. But the affection between them would not be obstructed due to a heavenly river. On every seventh day of the seventh month of the lunar calendar, thousands of magpies would fly to form a long bridge for the couple to reunite. Currently, such a date has become the day when many lovers date with each other, present gifts for each other and show their affection. Thus, this day can be considered as the oriental Valentine's Day. As the story goes, if you sit under the grapevine on this day and listen silently, you may hear the couple and their children having a private conversation.

Liang Shanbo and Zhu Yingtai (The Butterfly Lovers: Leon and Jo)

Once upon a time, there was a clever and beautiful girl named Zhu Yingtai. Although girls were not allowed to study in the school, Zhu Yingtai persuaded

her parents into permitting her to study and disguised herself as a male with her servant girl, then went to Hangzhou to pursue her studies.

In the school, Zhu Yingtai met Liang Shanbo, who was simple and honest as well as having a profound acquirement. Therefore, they became blood brothers and had a profound affection for each other.

After three years of study, Zhu Yingtai finished "his" studies and returned to her hometown. At that time, she actually fell in love with Liang Shanbo. Although Liang was unaware of Zhu's real identity, he also adored Zhu Yingtai. On departure, they were so reluctant to part with each other. Zhu invited Liang to visit

"his" family, and told him "he" would ask parents to marry "his" sister to Liang. Zhu hoped that Liang could marry "his" sister as early as possible. However, when Liang Shanbo visited Zhu's family, Councilor Zhu betrothed Zhu Yingtai to the child Ma Wencai, the son of the moneyed Procurator Ma. Liang Shanbo and Zhu Yingtai met each other at the balcony and were remorseful when they realized that they couldn't get married. After Shanbo returned home, he was utterly disheartened and therefore fell ill and soon succumbed to disease.

Zhu Yingtai was unable to resist reality and was forced to get married with child Ma. On the day of the wedding, Zhu Yingtai asked carriers of the bridal sedan to pass Liang's tomb so

that she could hold a memorial ceremony for Shanbo. When Zhu arrived at Liang's tomb, there came a fresh gale, which caused the wave to surge. Suddenly, the skies fell and the earth cracked, Liang's tomb split open. Seizing this opportunity, Zhu happily jumped into the tomb. Immediately, the rain passed off and the sky cleared up; the wind abated and waves calmed down; flowers bloomed. Zhu Yingtai and Liang Shanbo became a couple of butteries, dancing gracefully among the wild flowers.

The story of "Leon and Jo" reflects the courage of young people who were pursuing true love in ancient times, showing that most people hate arranged (forced) marriages and long for lives of happiness and liberty.

1	3
2	

1. 黄梅戏:《牛郎织女》
   The Cowherd and the Girl Weaver
   (Huangmei Opera)
2. 昆剧:《梁祝》
   Liang Shanbo and Zhu Yingtai (Kun Opera)
3. 越剧:《梁祝》
   Liang Shanbo and Zhu Yingtai (Yue Opera)

▶ 注解 Note

① 王母是中国古代传说中的女性天神，有极大的权力。
The Queen Mother of Heaven is the goddess of the Heaven with great power in Chinese ancient folklores.

中国古代科技

Science and Technology of Ancient China

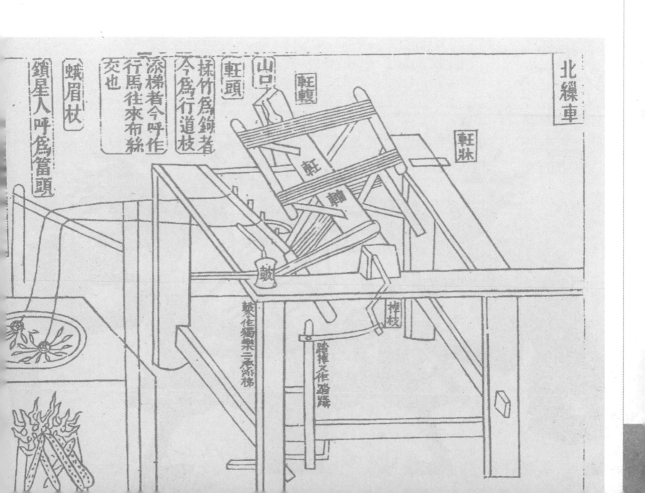

概 述

Introduction

中国是世界文明古国之一。古代中国的科技非常发达，国际著名学者李约瑟教授撰写的《中国科学技术史》很好地展现了中国灿烂的科技文化。勤劳智慧的中国人为世界贡献了许多发明创造，最为有名的无疑是指南针、造纸术、印刷术和火药这四大发明。

Introduction

China is one of the countries with ancient civilizations in the world. The ancient China was rather advanced in the fields of science and technology. The book *Science and Civilization in China* written by internationally noted scholar Professor Joseph Needham, presents an elegant picture of the splendid culture of science and technology in ancient China. The Chinese people, who are industrious and wise, have contributed to the whole world a great number of inventions and creations, of which the most well-known are undoubtedly the four great inventions, i.e. the compass, papermaking, the technique of printing and gunpowder.

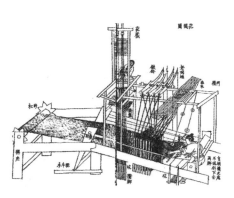

```
1 | 3
  |   4
2 |   5
```

1. 织布图
   Weavers at a loom
2. 浑天仪
   The armillary sphere
3. 抛石机
   The stone thrower
4. 古代宗教织锦
   An ancient braid with religious motif
5. 花织机
   The ancient spinning machine

指南针

The Compass

在指南针发明以前，人们在茫茫大海上航行，只能靠太阳和星星的位置辨认方向，如果遇上阴雨天，就会迷失方向。是中国人发明的指南针，帮助人们解决了这个难题。

指南针是指示方向的仪器。早在战国时期，中国人就发现了磁石指示南北的特性，并根据这种特性制成了指示方向的仪器——司南。司南由一把光滑的磁勺和刻有方位的铜盘组成，勺把指示的方向是南方，勺头指示的方向是北方。到了宋代，人们把经过人工磁化的指南针和方位盘结合起来，制成了"罗盘"。有了罗盘，无论在什么情况下，人们都能准确地辨认方向了。

北宋时，指南针已开始应用于航海事业。南宋时，指南针经由阿拉伯传到欧洲，当时的阿拉伯人亲切地称指南针为"水手之眼"。

指南针的发明，给航海事业带来了划时代的影响，世界航运史也由此翻开了新的一页。明朝初期郑和率领船队七下西洋，15世纪哥伦布发现新大陆和麦哲伦环绕地球航行等壮举，都是指南针用于航海事业的成果。

The Compass

Before the compass was invented, most people identified the direction at sea, only depending upon the position of the sun and stars. If it was cloudy or rainy, people would lose the direction in this way. It was the compass, invented by the Chinese people, that solved this problem.

The compass is the instrument used for indicating direction. As early as the Warring States Period (475 BC—221 BC), the Chinese discovered that a magnet could be applied to indicate the south or the north, and a direction-indicating instrument *sinan* was made on the basis of

this feature. The instrument comprised a smooth magnetic spoon and a copper plate carved with directions; the handle of the spoon pointed south, and the head north. In the Song Dynasty, people combined an artificially magnetized compass with an azimuth plate to create a proper

compass called *luopan*, which, in any cases, could tell sailors the accurate direction.

In the Northern Song Dynasty (960—1127), the compass was being applied to navigation. In the Southern Song Dynasty, the instrument was introduced to Europe via Arabia, and Arabs at that time called it affectionately "the Eyes of Sailor".

The invention of the compass had an epoch-making influence on navigation, thereby opening up a new era in the history of international navigation. Zheng He's fleets made seven voyages across seas to Southeast Asia and around Indian Ocean in the early Ming Dynasty, Christopher Columbus discovered the New World and Ferdinand Magellan sailed round the world in the 15th century, which was the consequence of the application of the compass to the navigation.

1	
2	3
	4

1. 罗盘
   Luopan (the ancient compass)
2、3、4. 司南
   Sinan (the ancient compass)

造 纸术

Papermaking

在造纸术发明以前，中国人把字刻在龟甲、兽骨上，写在竹片、木片和绢帛上。甲骨、木片都很笨重，用起来不方便；绢帛太贵，一般人用不起。大约在西汉初期，有人用大麻和苎(zhǔ)麻造出了纸。这种早期的纸比较粗糙，不太适合写字。

到了东汉时期，在朝廷做官的蔡伦，经过长期的试验，改进了造纸方法。他用树皮、破布、破渔网等多种植物纤维做原料，加水蒸煮，捣烂成浆，再均匀地摊在细帘子上晾干，造成了一种薄薄的纸。这种纸便于写字，而且便宜，受到了人们的欢迎。所以说蔡伦在造纸术方面的贡献是巨大的。

东汉以后，造纸技术得到不断改进，竹子、稻草、甘蔗渣等都逐渐成为造纸原料。因为原料不同，纸也有了各种不同的种类和用途。安徽省宣州生产的宣纸，就是闻名中外的上等纸张，是用于中国书法和绘画的珍品。

中国的造纸术于隋末唐初传到朝鲜和日本，后来又传到阿拉伯地区和其他国家，纸的发明，极大地方便了信息的储存和交流，对于推动世界文明的发展具有划时代的意义。

Before papermaking technology was invented, the Chinese carved or wrote characters on tortoise shells, animal bones, bamboo slices, wooden plates, and thin tough silk. Tortoise shells, animal bones and wooden plates were too heavy to use while silk was too expensive. In the early years of the Western Han Dynasty (206 BC—25 AD), someone used hemp and ramie to produce the paper, which was very rough and not suitable for writing.

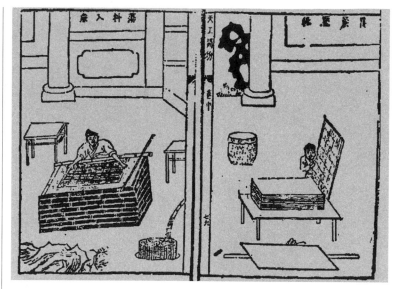

Papermaking

Till the Eastern Han Dynasty (25—220), an official named Cai Lun improved the papermaking technique after long-term experimentation. He used various kinds of plant fibers, bark, rags, and torn fishing nets as raw materials. He steamed and cooked all those materials with water, and pounded them into pulp, then rolled the pulp out evenly on a fine screen and dried it into a kind of thin paper. The paper was suitable for writing and was also very cheap so it became very popular. Therefore, Cai Lun's contribution to the papermaking was great.

After the Eastern Han Dynasty, the papermaking technology

had been gradually improved. Gradually, bamboo, straw and sugarcane residue could also be used as the raw materials for making paper. Due to different materials, various types of paper were produced for different uses. For example, the Xuan paper made in Xuanzhou of Anhui Province belongs to the high-quality paper exclusively adapted for use in Chinese calligraphy and painting.

The technology was introduced to Korea and Japan in the late Sui (581—618) and early Tang (618—907) dynasties, and later to Arabia and other countries. The invention of paper provides a more convenient way for the storage and communication of information, and also has an epoch-making significance on the promotion the development of global civilization.

1、2、3. 造纸流程图
The process of papermaking

印刷术

Printing

印刷术发明以前，读书人要得到一本新书，只有逐字逐句地抄写。隋唐时，发明了雕版印刷术，提高了印书的速度。但是每印一本书都要雕大量的版，还是十分费事。到了900多年前的北宋时期，平民发明家毕昇，经过反复试验，发明了活字印刷术。他把字刻在一小块一小块的胶泥上，放进火里烧硬，做成一个个活字。印书时，把活字按书稿排列，排成整版后印刷。印完后，把这些活字拆下来，以后还可以再用。毕昇发明的活字版印刷术，既经济又省时，使印刷技术进入了一个新时代。

中国的活字印刷术先向东传到了朝鲜、日本，接着向西传到波斯、埃及。印刷术的发明大大加快了世界各国文化发展、交流的速度。活字印刷术是中国对世界的一大贡献。

Printing

Before printing was invented, a scholar had to do the transcription word for word if he wanted to own a new book. In the Sui and Tang dynasties, the technology of block printing was invented, and therefore the speed of printing was increased. But when a book was to be printed, many wooden blocks had to be engraved so it was rather troublesome. Till the Northern Song Dynasty more than 900 years ago, Bi Sheng invented movable type printing after the repeating experimentations. He engraved the characters on small pieces of clay, and heated them until they became hard movable characters. In the course of presswork, the moveable characters were placed into a whole block in accordance with manuscripts to be delivered to the printing. All those moveable characters could be removed from the block after the presswork for the later reuse of them. This technique invented by Bi Sheng was both economical and timesaving, thus brought the technique of printing into a new era.

China's movable type printing was first introduced eastward to Korea and Japan, and then westward to Persia and Egypt. The invention of the technique of printing greatly sped up the international development of culture and exchanges. It is no doubt that the moveable type printing is one of the greatest contributions to the world.

	2
1	3
	4

1、4. 清代印刷用活字
   The movable types in the Qing Dynasty
2. 刻字
   The character carving
3. 印刷宗谱
   The genealogy printed by using movable types

火药

Gunpowder

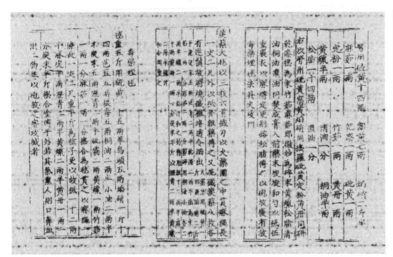

火药的配方最初是由中国古代炼丹家在炼制丹药的过程中发现的。后来，人们根据这个配方，将硝石、硫磺、木炭按一定比例配制在一起，制成了黑火药。唐朝中期的书籍里，记载了制造这种火药的方法。火药发明后，先是被制成了爆竹和焰火，到了唐朝末年，开始用于军事。北宋时，火药在军事上大量使用，那时候的火药武器有突火枪、火箭、火炮等。

公元1225—1248年之间，火药和火药武器经由阿拉伯传到欧洲。因为制造火药的主要原料硝石洁白如雪，所以火药被阿拉伯人称为"中国雪"或"中国盐"。火药传到欧洲后，被各国用来制造武器，还在开山、修路、挖河等工程中广泛使用，火药的使用促进了工业革命的到来。

```
      3
1  ┌──────
   │  4
2  │  5
```

1. 古代火药配方
   The ancient recipe of powder
2. 古代兵器：鸟铳
   An ancient weapon: bird blunderbuss
3. 古代兵器：火龙箭
   An ancient weapon: firedrake arrow
4. 明代虎蹲炮
   The squat tiger artillery in the Ming Dynasty
5. 古代火炮
   Ancient artillery

The formula of the gunpowder was initially discovered by Taoist alchemists of ancient China when they attempted to make pills of immortality. Afterward, according to the formula, some people produced black gunpowder using a mixture of niter, sulfur and charcoal in a certain proportion. In the middle years of the Tang Dynasty , some books recorded the method of producing this kind of gunpowder. After its invention, the gunpowder was first used to produce firecrackers and fireworks, and began to be applied to the military affairs till late years of the Tang Dynasty.

In the time between 1225 AD and 1248 AD, the gunpowder and weapons using gunpowder were introduced to Europe via Arabia. Since niter, the major raw material of the gunpowder, is as white as snow, Arabians called the gunpowder "Chinese Snow" and "Chinese Salt". After the introduction of gunpowder to Europe, the gunpowder was not only extensively applied to weapons industry, but also various projects such as exploding mountains, road construction, and river excavation. The invention of gunpowder accelerated the advent of the Industrial Revolution.

Gunpowder

In the Northern Song Dynasty, gunpowder had been in the extensive application to the military affairs, and then weapons such as firelock, rocket and cannon already emerged.

《甘石星经》

Gan and Shi's Celestial Book

哈雷彗星
Halley's Comet

中国人很早就注意观察天象。

春秋战国时期，天文学已经取得了相当高的成就。鲁国的天文学家在对天象的观测中，观测到37次日食，其中33次已经被证明是可靠的。现在世人通称的哈雷彗星，早在公元前613年就被载入鲁国的史书《春秋》中，这是世界上关于哈雷彗星最早的记录。

战国时期还出现了天文学专著，如齐国的天文学家甘德著的《天文星占》，魏国人石申著的《天文》，后人将这两部著作合为一部，称作《甘石星经》。这是中国、也是世界上现存最早的一部天文学著作。

《甘石星经》记录了水、木、金、火、土五大行星的运行情况以及它们的出没规律。书中还测定了121颗恒星的方位，记录了800颗恒星的名字。

甘德还用肉眼发现了木星的卫星。石申则发现日食、月食是天体相互掩盖的现象，这在当时也是难能可贵的。为了纪念石申，月球上有一座环形山就是用他的名字命名的。

后世许多天文学家在测量日、月、行星的位置和运动时，都要用到《甘石星经》中的数据。因此，《甘石星经》在中国和世界天文学史上都占有重要地位。

Gan and Shi's Celestial Book

Early in ancient China, some people had begun to observe astronomical phenomena.

In the Spring and Autumn Period and the Warring States Period, China had made great achievements in the field of astronomy. In the observation of astronomical phenomena, the astronomers of the State of Lu had observed a solar eclipse 37 times, 33 of which were proved to be reliable. The observation of what we have termed as Halley's Comet currently had been recorded in one of the history records of the State of Lu, *The Spring and Autumn Annals* as early as in 613 B C. It has been recognized that the record related to Halley's Comet is the first one all over the world.

In the Warring States Period, the astronomical monographs also came out. For instance, the astronomer of the Qi State, Gan De, wrote *Astronomic Auspice*, and Shi Shen from the Wei State wrote *Chronometer*. Afterwards, those masterpieces were integrated into one and got the name *Gan and Shi's Celestial Book*, which is the earliest still existing astronomical masterpieces of China and the world.

Gan and Shi's Celestial Book recorded how five planets including Mercury, Jupiter, Venus, Mars and Saturn moved and the rules concerning when and how they appeared and disappeared. The book also recorded the azimuth of 121 fixed stars measured by ancient astronomers and the names of 800 fixed stars altogether.

Gan De discovered the satellite of Jupiter with his naked eyes. However, Shi Shen found out that the solar eclipses and the lunar eclipses could be regarded as the phenomenon in which celestial bodies hide each other when they move. Therefore, in memory of Shi Shen, a crater on the moon is named after him.

In later generations, many astronomers referenced the data from *Gan and Shi's Celestial Book* when they measured the place and movement of the sun, the moon or other planets. Thus, *Gan and Shi's Celestial Book* holds a very important place in the history of astronomy of China and the whole world.

张衡 与地动仪

Zhang Heng and the Seismograph

在北京中国历史博物馆的展览大厅里，陈列着世界上第一架地动仪的复原模型。这架地动仪的发明者是中国东汉时著名的科学家张衡。

张衡（78—139），河南南阳人。他勤学好问，博览群书，特别爱好天文、历法和数学，是一位博学多才的科学家。

公元132年，张衡在京城洛阳制成了可以测定地震方向的"候风地动仪"。地动仪全部用精铜铸成，外形像一个带盖的大茶杯。仪器表面铸有八条垂直向下的龙，龙头分别对准东、南、西、北、东南、东北、西南、西北八个方向，每条龙的嘴里都含有一个铜球。在正对龙嘴的地上，蹲着八个仰头、张嘴的铜蟾蜍(chánchú)。地动仪的内部结构非常精细巧妙，当某个方向发生地震时，仪器上对着那个方向的龙嘴就会张开，铜球就会掉进铜蟾蜍的嘴里，自动报告发生地震的方向。公元138年的一天，地动仪西边的龙嘴吐出了铜球。果然，远在千里之外的陇西（今甘肃省）在这一天发生了地震。这是人类第一次用仪器测报地震。

张衡还制造出了世界上第一架测量天体位置的水运浑天仪，凡是已知的重要天文现象，都刻在这架仪器上。人们可以通过浑天仪观测到日月星辰运行的情况。张衡又是一位机械工程师，制造过能飞的"木雕"和能计算里程的"计里鼓车"等。

人们非常敬重张衡，经常举行纪念活动，表示对他的敬意。月球上有一座环形山是以他的名字命名的。

Zhang Heng
and the Seismograph

In the Exhibition Hall of the Museum of Chinese History in Beijing, there is a restored model of the first seismograph of the world, whose inventor is Zhang Heng, a famous scientist in the Eastern Han Dynasty (25—220).

Zhang Heng (78—139) was from Nanyang in Henan Province. He studied diligently, and was especially keen on astronomy, calendars and mathematics. As a whole, Zhang Heng can be regarded as an erudite and talented scientist.

In 132 AD, Zhang Heng made a seismograph named Houfeng used for measuring the direction of a certain earthquake in the capital city of Luoyang. It was made of fine copper, and looked like a big cup with a lid. The surface of the instrument was cast with eight dragons,

whose bodies were downward vertically and heads pointed to eight directions (east, south, west, north, southeast, northeast, southwest, and northwest), and each dragon had a copper ball in the mouth. On the ground vertically below the mouths of dragons, there were eight copper toads raising their heads and opening their mouths. The inner side of the seismograph was elaborately constructed. When an earthquake occurred in a place at a certain direction, to which the dragon pointed would open its mouth, and the ball would fall into the toad's mouth, automatically indicating the earthquake occurring at that direction. One day in 138 AD, the dragon pointing to the west expelled its ball. As expected, an earthquake had occurred on that day in Longxi (in present-day Gansu Province) a thousand miles away from Luoyang. It was the first time that mankind had used the instrument to sense an earthquake.

Zhang Heng also made the first water-driven armillary sphere in the world to measure the position of celestial bodies. All the important astronomical phenomena known to all had been carved on this instrument, which can be used for observation of the movement of the sun, the moon and stars. Meanwhile, Zhang Heng was also a mechanical engineer, who had made a flying wooden vulture and a mileage-counting drum car.

Most people highly esteem Zhang Heng, and therefore they often hold commemorative activities to show respect for him. A crater on the moon was named after him.

1. 浑天仪
   The armillary sphere
2. 地动仪
   The seismograph

祖冲之与圆周率

Zu Chongzhi and *Pi*

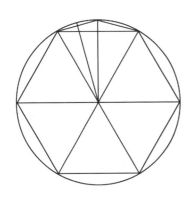

月球背面有一座环形山，被命名为"祖冲之环形山"。

祖冲之（429—500）是中国南北朝时著名的数学家、天文学家和机械制造家。他从小聪明好学，爱好自然科学、文学和哲学，经过刻苦的学习钻研，终于成为一位享誉世界的科学家。

祖冲之在圆周率计算方面的成就为世界所公认。他在前人研究的基础上，采用"割圆术"，经过1 000多次计算，得出圆周率在3.1415926和3.1415927之间。祖冲之还提出 π 的近似值为355/113，称为"密率"，把数学中关于圆周率的计算推进到一个新阶段。日本数学家尊称它为"祖率"。

1 | 2

1. 割圆术
   The "Cutting Circle Method"
2. 祖冲之
   Zu Chongzhi

Zu Chongzhi and *Pi*

There is a crater on the back of the moon, which has been named after Zu Chongzhi.

Zu Chongzhi (429—500) was a famous mathematician, astronomer and mechanic in the Northern and Southern dynasties (420—589). Being smart and fond of learning since his childhood, Zu was keen on natural science, literature and philosophy. Through his assiduous study, Zu Chongzhi finally became a world-famous scientist.

The achievement Zu Chongzhi had made in the calculation of the value of *pi* has been internationally acknowledged. Based on earlier research, he resorted to the "Cutting Circle Method" and concluded that the value of *pi* falls between 3.1415926 and 3.1415927 after more than 1 000 times of calculation. Zu Chongzhi also put forward the viewpoint that the approximate value of *pi* was 355/113, which was called "*milü*", which had boosted the calculation of *pi* to a new phase. Japanese scientists respectfully called the approximate value of *pi* "Zu Ratio".

纺织技术

Textile Technique

黄道婆生活在宋末元初，是松江乌泥泾人。她年轻时因为受不了公婆的虐待，离开家乡流落到海南岛。海南岛盛产棉花，那里的黎族同胞很早就从事棉纺织业。黄道婆和黎族姐妹一起生活，结下了深厚的友谊，也学到了一整套种植和纺织棉花技术。

30年后，两鬓斑白的黄道婆回到家乡。她把在海南岛学会的纺织技术教给松江的兄弟姐妹，同时还推广和改进了很多纺织机械，大大提高了劳动效率。她改进了弹棉花的弹弓，并成功地制成了当时世界上最先进的纺纱工具——三锭脚踏纺棉车；她还把黎族先进的纺织技术和汉族传统的织造工艺结合在一起，织成了配有各种图案的被褥等物品，被人们称为"乌泥泾被"。

黄道婆逝世后，当地人民把她安葬在乌泥泾镇旁，还编了歌谣来纪念这位平凡而伟大的古代巧妇。这首广为流传的歌谣是："黄婆婆，黄婆婆，教我纱，教我布，两只筒子两匹布。"

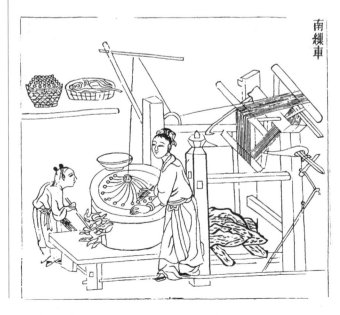

南缫車

Textile
Technique

Huang Daopo lived in late years of the Song Dynasty (960—1279) and the early years of the Yuan Dynasty (1206—1368) and was from Wunijing of Songjiang. Since she could not bear the maltreatment of her parents-in-law when she was young, she left her hometown and wandered to Hainan Island, where there was abundant cotton, and the local Li people had been engaged in the textile industry long before. Huang Daopo lived with the Li women, with whom she had established deep friendship. Meanwhile, Huang had learnt from them a series of techniques of planting as well as cotton spinning and weaving.

Being gray at her temples, Huang Daopo returned to her hometown 30 years later. She taught the Songjiang people the textile technique she had learnt in Hainan Island. At the same time she also popularized and improved many textile machines so that the efficiency of labor was greatly increased. She improved on the cotton fluffer and successively invented a tool for cotton-spinning, a pedal spinning wheel with three spindles, which was the most advanced one at that time. Integrating the advanced textile techniques of the Li people into the traditional weaving techniques of the Han nationality, she made many textiles including "Wunijing Bedding" with various patterns.

After Huang Daopo's death, the local people buried her near Wunijing Town, and also produced a ballad to commemorate the ancient clever woman who was ordinary but great. The popular ballad is as follows: "Granny Huang, Granny Huang, teach me to spin, teach me to weave, two spindles and two bolts of cloth."

1	3
2	

1. 纺织图
   A painting of spinning
2. 南缫车
   The filature
3. 中国皇帝穿的龙袍
   The Chinese emperor's dress with dragon patterns

日晷 和铜壶滴漏

Sundial and Copper Kettle Clepsydra

今天，各式各样的钟表为人们计时提供了方便。在没有钟表的古代，中国人用什么工具计时呢？

最初，人们根据日月星辰在天空中的位置来判断时间，但是这种判断并不准确。后来，人们设计了一种利用太阳测定时刻的定时器——日晷（guǐ）。秦汉时，日晷已在民间流行。日晷是个大圆盘，晷面上刻着"子丑寅卯辰巳午未申酉戌亥"12个时辰，晷面中间插着一根铜针。在太阳的照射下，铜针的影子随着太阳的移动在晷面上慢慢地移动。移到哪个刻度上，就是到了哪个时辰。这样，计算时间就准确多了。

但是到了阴天和夜晚，日晷就起不了作用了。后来，人们又用滴水、漏沙的方法计时，发明了一种新的计时工具——铜壶滴漏。

铜壶滴漏又叫"漏刻"、"刻漏"、"壶漏"、"漏壶"。最早的漏壶用一只铜壶盛水，壶底有一个小洞，壶中插一根刻有刻度的标杆，水从小洞滴出后，人们根据水位降低后标杆上的刻度来判断时

月壶、星壶的下面各有一个滴水的铜嘴，授水壶内有一个标尺。水从日壶滴入月壶，再到星壶，最后滴入授水壶。授水壶内的水越来越多，标尺受到水的浮力作用逐渐上升，人们通过标尺浮出水面的刻度，就可以知道时间了。漏壶的级数越多，计时就越准确。现在，在北京的中国历史博物馆和故宫博物院里还分别保存着元代和清代的四级漏壶。

日晷和铜壶滴漏是中国古人聪明才智的结晶，它们不仅告诉了我们古人计时的方法，也留下了中国古代科学技术发展的宝贵资料。

间。这种漏壶计时的准确性仍然比较差。

漏壶历代相传，由单只逐渐发展成为后来四只一套的漏壶。人们把四只漏壶依次放在一个四级木架上，上面的一只叫日壶，下面的三只分别叫月壶、星壶、授水壶。日壶、

1、2. 日晷
   The sundial
3. 北京故宫铜壶滴漏
   The copper kettle clepsydra in the Palace Museum in Beijing

Sundial and
Copper Kettle Clepsydra

Today, all kinds of clocks and watches give people the convenience for calculation of time. But in ancient China without clocks and watches, how did people calculate the time?

Initially, most people identified the time according to the position of the sun, the moon and stars in the sky. However, such method was not very accurate. Afterwards, by watching the sun, someone designed a kind of time-counter to identify the time, i.e. the sundial. In the Qin and Han dynasties, the sundial had become popular among people. The sundial is a round plate, whose surface is carved with 12 degrees indicating 12 hours, i.e. *zi, chou, yin, mou, chen, si, wu, wei, shen, you, xu* and *hai*, with a copper needle erected in the center of the sundial's surface. Under the sun, the shadow of the copper needle moves slowly on the surface with the movement of the sun, that is, when the shadow of the copper needle moves to a certain degree, it is the time that the degree indicates. In this way, the calculation of time is more accurate.

But when it is cloudy or at night, the sundial doesn't function. Later, some people resorted to the method of dropping water or sand to calculate the time, and thereby invented a new tool "the copper kettle clepsydra".

The copper kettle clepsydra was also called "clepsydra" or "kettle clepsydra". The earliest clepsydra was a copper pot holding water with a small hole at the bottom and a pole with scales inserting in the center. When the water dropped through the small hole, people would determine the time by the scale on the pole with the decline of the water level. However, the accuracy of this method of calculating the time through clepsydra was still unsatisfactory.

As the clepsydra was passed on from generation to generation, it gradually evolved into a set of four pots, which were placed in order on a four-level wooden stand. The one on the highest level is called "the Sun Pot", and the other three pots below it are named "the Moon Pot", "the Star Pot" and "the Water-receiving Pot" respectively. The Sun Pot, the Moon Pot and the Star Pot all have a hole at the bottom so that water can drop through it and the Water-receiving Pot has a gauge inside. The water drops from the Sun Pot into the Moon Pot and then into the Star Pot and finally into the Water-receiving Pot. As more and more water drops into the Water-receiving Pot, the gauge gradually rises due to the buoyancy of water. Thus people could identify the time by observing the very scale of the gauge emerging above the water. The more levels a clepsydra has, the more accurate it is to calculate the time. Now, the four-level clepsydra of the Yuan and Qing dynasties are preserved respectively in the Museum of Chinese History and the Palace Museum in Beijing for the exhibition.

The sundial and copper kettle clepsydra are the crystallization of the ancient Chinese' wisdom and creativity. They not only show us how the ancient Chinese calculated time, but also provide precious materials for research on the development of science and technology in ancient China.

1
   2

1. 日晷
   The sundial
2. 铜壶滴漏
   The copper kettle clepsydra

算盘 和珠算

Abacus and Abacus Calculation

算盘是中国人在长期使用算筹的基础上发明的。古时候，人们用小木棍进行计算，这些小木棍叫"算筹"，用"算筹"作为工具进行的计算叫"筹算"。后来，随着生产的发展，需要计算的数目越来越大，用小木棍计算受到了限制，于是，人们又发明了更先进的计算器——算盘。

算盘是长方形的，四周是木框，里面固定着一根根小木棍，每根木棍代表一位，小木棍上穿着木珠，中间有一根横梁把算盘分成两部分：每根木棍的上半部有两个珠子，每个珠子代表五；下半部有五个珠子，每个珠子代表一。

随着算盘的使用，人们总结出许多计算口诀，加上熟练的手指技巧，使计算的速度大大快于笔算。这种用算盘计算的方法，叫珠算。到了明代，珠算已能进行加减乘除的运算，广泛用于计算物体的重量、数量、面积、体积等。

由于算盘制作简单，价格便宜，珠算口诀便于记忆，运算又简便，所以算盘曾在中国被广泛使用。算盘后来陆续流传到了日本、朝鲜等周边国家和地区。

Abacus and Abacus Calculation

The abacus was invented on the basis of Counting Rod that Chinese had used for a long period. In ancient times, people used small rods to count numbers. The small rod was called "Counting Rod" and calculation using counting rods was called "Rod Counting". Later, with the development of productivity, the number requiring calculation was bigger and bigger, and the limitation of calculation with rods was more and more apparent. Thereby, some people invented a kind of more advanced counter: the abacus.

The abacus is rectangular with wooden frame on the four sides and small rods fixed inside, each one representing one digit. The rods are strung with wooden beads, and a girder across the middle separates the abacus into two parts: the upper part, in which each rod has two beads, each representing the number "five"; and the lower part, in which each rod has five beads, each representing the number "one".

With the use of the abacus, people had summarized many abacus rules. Together with proficient digital skills, the rules had made the calculating speed increase greatly. By the time of the Ming Dynasty (1368—1644), people could use the abacus to deal with addition, subtraction, multiplication and division, and thus abacus calculation was widely used in calculating weight, amount, space and volume of an object.

Since the abacus is inexpensive and simple to make, it is easy to remember abacus rules, and the abacus calculation is so simple

and convenient that the abacus is widely used in China. Afterwards, the abacus was gradually introduced to Japan and Korea as well as circumjacent countries and regions.

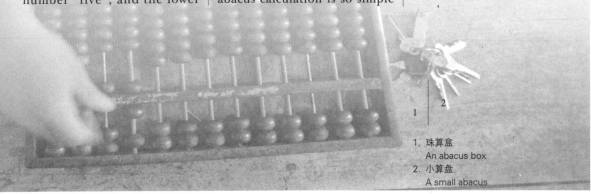

1. 珠算盒
An abacus box
2. 小算盘
A small abacus

中国传统艺术
Traditional Chinese Art

概 述

Introduction

中华民族是一个古老的民族，也是一个有深厚文化底蕴的民族。中国的传统艺术门类繁多、雅俗共赏，从悠扬动人的民间音乐到细腻缠绵的地方戏曲，从疏洁淡雅的水墨画到刚柔并济的书法，无不闪烁着智慧之光，令世人赞叹不已。

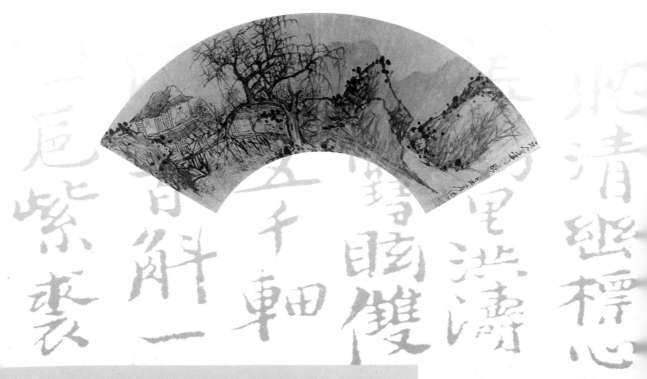

Introduction

China, a nation of long history with profound culture, inherited and developed a great variety of traditional art forms which suit both refined and popular tastes. From the melodious and pleasant folk music to the elaborate and touching local dramas, from the simple but elegant inkwash painting to the flexible and powerful calligraphy, one can always discern the light of sparkling wisdom. Traditional Chinese arts have tremendously impressed the world.

1. 篆刻：大江东去……
   Seal cutting: *dajing dongqu* (The mighty river flows eastward ...)
2. 篆刻：水滴石穿
   Seal cutting: *shuidi shichuan* (Dropping water wears a stone.)
3. 书画扇面
   Fan painting and calligraphy
4. 秦华阳丞印封泥
   The Seal Earth of the Qin Dynasty
5. 京剧
   Beijing Opera

1	4
2	
3	5

民乐

Folk Music

中国民乐具有浓郁的民族特色，是中华文化宝库中的瑰宝。

中国在原始社会时就已经有了乐器。中国民族乐器种类繁多，可分为吹、拉、弹、打四大类。吹的有箫、笛子、唢呐等；拉的有二胡、京胡、板胡等；弹的有古筝、古琴①、琵琶等；打的有锣、鼓等。

千百年来，中国音乐家创造了不少优秀的曲目，遗憾的是有很多曲目没能保留下来，流传至今的著名曲目有：《十面埋伏》、《阳春白雪》、《百鸟朝凤》、《广陵散》、《梅花三弄》、《春江花月夜》、《二泉映月》、《雨打芭蕉》、《步步高》、《旱天雷》等。这些名曲现已广泛流传于海内外，有的还在国际舞台演奏时获得了大奖，如《百鸟朝凤》曾在第四届世界青年联欢会上，荣获民间音乐比赛二等奖。

中国民乐以独特的魅力受到中国人民的喜爱。在中国，几乎每个地区都有民乐团，有的还是民间音乐爱好者自发组织的。中国民乐团经常接受邀请，到世界各国访问演出。最近几年，每到春节，中国的民乐团都应邀到著名的音乐之都维也纳访问，并在举世闻名的金色大厅演奏优秀的中国民族乐曲。这些优美动听的乐曲，深深地打动了当地的听众。中国的民乐受到了世界各国人民的欢迎。

Chinese folk music, with strong nationalistic features, is a treasure of Chinese culture.

As early as in the primitive times, Chinese people began to use musical instruments, which evolved today into four main types categorized by the way they are played. The first type is wind instrument, as shown in *xiao* (a vertical bamboo flute), flute, *suona* horn, etc. The second type is string instrument, represented by *urheen*, *jinghu* (a two-string musical instrument similar to *urheen*), *banhu* fiddle, etc. The third type is also string instrument, but played unconventionally by striking the strings with fingers, represented by *guzheng* (a Chinese zither with 25 strings), *guqin*, *pipa* (a plucked string musical instrument), etc. The fourth type is percussion instrument, as seen usually in gong, drum, etc.

For centuries, Chinese musicians have created numerous excellent songs and lyrics, but, unfortunately, many were lost. The extant melodies include "The Ambush on All Sides", "Spring Snow", "Hundred Birds Worshipping the Phoenix", "Guangling Verse", "Three Variations on Plum Blossom", "Spring River Moon Night", "The Moon Reflected on the Erquan Spring",

Folk Music

"Rain Pattering at Plantain Leaves", "Higher Step by Step", "A Thunder in the Dry Season", etc. Those well-known melodies are often performed at home and abroad, and some have won international awards. "Hundred Birds Worshipping the Phoenix", for example, won the second prize in the folk music contest, at the Fourth World Youth Festival.

▶ 注解 Note

① 古琴又叫七弦琴、丝桐等，是中国最古老的弹拨乐器，已有3 000多年的历史。琴体由面板和底板胶合而成，形狭长。古琴演奏形式丰富，音色含蓄、深沉。

Guqin, also named seven-stringed *qin* or *sitong*, etc., with a history of over 3 000 years, is the oldest string instrument in China. Its long narrow body is made of two pieces of boards at the top and with the bottom glued together. *Guqin* can be played in many forms, and can produce a deep, restrained sound.

Chinese people love folk music for its unique charm. In China, almost every region has its own folk music troupes, some of which are self-organized by folk music fans. Chinese folk music troupes are often invited to perform internationally. In recent years, they have been invited to visit Vienna—the world music capital, and perform in the famous Golden Hall during the Chinese Spring Festival. The pleasant melodies not only impress the local audiences, but also win international popularity.

1	2
	3

1. 吹箫
   Playing *xiao*
2. 民乐队
   Folk music *ensemble*
3. 琵琶
   Pipa

京剧

Beijing Opera

京剧是中国流行最广、影响最大的一个剧种，有近200年的历史。京剧在形成过程中，吸收了许多地方戏的精华，又受到北京方言和风俗习惯的影响。京剧虽然诞生在北京，但不仅仅是北京的地方戏，中国各地都有演出京剧的剧团。

京剧是一种唱、念、做、打并重的艺术。唱，指按照一定的曲调演唱。念，是剧中角色的对话和独白。做，指动作和表情的表演。打，是用舞蹈化的武术表演的搏斗。

在长期的发展过程中，京剧形成了一套虚拟表演动作。如：一

只桨可以代表一条船；一条马鞭可以代表一匹马；演员不需要任何道具，能表现出上楼、下楼、开门、关门等动作。这些动作虽经过了夸张，但是能给观众既真实又优美的感觉。

京剧演员分生、旦、净、丑四个行当。"生"所扮演的是男性人物，根据角色年龄、身份的不同，又分老生、小生和武生。著名演员有马连良、周信芳、叶盛兰、盖叫天、李少春等。"旦"所扮演的都是女性人物，又分青衣、花旦、武旦、老旦。最著名的旦角演员有20世纪20年代出现的四大名旦——梅兰芳、程砚秋、尚小云、荀慧生。"净"扮演的是性格豪爽的男性，特征是要在脸上勾画花脸，所以也叫"花脸"，著名花脸演员有裘盛戎、袁世海等。"丑"扮演

的是幽默机智或阴险狡猾的男性，著名丑角演员有萧长华、马富禄等。

京剧的化妆也很有特点。"生"、"旦"的化妆要"描眉"、"吊眉"、"画眼圈"，"净"、"丑"的化妆要根据京剧的脸谱①勾画，比如忠勇的人要画红脸，奸诈的人要画白脸。

京剧的剧目很多，据说有3 800出。目前上演的主要有传统剧、新编历史剧和现代戏三大类。

京剧作为中国民族戏曲的精华，在国内外都有很大的影响。许多外国人专门到中国来学唱京剧。许多京剧表演艺术

家也曾到世界各地访问演出，受到了各国人民的喜爱。

1	3
2	

1. 京剧演员在化妆
   A performer of Beijing Opera is putting on makeup.
2. 孙悟空
   The Monkey King
3. 净
   Jing (painted-face role)

Beijing Opera

Beijing Opera is the most popular and influential opera in China with a history of almost 200 years. In the course of its formation, it assimilated the best from many other local operas and was affected by Beijing local dialect and customs. Though Beijing Opera originated from Beijing, it is not a localized opera exclusive to Beijing only. Beijing opera troupes can be found in most regions of China.

Beijing Opera combines singing, recital, acting and acrobatic fighting. Singing refers to the singing according to certain tunes. Recital refers to monologues by performers and dialogues between performers. Acting refers to body movements and facial expressions. Acrobatic fighting refers to choreographed martial art.

In the long term of development, Beijing Opera has formed a number of fictitious props. For instance, a pedal means a boat, a whip in the hand means

riding on a horse. Without any physical props involved, an actor may perform going upstairs or downstairs, opening or closing a door by mere gestures. Though rather exaggerated, those actions would, with their graceful movements, give audience a deep impression.

There are four main roles in Beijing Opera: *sheng*, *dan*, *jing* and *chou*. *Sheng* are the leading male actors, and are divided into *laosheng* who wear beards and represent old men, *xiaosheng* who represent young men, and *wusheng* who are acrobats playing military men and fighters. These roles usually wear no facial paintings. Famous actors playing this type of role include Ma Lianliang, Zhou Xinfang, Ye Shenglan, Gai Jiaotian and Li Shaochun. *Dan* are female roles.

注解 Note

① 戏曲中某些角色脸上画的各种图案，用来表现人物性格和特征。
Facial makeup refers to the various designs of lines and colored patches painted on the faces of certain opera characters. They follow traditionally fixed patterns for specific types to highlight the disposition and quality in the personages so that the audience may immediately know whether they are heroes or villains, whether they are kind or treacherous and wicked.

1
　　2

1. 生
   Sheng (male role)
2. 旦
   Dan (famale role)

Formerly, the term meant female impersonators. It is further divided into several categories. The most important category, *qingyi*, usually play respectable and decent ladies in elegant costumes. *Huadan* represent lively and clever young girls, usually in short costumes. *Wudan* usually play military or non-military women capable of martial arts. *Laodan* are the old ladies. Mei Lanfang, Cheng Yanqiu, Shang Xiaoyun and Xun Huisheng were the celebrated Four Major *Dan* Roles in the 1920s. *Jing*, mostly male, are the face-painted roles who represent warriors, heroes, statesmen, adventures and demons. Famous actors playing this role include Qiu Shengrong and Yuan Shihai. *Chou*, most of time, play roles of wit, alert and humor. It is these roles who keep the audience laughing and improvise quips at the right moments to ease tension in some serious plays. Renowned actors playing this role include Xiao Changhua and Ma Fulu.

Facial makeup in Beijing Opera has its own pattern. A *sheng* or a *dan* has to have his or her eyebrows painted in a way that they look slanted with the outer ends of eyebrows going upward, and their eyes circled with black color. As for a *jing* and *chou*, the pattern is in accordance with the disposition of the characters according to the rule of facial makeup in Beijing Opera. For example, a red face usually depicts the role's loyalty and bravery; while a white face symbolizes a sinister role's treachery and guile.

It is said that the complete Beijing Opera repertoire includes more than 3 800 plays. What are staged today are primarily three types, namely, traditional Beijing Operas, newly composed historical ones and modern ones.

Beijing Opera, as the national opera, enjoys a high reputation both inside and outside China. Many foreigners have come to China to learn Beijing Opera, while many Beijing Opera troupes and famous opera actors and actresses have frequently been invited to perform abroad and have been highly appreciated by foreign audiences.

地 方戏

Local Operas

中国由于地域辽阔，民族众多，各地的方言不同，除了京剧以外，还形成了丰富多彩的地方戏。

据统计，中国的地方戏有360多种，其中影响较大的有评剧、越剧、豫剧、黄梅戏、粤剧、川剧等。

评剧发源于河北唐山，流行于北京、天津和华北、东北各地。评剧具有活泼、自由、生活气息浓郁的特点，擅长表现现代生活。著名演员有小白玉霜、新凤霞等，代表剧目有《秦香莲》、《小女婿》、《刘巧儿》等。

越剧发源于浙江绍兴，流行于浙江、江苏、江西、安徽、上海等地。最初男女角色全部由男演员扮演，20世纪30年代变成全部由女演员扮演。越剧唱腔委婉、表演细腻，已成为仅次于京剧的一个大剧种。著名演员有袁雪芬、王文娟、徐玉兰等,代表剧目有《梁山伯与祝英台》、《红楼梦》等。

豫剧是河南省的地方戏,也叫河南梆子、河南高调,流行于河南及邻近各省。豫剧的声腔,有的高亢活泼,有的悲凉缠绵。传统剧目有650多出。著名演员有常香玉、马金凤、牛得草等,代表剧目有《花木兰》、《穆桂英挂帅》、《七品芝麻官》等。

黄梅戏是安徽省的地方戏,旧时称黄梅调,流行于安徽及江西、湖北的部分地区。黄梅戏载歌载舞,唱腔委婉动

听,表演朴实优美,生活气息浓厚。著名演员有严凤英、马兰等,代表剧目有《天仙配》、《女驸马》、《牛郎织女》等。

粤剧是广东省的地方戏,主要流行于广东、广西、福建南部一带。居住在东南亚、美洲、欧洲和大洋洲的华侨、

华人及港澳同胞也十分喜爱粤剧。粤剧用广东话演唱,形成了独特的风格。著名演员有红线女、马师曾等,代表剧目有《搜书院》、《关汉卿》等。

1	2
	3

1. 越剧:《穆桂英》
   Mu Guiying the Marshal (Yue Opera)
2. 越剧演员在化妆
   A Yue Opera performer is making up.
3. 川剧
   Sichuan Opera

Local Operas

China is a country with vast land and various nationalities. People in different regions speak different dialects. As a result, many local opera forms have appeared alongside Beijing Opera.

Statistics show that there are more than 360 types of local operas, of which the best-known are Pingju Opera, Yue or Shaoxing Opera, Yu or Henan Opera, Huangmei Opera, Guangdong Opera, and Sichuan Opera, etc.

Pingju Opera originated in Tangshan city, Hebei Province and is popular in Beijing, Tianjin, North and Northeast of China. Pingju Opera is lively, free in style and close to life. It is a perfect form to reflect the modern life. The best-known performers include Xiao Bai Yushuang and Xin Fengxia. The representative plays are *Qin Xianglian*, *Small Son-in-Law* and *Liu Qiao'er*, etc.

Yue or Shaoxing Opera origi-

1	3
2	4

1. 越剧:《梁祝》
   Butterfly Lovers (*Liang Zhu*)
   (Yue Opera)
2. 河南农村豫剧演员
   Henan Opera performers from the
   country of Henan Province
3. 秦腔
   Qin Opera
4. 越剧
   Yue Opera

Ma Lan. The representative plays are *Marrying a Fairy, Emperor's Female Son-in-Law, The Cowherd and the Girl Weaver*, etc.

Guangdong Opera is the local opera form of Guangdong Province and is also popular in Guangxi Province and southern Fujian Province. Overseas Chinese in Southeast Asia, America, Europe and Oceania, and the people of Hong Kong and Macao SARs are also very fond of this type of local opera. Guangdong Opera is sung with the Cantonese dialect and is rather unique in its singing style. The best-known performers include Hong Xiannü and Ma Shizeng. The representative plays are *Searching the Study, Guan Hanqing*, etc.

nated in Shaoxing of Zhejiang Province and is popular in Zhejiang, Jiangsu, Jiangxi, Anhui provinces and Shanghai. At first, all of the performers were male. But since the 1930s, all the roles were played by female performers. The tunes of this opera are mild and roundabout, and the acting is meticulous. It became the second largest opera form next to Beijing Opera. Renowned performers include Yuan Xuefen, Wang Wenjuan and Xu Yulan. The representative plays are *Butterfly Lovers* (or *Liang Shanbo and Zhu Yingtai*), *A Dream of Red Mansions*, etc.

Yu or Henan Opera is the local opera of Henan Province and prevalent in Henan and neighboring areas. Yu Opera is played with a bright, loud sound, alternating with sorrowful tone. There are about 650 traditional plays, of which *Hua Mulan, Mu Guiying Takes Command, A Petty Official*, etc. are the most famous. Well-known performers include

Chang Xiangyu, Ma Jinfeng and Niu Decao.

Huangmei Opera is the local opera of Anhui Province and is popular in Anhui and Jiangxi provinces, and part of Hubei Province. This opera is characterized by dancing while singing. Its tunes are mild and pleasant, and its movements are natural and graceful. It is also very close to real life. Renowned performers include Yan Fengying and

曲艺

Quyi (Folk Art)

"曲艺"是各种说唱艺术的总称，是由古代民间的口头文学和说唱艺术发展演变形成的。它的主要艺术手段是用带有表演动作的说和唱来叙述故事、表达思想感情、反映社会生活。

现在流行于中国的曲艺种类有300多个，包括相声、大鼓①、快板②、二人转③、弹词④、双簧⑤等。其中最为人们所喜闻乐见的曲艺形式是相声。

中国的相声是一种笑的艺术，是以语言为主要表演手段的一种喜剧性曲艺艺术，它是在古代笑话和民间笑话的基础上发展起来的。现代的相声，是100多年前在北京和天津地区产生的。

相声表演的艺术手段是说、学、逗、唱。相声的笑料来自那些巧妙安排在相声中的"包袱"。"包袱"是相声演员的行话，意思是把可笑的东西像包东西一样一件一件地包在包袱里，到了一定的时候，突然抖出里面的东西，既出乎观众的意料，又合情合理，使观众忍不住大笑起来。

相声说的内容，大多数是我们生活中的事情，也有的是根据民间笑话、历史人物、历史故事和语言文字游戏编写的。表演相声所用的道具非常简单，一张桌子、一把扇子或一块手绢就可以了。一个人说的叫单口相声，两个人说的叫对口相声，三个人或多人合说的叫群口相声。其中，最常见的是对口相声。它由两个演员采用问答的方式表演，一个逗，另一个捧。

著名的相声演员有马三立、侯宝林、马季、姜昆等。在一代一代相声艺人的努力下，相声已成为雅俗共赏的全国性艺术形式。

Quyi

(Folk Art)

Quyi is a general term for all kinds of talking and singing arts. It derived from oral literature, the talking and singing performances of ancient people. It refers primarily to storytelling accentuated by body movements to tell stories, express feelings and reflect the social conditions.

There are still about 300 types of *quyi* being performed in China, including comic dialogue, *dagu*, *kuaiban*, *errenzhuan*, *tanci*, *shuanghuang*. Of these, the most popular is comic dialogue.

Comic dialogue is a kind of folk art with the "comic" dialogue as the main form of performance. It evolved on the basis of ancient folk jokes. Comic dialogue of today originated in Beijing and Tianjin over a century ago.

Comic dialogue realizes its artistic presentation by means of talking, imitating, teasing and singing. The jokes are skillfully hidden in the *baofu*, or "package", a jargon used by the comic dialogue performers. When the right time comes, they are suddenly spilled out, just like the funny stuffs being tossed out of a carefully wrapped package, so unexpectedly, but logically with a second thought, causing the audiences to laugh.

Most of the comic dialogue stories come from daily life. Others are based on folk jokes, historic legends, events, and word games. The stage props is quite simple, a table, a fan, or a handkerchief will be adequate. It could be performed either by one person or two, or even by a group. However, normally, a comic dialogue is performed by two people. The usual pattern is that one is a straight man that asks questions and the other gives funny answers.

The best-known comic dialogue performers are Ma Sanli, Hou Baolin, Ma Ji, Jiang Kun, etc. With the concerted effort of performers generation after generation, comic dialogue has become a national entertainment loved by highbrows and lowbrows alike.

▶ 注解 Notes

① 以唱为主，说唱故事，用鼓、板、三弦伴奏。
Versified storytelling accompanied by drum and other instruments.

② 用有韵律的语言讲故事，说时用竹板伴奏，节奏较快。
Telling stories to the rhythm created by bamboo castanets.

③ 流行于中国的东北地区。用板胡、唢呐等乐器伴奏，一般由两人边舞蹈边说唱故事。
It consists of two people — one male and one female — singing and dancing, as well as telling jokes, usually accompanied by *banhu* or *suona* horn.

④ 流行于中国南方各地，有说有唱，用三弦伴奏，或再加琵琶陪衬。
Storytelling accompanied by *sanxian* fiddle or *pipa* fiddle.

⑤ 一个人表演动作，一个人藏在后面或说或唱，互相配合。
One man acting in the front and another hidden behind talking or singing.

1
2

1. 曲艺表演
   Folk art performance
2. 双簧
   Shuanghuang

围棋

The Game of Go

1
2
3

1. 围棋棋子和棋盘
   Go pieces and the board of the game of go
2. 观棋图
   Watching the Go Play
3. 弈棋图
   Playing the Game of Go

围棋起源于中国，是世界上最古老的棋类。

围棋的棋盘面由纵横的19条交叉线组成，构成361个交叉点，棋子就下在这些交叉点上。围棋棋子分黑白两色，各有180枚。围棋对弈（yì），千变万化，紧张激烈。双方动用各种技术、战术攻击对方，非常富有战斗性。由于围棋奥妙无穷，古人曾经夸张地说，只有神仙才能发明它。

围棋是一种智力型运动，学围棋既可锻炼提高人们的逻辑思维能力，又能陶冶性情，培养人们顽强、冷静、沉着的性格。因此，它越来越受到现代人的欢迎。

隋唐时期，围棋传到日本，19世纪时又传到欧洲。现在，世界上已有40多个国家和地区开展了围棋运动。其中，以中国、日本、韩国的围棋运动水平最高。中国的围棋选手聂卫平、马晓春等，都是国际著名的选手。围棋已发展成为一种重要的国际体育竞赛项目。

The Game of

Go

观棋

ic. At the same time, it can also cultivate temperament, build up character of perseverance and calmness. Therefore, go has become more and more popular with young people.

Go was introduced into Japan during the Sui (581—618) and Tang (618—907) dynasties and into Europe in the 19th century. Today, it has spread to more than 40 countries and regions. Players from China, Japan and The Republic of Korea are of the highest skill in the world, and Chinese competitors like Nie Weiping and Ma Xiaochun enjoy international fame. Go has been developed into a very important international contest.

The game of go, originated in China, is the earliest form of chess in the world.

The board of go consists of a grid 19 by 19 resulting in, 361 intersections. The pieces are placed on the intersections in such a way as to gradually command more territory by surrounding and eliminating the opposition. Each of the two sides, one with black pieces and the other with white pieces, possesses 180 of them. It is an exciting and intense competition and the situation on the board keeps changing and unpredictable. Players have to resort to all sorts of tactics in order to defeat the opponent. As the tactics used in the go are so variable and profound, the ancient Chinese said in an exaggerated manner that only deities can invent such a game.

Playing go exercises the brain and enhances one's sense of log-

中国 象棋

The Chinese Chess

中国象棋，古代叫"象戏"，大约起源于战国时代，是根据春秋战国时两军对垒的战阵创造的战斗游戏。唐朝时，象棋已很普及。到了宋代，中国象棋基本定型，并且在全国流行。

中国象棋的棋盘是正方形的，棋盘的中间有一条"界河"，把对垒的双方隔在两边。两边画有交叉线的地方共有90个交叉点，棋子就摆在这些交叉点上。中国象棋共有32枚棋子，分为黑红两组，下棋的双方各用一组，每组各有一帅（将）、两士、两相（象）、两马、两车、两炮、五兵（卒）。两人对局时，按照规定的位置将各自的棋子摆好，红方先走，然后轮流下棋子。各种棋子走法不同，如：马走日字，相走田字，车可以"横冲直撞"，兵只可前行……最后以把对方将[①](jiāng)死为胜，不分胜负为和棋。

1949年以后，中国象棋被列入全国正式体育比赛项目。20世纪70年代后，中国象棋开始走出亚洲，走向世界。现在，世界上已经有40多个国家和地区建立了中国象棋组织。

1 | 2
| 3

1. 中国象棋棋盘
   The board of Chinese chess
2. 中国象棋棋子
   The piece of Chinese chess
3. 下象棋
   Playing Chinese chess

The Chinese Chess

The Chinese chess, originated from the Warring States Period, is a game created on the basis of two confronting military formations of that period. By the time of the Tang Dynasty (618—907), it had already become very popular, with its style of play basically fixed by the Song Dynasty (960—1279).

The chessboard is square in shape, with a border called the Chuhe River in the middle that separates the two sides. On either side, vertical and horizontal lines are drawn forming 90 intersections, where pieces are placed. There are altogether 32 pieces, which are divided into two groups. Characters engraved in chessmen are painted red or black respectively to represent the two sides. Each side has a Marshal (King), two Mandarins (Assistants), two Elephants, two Horses, two Chariots, two Cannons and five Soldiers, each with its designated move. At the start of play, all the chessmen must be placed in fixed positions. The red side moves first, then the players take alternate turns. Different pieces have different rules to move, for example, the Horse moves one point orthogonally followed by one point outward-diagonally, the Elephant moves exactly two points diagonally, the Chariot moves any number of points either horizontally or vertically but not diagonally, etc. When the Marshal is checked and there is no way to save him, that side is lost, but sometimes there can be a stalemate.

Since 1949, Chinese chess has been listed as an event in the national sport games. In the 1970s, Chinese chess players began to promote the game abroad. Today, more than 40 countries and regions have established their own Chinese chess clubs.

▶ 注解 Note

① 将：下象棋时攻击对方的"将"或"帅"。如把对方的"帅"或"将"攻下，即获胜。
In Chinese chess, one player tries to make the other player's Marshal unmovable. When the Marshal is checked and there is no way to save him, that side is lost.

汉字

Chinese Characters

汉字是世界上最古老的文字之一，也是世界上使用人数最多的文字。汉字的数量很多，总数约60 000个，其中常用字约6 000个。汉字历史悠久，它起源于记事图画，目前发现的最古老的汉字，是距今3 400多年前的甲骨文，它们已是很成熟的文字。

汉字从古到今形体发生了很大的变化，由图形变为由笔画构成的方块形符号，所以汉字一般也叫"方块字"，经历了甲骨文、金文、小篆①、隶书②、楷书③等字体的演变。

汉字的造字方法，主要有以下四种：

象形：是指画出事物形状的造字法。如："月"，"月"写起来像一个弯弯的月亮。

指事：在象形字上加指事符号，或完全用符号组成字的造字法。如："刃"，在刀锋上加一点儿，指出这个位置就是刀刃所在。

会意：把两个或两个以上的符号组合起来，表示一个新的意义的造字法。如"明"，是由"日"和"月"组成，太阳和月亮在一起，怎么能不明呢。

形声：用形旁和声旁组成新字。形旁，是表示字的意义；声旁，是表示字的读音。如："湖"字，"水"是形旁，告诉大家，这是一个与水有关的字，"胡"是声旁，告诉大家，这个字的读音和"胡"一致。

千百年来，中国人都是用繁体字来书写，但是，笔画繁多的繁体字，难认、难记，也难于书写。1949年以后，为了普及教育的需要，中国政府统一对汉字进行了较大规模的简化工作，先后有2 000多个繁体字被简化字取代。现在，简化字是联合国的工作文字之一。

历史上，汉字曾被朝鲜、日本、越南等国家长期借用，汉字正以其旺盛的生命力和独特的魅力走向世界。

▶ 注解 Notes

① 小篆是秦朝使用的标准字体。特点是字体呈长方形，笔画横平竖直，讲究上紧下松、平衡对称。
Xiaozhuan was the standard script of the Qin Dynasty (221BC—206 BC). This script, often used in seals, is translated into English as "the seal character". A passage written in *xiaozhuan* appears as a balanced and wellspaced series of neat columns and rows of equal squares.

② 隶书是汉代使用的标准字体，是汉字演变史上的一个转折点，奠定了楷书的基础。隶书结构扁平、工整、精巧。
Lishu was the standard script of the Han Dynasty (206 BC—220 AD). Being the turning point of Chinese character evolvement history, it established the foundation of *kaishu*.

③ 楷书，也叫真书、正书，产生于汉末。因其形体方正，可作楷模而故名，一直通行至今。
Kaishu, also called *zhenshu* and *zhengshu*, appeared in the late Han Dynasty, and has been in use till now.

Chinese Characters

The Chinese characters constitute one of mankind's oldest systems of writing, and have the most users in the world. There are numerous Chinese characters, totaling about 60 000, with about 6 000 basic ones. Chinese characters have a long history. It derived from the pictorial recording of events, known as hieroglyph. The earliest Chinese characters discovered up to now are *jiaguwen* (ancient Chinese characters inscribed on tortoise shells or animal bones), dating back 3 400 years, which were already mature characters.

Chinese characters have undergone tremendous changes over the ages. From the earliest form of hieroglyph to the more advanced symbol character composed of strokes, it has experienced a process of *jiaguwen*, *jinwen* (ancient language used in inscriptions on ancient bronze objects), *xiaozhuan* (small seal character), *lishu* (official script), and *kaishu* (regular script).

There are mainly four ways of creating a word as follows:

Hieroglyph refers to the method by drawing the profile of the involved subject, such as 月 which looks like a curve moon.

Self-explanatory characters are made up by adding self-explanatory symbols on pictographs, or totally made up of symbols, such as 刃 (blade), which is made up by adding a point on the cutting edge of a knife, pointing out the position of the blade.

Associative compounds are combination of two or more symbols to represent a new character with a new meaning. For instance, the character 明 (bright) is composed by 日 (sun) and 月 (moon). Definitely, it will be bright when the sun and the moon appear in the same place.

Pictophonetic method is a word-formation method combining one element of a character indicating meaning and the other, pronunciation, into a new word. Form element indicates the word's meaning and characteristic. Phonetic element indicates the pronunciation of the word. For example, 湖 (lake) is composed of three dots indicating water, and 胡 indicating the pronunciation.

For thousands of years, Chinese people had been writing in Complex Chinese Characters (Traditional Chinese). However, the Complex Chinese Characters are difficult to identify, memorize and write due to their complicated strokes. From 1949, for the sake of the popularization of education, the Chinese government simplified the Chinese Characters on a large scale. There were more than 2 000 Complex Chinese Characters that were simplified to today's appearance. Nowadays the Simplified Chinese Character is one of the official characters used by the UN.

In history, Chinese characters were borrowed by Korea, Japan, and Vietnam for a long time. It has been borne out that Chinese characters are of vigorous vitality.

1	2
	3

1. 楷书千字文
   Thousand-Character Classic in regular script
2. 象形文字：月
   Pictography: *yue* (moon)
3. 象形文字：雨
   Pictography: *yu* (rain)

书法

Calligraphy

书法是中国传统的汉字书写艺术，经过千百年的创作和发展，已成为一门风格独特的艺术。

常见的书法字体有篆书、隶书、楷书、草书和行书。篆书是秦代的代表字体；隶书是汉代的通行字体；楷书由隶书发展而来；草书是隶书和楷书的快写体；行书是介于楷书、草书之间的字体，它既不像楷书那么工整，也不像草书那么难认，是一种最常用、最方便的手写体。

中国历史上出现了许多著名的书法家，如：王羲之[1]、欧阳询[2]、颜真卿[3]、柳公权[4]、赵孟頫[5]等。他们经过多年的勤学苦练，形成了不同的风格和流派，使中国的书法艺术达到了很高的水平。

书法的书写工具，是被人们称为"文房四宝"的笔、墨、纸、砚。学书法，首先要学会使用毛笔，初学的人应该先从楷书学起。

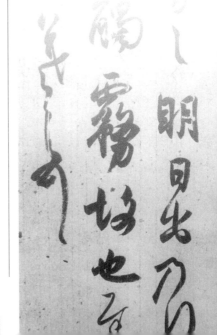

1	3
2	

1. 书法
   Calligraphy
2. 王羲之草书
   The cursive script of Wang Xizhi
3. 毛笔
   Chinese brushes

Calligraphy

Calligraphy is the traditional art of writing Chinese characters. After centuries of creation and evolution, calligraphy has become a unique form of art.

Chinese scripts are generally divided into five categories: the seal script (*zhuan*), the official script (*li*), the regular script (*kai*), the cursive hand (*cao*) and the running hand (*xing*). The seal script was the representative script of the Qin Dynasty (221BC—206 BC). The official script was popularly used in the Han Dynasty (206 BC—220 AD). The regular script was the result of development of the official script. The cursive hand is a fast way of writing the regular and official scripts. The running hand is the script between the regular and cursive. Neither as neat as the former nor as difficult to recognize as the latter, it is the most commonly used, and is the easiest way of handwriting.

There have been many famous calligraphers, such as Wang Xizhi, Ouyang Xun, Yan Zhenqing, Liu Gongquan and Zhao Mengfu, to name but a few. Each, after years of hard practice, has formed a unique calligraphic style, elevating the Chinese calligraphy into a higher level.

Chinese brush, ink stick, paper and ink stone are the necessary tools and materials for writing and painting and have always been named collectively as the "Four Treasures of the Study". To learn calligraphy, one first has to learn how to use a Chinese brush. Beginners should start by copying the regular script.

注解 Notes

① 王羲之（303—361 或 321—379），东晋著名书法家，被誉为"书圣"。
Wang Xizhi (303—361 or 321—379) was a famous calligrapher of the Eastern Jin Dynasty and enjoyed the reputation of "the saint of calligraphy".

② 欧阳询（557—641），字信本，唐代著名书法家，被称之为唐人楷书第一。
Ouyang Xun (557—641), with personal name as Xinben, was a famous calligrapher of the Tang Dynasty, called "the regular script top one of the Tang Dynasty".

③ 颜真卿（709—785），字清臣，唐代著名书法家。他彻底摆脱了初唐的风范，创造了新的书法风气。
Yan Zhenqing (709—785), with the personal name as Qingchen, was a famous calligrapher of the Tang Dynasty. He totally got rid of the early Tang Dynasty writing style and created a new calligraphy style.

④ 柳公权（778—865），字诚悬，唐代著名书法家。书法风格自成一体，与颜真卿齐名，人称"颜柳"。
Liu Gongquan (778—865), with the personal name of Chengxuan, was a famous calligrapher of the Tang Dynasty. He was famous for his unique script equally with Yan Zhenqing and they were called "Yan & Liu".

⑤ 赵孟頫（1254—1322），号松雪，别号欧波，元代著名书画家，在绘画史、书法史上，都占有重要的地位。
Zhao Mengfu (1254—1322), with the personal name of Songxue or Oubo, was a famous calligrapher and painter of the Yuan Dynasty.

篆刻

Seal Cutting

篆刻，就是以刀代笔，在印材上按照已经写好的书法或画好的图像，进行刻写。它是中国的书法和雕刻相结合的独有的一门传统工艺美术，具有实用与欣赏的双重价值。

篆刻产生的艺术品叫印章。印章的文字刻成凸状的称为"阳文"；刻成凹状的称为"阴文"。在印面左侧面上刻制作者姓名、治印年月等，叫做刻"边款"，边款多用阴文。

印章最初仅是一种"信物"和"权力"的象征，到了唐代才由实用品转变成为一种艺术品。篆刻艺术形成于宋元年间，兴盛于明末清初。这期间，出现了许多篆刻家和篆刻流派。著名的篆刻艺术家有"篆刻之祖"文彭① 及何震②、丁敬③、邓石如④、齐白石⑤等。

篆刻最常用的字体是篆字。此外，还有隶书、楷书、行书等。篆刻的材料有水晶、玉、金属、兽角、象牙、竹、木、石料等。其中，使用最广泛的是石料。最受篆刻家喜爱的石料有青田石、寿山石、昌化石、巴林石等。

在当今的中国，篆刻艺术受到各界的重视，也受到了广大青少年的喜爱。

Seal Cutting

Seal cutting refers to the art of carving on a block of certain material following a diagram of calligraphy or painting already drawn on it. A unique form of traditional art in China, it is of both practical and appreciative functions.

A block thus carved is called a seal. Characters can be carved in relief or deep into the carving material. The latter is called intaglio. The edge face on the left of the seal normally show the name of the carver and the date of the carving mostly in intaglio.

At the very beginning, a seal was only used as a token of pledge or a symbol of power. It was not until the Tang Dynasty (618—907) that the seal was gradually transformed from a practical item into a piece of art. Seal cutting, as a new form of art, started in the Song (960—1279) and Yuan (1206—1368) dynasties and flourished in the late Ming Dynasty (1368—1644) and early Qing Dynasty (1644—1911). During this period, many carving artists and schools appeared. The renowned carving artists included Wen Peng, He Zhen, Ding Jing, Deng Shiru and Qi Baishi.

In seal cutting, seal style cutting is commonly used. Besides that, regular, official, running styles can also be seen. The seal itself can be made of crystal, jade, metal, animal horn, ivory, bamboo, wood, stone, etc. Stone is most extensively used, among which, Qingtian, Shoushan, Changhua and Balin seal stones are the most favorable.

In China, seal cutting is recognized by all circles and is popular today among young people.

▶ 注解 Notes

① 文彭（1498—1573），明代篆刻名家。
Wen Peng (1498—1573) was a famous seal cutting artist of the Ming Dynasty.

② 何震（？—1604左右），明代篆刻名家。
He Zhen (?—1604) was a famous seal cutting artist of the Ming Dynasty.

③ 丁敬（1695—1765），清代篆刻名家。
Ding Jing (1695—1765) was a famous seal cutting artist of the Qing Dynasty.

④ 邓石如（1743—1805），清代篆刻名家。
Deng Shiru (1743—1805) was a famous seal cutting artist of the Qing Dynasty.

⑤ 齐白石（1864—1957），现代著名篆刻家、书画家。
Qi Baishi (1864—1957) was a famous seal cutting artist, calligrapher and painter of modern times.

中国画

Traditional Chinese Painting

中国画又叫国画，它是用毛笔、墨及颜料，在宣纸或绢上画出的画。中国画与中医、京剧一起，被誉为中国的"三大国粹"。

中国画按内容分，主要有人物画、山水画、花鸟画三大类。

战国时，中国已经有了比较成熟的人物画，唐朝时达到了顶峰。著名的人物画家有顾恺之①、吴道子②等。

山水画是表现山川美景的画种。它产生于秦代，隋唐时成为独立的画种，宋代达到了很高的水平，工整富丽，佳作纷呈。著名的山水画家有李思训③、范宽④、唐寅⑤等。

花鸟画画的是自然界中的花卉、鸟兽、鱼虫。南北朝时出现了花鸟画，宋代走向

成熟。著名的花鸟画家有擅长画花鸟的朱耷⑥、擅长画竹子的郑燮⑦、擅长画鱼虾的齐白石等。

中国画按画法分，主要有工笔画和写意画。它不像西画家的素描，如实描写，而是重神韵、重意境，推崇"画中有诗"，比如徐悲鸿先生画马，对马的形态特征了然于心后，简单数笔，画出的马却要比真马更真、更美。再如写意画家齐白石先生在一幅画上，画两个小鸡在争食一条蚯蚓，互不相让，题曰："他日相呼"，意思是"两个小家伙现在不懂事，为一条小虫打得不可开交，他日长大了，手足情谊依然深厚，还是要相呼相唤的"，把小鸡完全拟人化了，寄寓了他对人生的感悟。总体而言，中国画画风往往气魄宏大，笔势流动，既有粗犷豪放的一面，又有细密瑰丽的一面，内容丰富博杂，形式多姿多彩。

一幅中国画作品，除了图画以外，还有诗文和印章。因此，中国画是诗、书、画、印相结合的艺术。它的艺术成就和民族风格早已受到世界人民的赞誉。中国画不仅能美化人们的生活，而且能给人们带来高雅的情趣和艺术享受。

1. 洛神赋图
   The Goddess of Luo River
2. 风雨归牧图
   Returning in the Storm After Herding
3. 清明上河图
   Along the River During the Ching Ming Festival
4. 仙山楼阁图
   The Pavillion in a Fairy Land

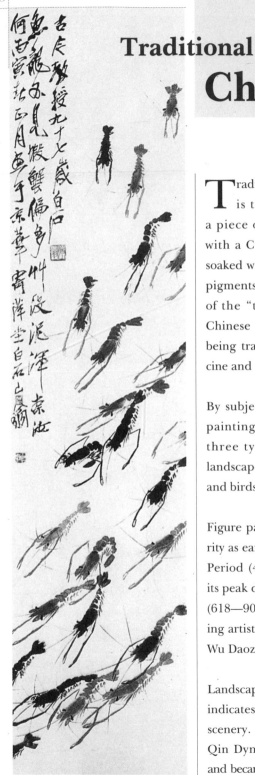

Traditional
Chinese Painting

Traditional Chinese painting is the art of painting on a piece of Xuan paper or silk with a Chinese brush that was soaked with black ink or colored pigments. It is regarded as one of the "three quintessence of Chinese culture", the other two being traditional Chinese medicine and Beijing Opera.

By subject, traditional Chinese painting can be classified into three types, figure painting, landscape painting, and flowers and birds painting.

Figure painting came into maturity as early as the Warring States Period (475—221) and reached its peak during the Tang Dynasty (618—907). Famous figure painting artists include Gu Kaizhi and Wu Daozi.

Landscape painting, as the name indicates, delineates the outside scenery. It first appeared in the Qin Dynasty (221BC—206 BC) and became an independent genre during the Sui (581—618) and Tang dynasties. By the time of the Song Dynasty (960—1279), it had reached a very high level. Representative artists of landscape painting include Li Sixun, Fan Kuan and Tang Yin.

Flowers and birds painting concentrates on the drawing of flowers, birds, animals, fishes, and insects, etc. in their natural state. It came into being in the Northern and Southern dynasties (420—589) and became a mature art during the Song Dynasty. Celebrated artists include Zhu Da, who excelled in execution of flowers and birds, Zheng Xie, who was good at bamboo, and Qi Baishi, who excelled in fish and shrimp.

By styles of brushwork, traditional Chinese painting can be categorized into "*gongbi*" (realistic painting characterized by fine brushwork and close attention to details) and "*xieyi*" (freehand brushwork aimed at catching the spirit of the object and expressing the author's impression or mood). Unlike Western sketches which focus on truthful regeneration of subject, traditional Chinese painting pays more attention to verve and artistic conception, canonizing the idea that painting should contain more meaning than what it depicts. For instance, when Xu Beihong began to draw horses, he would firstly have shape features in his mind, and then draw a painting of horses that were more beautiful and real than horses in real life in the simple brushwork. To take "*xieyi*" painter Qi Baishi as another example, in one of his paintings there were two chickens scrabbling for an earthworm. However, he named the painting "Say 'Hello' Afterwards", meaning that although the bubs were

not so sensitive that both of them scrabble for the same food, they would have deep friendly feelings and say "Hello" to each other afterwards. The whole personification of little chickens reflected Qi's comprehension of the whole life. In general, the style of traditional Chinese paintings is grandiose, containing ruggedness as well as detail and magnificence. In addition, its contents are rich with colorful forms.

In a finished works of traditional Chinese painting, inscriptions, poems, and stamps often come side by side. Therefore, traditional Chinese painting is an art form combining poetry, calligraphy, painting and seal carving. Its artistic achievement and national features have won recognition of the people all over the world. Thus, traditional Chinese painting brings decorous sentiment and artistic enjoyment for people.

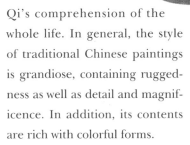

1	2
	3

1. 虾
   A painting of shrimps
2. 瑶台步月图
   A painting depicting ancient people admiring the moon at *Yaotai*
3. 布袋和尚图
   A painting of a monk

▶ 注解 Notes

① 顾恺之（约345—409），东晋著名画家。
Gu Kaizhi (c. 345—409) was a famous painter of the Eastern Jin Dynasty.

② 吴道子（约为8世纪前期人），唐代著名画家。他画的人物衣服的带子好像在飘动，被人们称赞为"吴带当风"。
Wu Daozi (c. early 8th century) was a famous painter of the Tang Dynasty. The belts of the clothes feel like waving by his painting.

③ 李思训（651—716），唐代著名画家。
Li Sixun (651—716) was a famous painter of the Tang Dynasty.

④ 范宽，具体生卒年月不详，宋代杰出画家。
Fan Kuan (? — ?) was a famous painter of the Song Dynasty.

⑤ 唐寅（1470—1523），字伯虎，明代著名画家。
Tang Yin or Tang Bohu (1470—1523) was a famous painter of the Ming Dynasty.

⑥ 朱耷（1626—1705），号八大山人，清初著名画家。
Zhu Da, or Bada Shanren (1626—1705) was a famous painter of the early Qing Dynasty.

⑦ 郑燮（1693—1765），号板桥，清代著名书画家。
Zheng Xie or Zheng Banqiao(1693—1765) was a famous painter of the Qing Dynasty.

中国文物

Chinese Cultural Relics

概 述

Introduction

中国文物多如繁星。它们包含丰富的时代和文化信息，形象地展示了中国文化发展的历程。它们在艺术和技术上所达到的高度，常常令世人惊叹不已。

2	3	4
1		5 6

1. 兵马俑
   Terracotta warrior
2. 甲骨文文字
   Inscriptions on tortoise shells or animal bones
3. 甲骨文碎片
   Pieces of inscriptions on tortoise shells or animal bones
4. 铜马车
   Bronze chariot
5. 三星堆青铜面具
   A bonze mask of Sanxingdui
6. 敦煌壁画
   The Dunhuang fresco

Introduction

There are myriads of ancient cultural relics in China. They embody rich information about history and culture and vividly display the process of Chinese cultural development. The astounding artistic and technological levels shown in those relics continue to impress people today.

甲骨文

Jiaguwen

在中国中部河南省安阳市，有一片面积约24平方公里的都城废墟，俗称殷墟，这是个注定要被永远载入世界文明史册中的名字。

据记载，公元前14世纪，商王盘庚将都城迁到这里，此后近300年，这里一直是商朝的政治、文化、经济中心。殷墟的发现和发掘，是20世纪中国最重大的考古发现。自从1928年首次发掘以来，这里出土了包括甲骨、青铜器在内的大量文物，其中甲骨文的发现则是世界考古史上的大事之一。

甲骨文是刻在龟甲和兽骨上的古老文字。商代统治者迷信鬼神，行事以前往往用龟甲兽骨占卜吉凶，之后把其相关内容在甲骨上记录下来，其文字称甲骨文。经过占卜应验之后，这些刻有卜辞的甲骨就成为一种官方档案被保存下来。

甲骨文一开始并没有被认识，刻有文字的甲骨人们一直以为是龙骨，用来当药材治病，直到1899年，一个叫王懿荣的商人意识到它可能是一种古代文字，从此引起考古学家和语言学家的注意，并开始了研究。目前甲骨出土数量在150 000片之上，发现的单字共有4 500个，已识的字公认有1 000余个，这已经是相当成熟的文字了。

甲骨文记载了3 000多年前中国社会政治、经济、文化等各方面的资料，是现存最早最珍贵的历史文物。甲骨文一直是研究中国古代历史特别是商代历史的最重要的直接史料，今天研究甲骨文已经成为一门世界性的学问。

Jiaguwen

In Anyang, in central China's Henan Province, there is a capital city ruins of 24 square kilometers called the Yin Ruins, whose name is destined to make a difference in the history.

According to the record, Pan Geng, a king of the Shang Dynasty, moved the capital to this area which had been the political, cultural and economic center of the Shang Dynasty for nearly 300 years. Since its first excavation in 1928, the Yin Ruins has provided the world with numerous cultural relics including bronze wares and tortoise shells and animal bones with inscriptions on them, i.e. *jiaguwen*, which is a great discovery in the history of archaeology.

Jiaguwen is the ancient character that is carved on tortoise shells or animal bones. The rulers of the Shang Dynasty were so superstitious that they would resort to divinity before going on a great activity. The predicted outcomes were carved on the tortoise shells and animal bones with the characters called *jiaguwen*. When the augural result came true, the very shell or bone would be saved as the official records. Therefore, these collections became the earliest recorded historical materials in China.

Jiaguwen was not recognized when it was first found. The tortoise shells and animal bones carved with *jiaguwen* were considered to be dragon bones, and were regarded as medicines to cure sickness. This happened until 1899, when a business man named Wang Yirong realized that these may be a sort of ancient characters. It drew archaeologists and linguists' attention, so they began to study on them. So far, more than 150 000 pieces of tortoise shells and animal bones have been excavated; about 4 500 different characters have been discovered, and more than 1 000 of them recognized, which show that a well-developed script with a complete system of written signs had already formed in that early age.

As the earliest and most precious culture relic, *jiaguwen* recorded the information of 3 000 years ago about Chinese social politics, economics, culture and so on. *Jiaguwen* has been the most important direct historical materials for us to study on Chinese ancient history, especially the Shang Dynasty history, and has become the worldwide knowledge.

1. 甲骨文碎片
   Pieces of inscriptions on tortoise shells or animal bones
2. 甲骨文文字
   Inscriptions on tortoise shells or animal bones
3. 殷墟
   Yin ruins

三星堆文化

　　1929年春季的一个傍晚，中国四川省几个农民在田间耕作时，意外地将一座人类文化的宝库打开了。它的发现地有一个美丽的名字——月亮湾，这就是后来震惊世界的三星堆文化。

　　三星堆文化诞生于四川省广汉地区，距今5 000至3 000年。在1929年首次发现后，经过了数十次发掘，其间有数不清的青铜器、玉器、象牙、金器相继出土，轰动一时。

　　在出土器物中以青铜面具尤为引人注目，其中，有一个巨大的青铜面具，宽138厘米，高65厘米，令人惊异的是其狭长的眼球竟然凸出眼眶长达16厘米，而且有一个巨大的鹰钩鼻和上翘至耳根的大嘴，

一双猪耳状的大耳朵，在世界各地从未出土过这般离奇怪异的面具青铜像。在三星堆文物中还有一个高2.6米的大立人铜像。另外还发现了6件由青铜制造的树木。其中 件残品高近4米，全部高度应该在5米左右，这是世界上迄今发现的最高的青铜器。

三星堆文化在工艺上也达到了一个让人吃惊的高度，铜树的树干和树枝采用了筒接的方法，套接部位历经数千年在今天还抽不出来；树上小鸟的爪子是用膏药状的东西粘上去的，比焊接还牢，具体的成分至今还没有完全分析清楚；三星堆出土的部分青铜头像后面，竖有一个弯弯的管子，这个弯管是焊接上去的，而焊接技术的历史尚不足百年，5 000—3 000年前，何以会有这种技术？这令现代人难以想象。

三星堆出土的每一件文物无不精湛到极致，正如国际著名的考古学家卡尔博格所说的："（三星堆出土的文物）与同时代世界任何地方的文化相比，都过于精致了。"

1	2
	3

1. 金面罩人头像
   Bronze human-head figure with gold mask
2. 三星堆博物馆
   Sanxingdui Museum
3. 凸目面具
   Bronze mask with protruding eyes

Sanxingdui Culture

In one evening of the spring in 1929, several farmers of Sichuan Province dug up a few pieces of jade when they were doing farming. Inadvertently, they had opened a door of human culture ever since. This is the world-shaking Sanxingdui Civilization. The site has the beautiful name of "Moon Bend".

Situated in the area of Guanghan in Sichuan Province, Sanxingdui Culture existed almost 3 000 to 5 000 years ago. Since its first appearance in 1929, dozens of excavation has been done. During this period, numerous bronze wares, jade wares, ivory and gold wares were unearthed one after the other and drew the eyes of the world.

Among the unearthed relics, the bronze masks caught most people's eyes. The largest one of the vertical-eyed masks is 65 cm high and 138 cm wide. Its most surprising part is the eyeballs, which are extremely exaggerated, bulging forward to 16cm. Furthermore, it has a huge hooknose, a big mouth with the mouth corners lifted upward to the ear root, and a couple of ears like that of pig. This is the first bronze mask with such an unearthly appearance among all the unearthed relics in the world. There was also a 2.6-meter-tall standing man sculpture. Besides, six bronze trees were taken out at the same time. The height of one destroyed tree of them is almost four meters, which is now the highest bronze ware unearthed in the world.

The craftwork of Sanxingdui Culture also reached a surprising height. The bell and spigot joint technique was used in the joint of trunk and branches of the bronze tree. The joint point still couldn't be pulled out after thousands of years. The claws of birds were stick onto the limbs with some plaster-like material of unknown composition, which was firmer than solder. There was a curving tube smelted onto the back of some bronze man-face masks. How did the bronze smelting technique come into being 5 000 to 3 000 years ago? This puzzles most people today since the history of the smelting technique is less than one hundred years.

All of the unearthed Sanxingdui cultural relics are so exquisite that the internationally distinguished archaeologist, Karlburg, says, "As for the exquisiteness, Sanxingdui culture is above any one of its contemporary culture around the world."

```
   |  2
1  |  3
   |  4
```

1. 青铜站立人像
   Standing bronze figure
2. 青铜坐跪人像
   Sitting and kneeling bronze figure
3. 青铜鸟头像
   Bronze bird-head figure
4. 青铜兽面像
   Bronze animal-face figure

司母戊方鼎

Simuwu Ding

司母戊方鼎
Simuwu Ding

鼎在古代是王权的象征，汉语里有些与鼎有关系的词语，也表达了这样的意思，比如："问鼎"指图谋夺取政权；"一言九鼎"指起决定作用的言论。

司母戊方鼎，是1937年在河南安阳发现的一件珍贵文物，它是中国商代晚期的遗物，距今已有3 000多年的历史。这个大方鼎是世界上已发现的最大的青铜器，现藏于中国历史博物馆。

鼎，在原始社会是煮食物用的炊具。那时的鼎是用陶土制成的。到了商周时代，中国的青铜铸造技术达到了很高的水平，人们就用青铜浇铸制鼎。这时的鼎，已不再是寻常百姓使用的东西，它成为一种祭祀用的礼器，代表着高贵的身份，是王权的象征。

司母戊方鼎是商王文丁为祭祀他的母亲而铸造的。"司母戊"原是这只方鼎内壁上的铭文。据考古学家解释，"司"是祭祀的意思，"母戊"就是商王文丁的母亲，后来，"司母戊"就成了这只大方鼎的名称。

司母戊方鼎高1.33米，长1.1米，宽0.78米，重832.84千克。在当时，需要1 000多千克的金属材料，二三百名工匠同时操作，才能铸成。它造型生动，气魄雄伟，制作工艺十分精巧。鼎下面有四根柱足支撑，显得粗壮有力。鼎身上的各种纹样，精美清晰，表现了丰收、吉祥的内容。司母戊方鼎集中代表了商周青铜铸造技术的最高成就。

Simuwu Ding

In ancient China, *ding* was a symbol of imperial power. Therefore *ding* is often used in phrases and expressions in the Chinese language to imply authority. For instance, *wending*, literally "enquiring about *ding*", means plotting to usurp political power; *yiyan jiuding*, literally "One word of promise is equal to nine *dings*", means a decisive comment.

Simuwu Ding was a very precious cultural relic, found in 1937 in Anyang of Henan Province. It was produced in the late Shang Dynasty more than 3 000 years ago. This square-shaped *ding* is the largest existing bronze ware in the world. It is now housed in the Chinese Historical Museum in Beijing.

Ding was a cooking vessel probably used to boil or cook food in the primitive society. At that time, dings were made of clay.

During the Shang and Zhou (11th century—771 BC) dynasties, bronze cast technology reached a very high level in China. Therefore, people used bronze to cast *ding*. However, *dings* were no longer cooking utensils in ordinary people's life but an object for important ceremonies to offer sacrifices. It was a symbol of imperial power.

Simuwu Ding was cast by Emperor Wending of the Shang Dynasty as a ritual object for a ceremony to offer sacrifices to his mother. The three characters *simuwu* form an inscription on the inside of the sidewall. According to archeologists, *si* means sacrificial ceremony and *muwu* is the name of the emperor's mother. Later on, Simuwu became the name of this huge *ding*.

Simuwu Ding is 1.33 m high, 1.10 m long and 0.78 m wide, weighing 832.84 kg. At that time, it needed 1 000 kg of metal and two to three hundred workers to produce it. This *ding* is solid in build, magnificent in appearance and was made with fine craftsmanship. The four pillar legs are thick and powerful. The motifs on its body are exquisite and clear, symbolic of harvest and auspiciousness. Simuwu Ding represents the highest level of bronze cast technology in the Shang and Zhou dynasties.

越王勾践剑

Sword of King Goujian of Yue

1965年，在中国湖北江陵的一座古墓中，出土了一把青铜剑，剑身上刻有"越王勾践自作用剑"八个字，原来，它是越王勾践使用过的宝剑。

勾践是2 000多年前春秋末期越国的国王。传说，越国被吴国打败后，越王勾践受到了吴王的羞辱。从此，他发愤图强，立志报仇雪耻。后来，日益强盛的越国，终于打败了吴国，成为当时的强国。

越王勾践剑全长55.6厘米，其中剑身长45.6厘米。剑与剑鞘吻合得十分紧密，拔剑出鞘，仍然寒光耀目，而且毫无锈蚀，用这把剑可以把20余层纸轻松地一划而破。剑身上刻满了菱形的暗纹，剑柄上缠着丝线，还镶嵌有蓝色琉璃和绿色的宝石，铸造得非常精细。

专家研究认为，那时中国的工匠就已经掌握了如此高超的铸剑技术，这在科学技术史上具有重要的意义。

Sword of
King
Goujian of Yue

In 1965, a bronze sword carved with eight characters meaning the sword of King Goujian of Yue, was discovered in an ancient tomb in Jiangling, Hubei Province.

King Goujian lived some 2 000 years ago, and ruled the State of Yue in the late Spring and Autumn Period. It is said that, when Goujian was defeated by the State of Wu, he was insulted by the King of that state. Goujian determined to take revenge. Later, the State of Yue grew stronger and finally defeated the State of Wu and became a superpower of the time.

The bronze sword is 55.6 cm in total length, and 45.6cm in length of the sword body. Though buried for more than 2 000 years, the sword shows no rust at all, and the sharp blade gleams with cold light as ever. It could lacerate more than twenty

pieces of paper in one time. It is decorated with veiled rhombus patterns. The hilt of the sword is wrapped with silk thread, and embedded on one side with a blue glaze and on the other a turquoise glaze.

According to research by experts, Chinese craft workers had mastered such superb technology of founding sword.

1	3
2	

1. 越王勾践剑
   Sword of King Goujian of the State of Yue
2. 越王勾践剑剑盒
   Box for King Goujian's sword
3. 越王勾践剑实物近照
   A near sight for King Goujian's sword

141

良渚美玉

中国有一句古话："金银有价玉无价"，中国人对玉自古就有着珍爱、膜拜之心。

良渚是中国新石器时代两大玉器中心之一，出土的玉器以其独特的材质、器型、纹饰、治玉工艺及其鲜明的文化特征著称于世。

良渚玉器主要集中出土在浙江、上海和江苏三地，其重大发现遗址有：草鞋山①、寺墩②、张陵山③、花厅④、福泉山⑤和反山⑥等。

据鉴定，良渚玉器的用材，多为就地取材的软玉。器型有礼器，有佩饰品，有工具。尤其是纹饰，繁密细致，和谐工整。最具神秘色彩的是神像纹图案，狰狞的人面，头戴高大豪华的羽冠，双手叉腰，骑于神兽之上，这种具象或抽象的氏族"神徽"成为良渚玉器上耐人寻味的特殊标记。宗教色彩显著而且具有权力象征的琮、璧等礼器的大量出现，则被学术界公认是中华文明曙光出现的重要象征。

外方里圆、造型独特的玉琮是所有玉器中最具代表性的，是至高无上的神权的象征。玉璧原本是古人祭天时用的礼器，在良渚时期，它往往是财富的象征。

在合金工具尚未出现的远古时代，这些细密的纹饰是如何加工雕刻的呢？至今仍然是一个谜，有的学者认为，良渚玉器上的纹饰是用鲨鱼牙齿雕刻的；有的学者估计是用玛瑙、水晶石等打制成雕刻玉石的工具；日本考古学者则认为在玉石上可以自如地刻画线条的工具应是钻石。真实的情况，暂时还无法确定，不过可以确定的是，良渚玉器是与中华民族历史文化传统血肉相连的，作为中华民族特有的文化，有着深厚的历史底蕴。

1 | 2

1. 良渚玉器
   Liangzhu jade ware
2. 神人面纹玉器
   Jade article with god-man face pattern

Liangzhu Jade

Jade has been highly treasured and prized by the Chinese people, as a Chinese saying goes "Gold has a value; jade is invaluable".

Liangzhu is one of the two major jade centers of the Neolithic Age. In terms of its unique material, type, carving decoration, working techniques and the distinct culture characteristic, the unearthed jades are well-known in the world.

Most Liangzhu jade items were excavated in Zhejiang Province, Jiangsu Province and Shanghai. The key culture sites include Caoxieshan, Sidun, Zhanglingshan, Huating, Fuquanshan, Fanshan, etc.

According to scientific identification, most Liangzhu jade works were made from local nephrite jade, could classified into ritual and insignia jade types, as well as implements. They are characterized by the fine work, especially the harmonious and exquisite carving decoration. The most mysterious is the god pattern.

With the ferocious face, he's wearing a huge and luxurious crown of feathers and sits akimbo on a mythical beast. This kind of concrete or abstract mysterious pattern of clan is regarded as a particular symbol of Liangzhu jade craftwork. The appearance of the great number of ritual jades with religious color, such as *cong* and *bi*, is recognized as the dawn of the Chinese civilization.

Cong jade is prominent for its unique shape of an oblong, squared tube with a round hole which symbolized the sovereign metaphysical power. *Bi* jade is a circle ring used to worship heaven. It was the token of fortune in Liangzhu Period.

In the ancient times when no alloy implements were discovered, how could such fine decorations be carved? It's still a mystery. Some scholars think that the decoration was carved using shark teeth, while some other scholars estimate that the instrument used for carving bowlders

were made of carnelian and crystal. Japanese archaeologists deem that the carving instrument should be diamond. For now, we have no idea of its real situation. However, what we can be sure of is that Liangzhu jade wares must have a rather close relation ship with the historical and cultural tradition of the Chinese nation. Being one of the culture elements unique to the Chinese nation, Liangzhu jade wares contain a great deal of information about history.

▶ 注解 Notes

① 草鞋山在江苏省吴县境内。
Caoxieshan is in Wu county, Jiangsu Province.
② 寺墩在江苏省境内。
Sidun is in Jiangsu Province.
③ 张陵山在江苏省吴县境内。
Zhanglingshan is in Wu county, Jiangsu Province.
④ 花厅位于江苏省新沂地区。
Huating is in Xinyi district, Jiangsu Province.
⑤ 福泉山位于上海市青浦地区。
Fuquanshan is in Qingpu district, Shanghai.
⑥ 反山在浙江省余杭地区。
Fanshan is in Yuhang district, Zhejiang Province.

长信宫灯

Changxin Palace Lamp

中国古代的灯具品种繁多，其中最精美的是专门为宫廷皇室制作的宫灯。汉代的长信宫灯，就是一件精美的灯中珍品。

长信宫灯是1968年从河北满城汉墓——刘胜[①]夫妇墓中出土的。因灯上刻有"长信家"等字，所以被称为长信宫灯。人们推测，这盏灯原本是放在汉代长信宫中的。现在，长信宫灯收藏在中国河北省博物馆。

长信宫灯是铜制的灯具，表面通体鎏（líu）金[②]，

长信宫灯
Changxin palace lamp

高48厘米，金光灿灿，设计构思颇具匠心。灯的外形是一个汉代宫女，宫女的表情非常文静，衣服的造型也相当生动。她左手拿灯，右手和衣袖笼在灯上，形成了灯罩。点灯时，蜡烛燃烧产生的烟尘可以通过右臂到达中空的体内，这样，就避免了烟尘污染室内的空气。宫女的头部和手臂可以拆卸，便于清洗。这盏灯的灯盘可以转动，灯罩可以开合，能够随意调节灯的亮度和照射的角度。宫灯不仅体现了高深的艺术造诣，更将实用功能、净化空气的科学原理和优美的造型有机地结合在一起，反映了古代高超的合金冶炼和制作工艺。

Changxin
Palace Lamp

There were a great varieties of lamps in ancient China, the best of which was the palace lamp for the imperial household. The Changxin Palace Lamp of the Han Dynasty (206 BC—220 AD) is a veritable treasure.

It was excavated from the tomb of Liu Sheng and his wife in Mancheng of Hebei, and was named for the fact that the characters *Changxin Jia* were carved on it. This lamp is believed to have been used in the Changxin Palace of the Han Dynasty. Now it is in the collection of the Museum of Hebei Province, China.

The Changxin Palace Lamp is made of bronze and is gold-coated. The shape of the lamp is that of a palace maid. The maid wears a calm and gentle expression, and her dress is rather impressive. She holds a lamp in her left hand, while the wide sleeve of her right arm covers the top of the lamp so as to create a shade. When the lamp is lit, candle smoke would go through the sleeve into the hollow body so as to prevent smoke from polluting the air of the room. The head and the right arm of the maid can be removed for cleaning. The lamp plate can be turned and the lampshade can be opened and closed to adjust the amount and direction of light.

> ▶ 注解 Notes
>
> ① 西汉第三个皇帝汉文帝的孙子。
> Liu Sheng was the grandson of the third emperor of the Western Han Dynasty, Han Wendi.
> ② 把溶解在水银里的金子用刷子涂在器物表面，用来装饰器物。
> To coat or cover with the thin gold melting in the mercury to decorate the ware.

秦始皇陵兵马俑

Terracotta Warriors and Horses of
Qinshihuang Mausoleum

在陕西省西安市往东数十公里处，有一座恢宏的地下军阵，这就是被称作世界第八大奇迹的秦始皇陵兵马俑。

秦始皇是中国历史上一位很有作为的帝王，他生前用了大量人力、物力为自己修造陵墓。秦陵兵马俑就是为陪葬这位皇帝而制作的陶兵和陶马。

秦始皇陵兵马俑发现于1974年。三个兵马俑坑占地约20 000多平方米，8 000多个与真人真马一般大小的陶俑陶马，排列成整齐的方阵，再现了秦始皇统一中国时兵强马壮的雄伟军阵。

秦始皇陵中的陶俑武士，个个身材魁梧，体态匀称，身高一般在1.80米左右。这些陶俑按照不同的兵种，又分为步兵俑、骑兵俑、车兵俑、弓弩手和将军俑等。他们身穿战

袍，手执兵器。有的牵战马；有的驾战车；有的单膝跪地，张弓搭箭；有的挺立阵前，凝视前方……兵马俑通体风格浑厚健美，细细观看，陶俑的脸型、发型、体态、神情都各有差异，似乎能令人感受到他们不同的遭遇和经历。军阵中的陶马，高1.50米，长2米，表情机警，仿佛马上就要奔向战场。

在秦始皇陵墓的附近，还出土了两套青铜车马，每辆车上都坐一个驾车的铜人，赶着四匹拉车的铜马。铜车马的大小是真车真马的一半。这样大的青铜器，在世界上也很少见。兵马俑为研究秦代的历史、军事和文化艺术，提供了重要的实物资料。

1、3. 兵马俑
Terracotta warriors and horses
2. 兵马俑坑
Pit of terracotta warriors and horses

Terracotta Warriors

and Horses of Qinshihuang Mausoleum

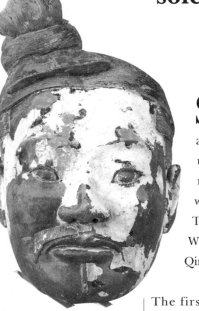

Several kilometers east of Xi'an, there is a grand terracotta army underground which is regarded as the eighth wonder of the world. This is the Terracotta Warriors and Horses of Qinshihuang Mausoleum.

The first emperor of the Qin Dynasty, known as Qinshihuang, made great achievements in Chinese history. While still alive, he mobilized huge manpower and used a great deal of materials to build his mausoleum. The terracotta warriors and horses were used as burial objects to accompany the emperor in the after world.

The terracotta warriors and horses were first discovered in 1974. Archaeologists, from three terracotta figurines pits occupying about 2 000 square meters, have since unearthed some 8 000 life-like soldiers and horses. Standing in formation, they indicate the powerful military might of Qin when it unified China.

All the warriors look robust and are physically well-proportioned. Normally, each one is about 1.80 m high. They are further divided into infantry, cavalry, archers, generals, etc. Dressed in armor, holding weapons, some lead horses, some ride in carriages, some have one knee on the ground pulling back their bow to release an arrow, while others stand aloof, gazing to the front. Each clay horse is 1.50 m in height and 2 m in length. They all look robust, beautiful and alert as if they are ready to

charge onto the battlefield at any moment.

Not very far from the Mausoleum of Qinshihuang, two sets of bronze horse-pulled chariots were found. On each chariot there sits a man driving a chariot pulled by four horses. The size of the bronze chariot is about half size of a true machine. Such big bronze wares are rarely seen in the world. The terracotta warriors and horses provide important material objects for the research on the history, the military, and the culture of the Qin Dynasty.

| 1 | 2 |

1、2. 兵马俑
Terracotta warriors and horses

曾侯乙编钟

Chime Bells

编钟，是中国古代一种打击乐器，由青铜制成。

人们按钟的大小、音律、音高，把钟编成组，悬挂在钟架上，制成编钟。演奏时用小槌或木棒敲打，钟声清脆响亮，幽雅柔美。

曾侯乙①编钟，是中国现存最大、保存最完整的一套大型编钟。1978年从湖北的一座战国古墓——曾侯乙墓中出土。出土时，整套编钟仍完好地挂在钟架上。

曾侯乙编钟共64件，分8组悬挂在铜、木制成的钟架上。钟架全长10.79米，高2.67米，分上、中、下3层，由6个佩剑的青铜武士和几根圆柱承托重量，设计精巧，结构稳定。64件编钟的总重量是2 500多千克，最大的一口钟高度超过1.5米，重量超过200千克。这套编钟的数量、重量和体积，在编钟中是很少见的。

曾侯乙编钟的制作非常精致美观。为便于人们敲击、演奏，每口钟上还刻有铭文，计有2 828字，记载了关于编钟的佩挂和音乐乐理方面的内容，被专家学者称为"一部珍贵的音乐理论论著"。这套编钟证明早在春秋战国时期，我国音乐就已发展到了相当成熟的阶段。

曾侯乙编钟出土后，仍然音色优美，音质纯正，演奏出的乐曲十分动听。中国音乐家创作的《编钟乐舞》，再现了中国古老音乐的迷人魅力。

Chime Bells

The chime bells, or *bianzhong*, are a kind of percussion musical instrument made of bronze.

Chime bells were divided into groups according to their size, temperament, pitch and were hung on a rack. A small hammer or wooden club is used to hit the bell to make a resonant and agreeable sound.

The chime bells of Yi, are the largest and the most complete ancient chimes existing today in China. They were unearthed from the tomb of Yi, the Marquis of Zeng, a small state of the Warring States Period (475 BC—221 BC), in 1978. When they were found, all bells were still hanging on their rack.

There are altogether 64 bells, hung in eight groups on wooden or bronze bars. The rack, 10.79 m long, 2.67 m high, is made of three bars, namely, the upper, middle and lower bars, held up by six bronze warriors and a few round, wooden posts. The 64 bells weigh 2 500 kg. The largest bell exceeds 1.5 m in height and weighs more than 200 kg. It is extremely rare to see a set with so many bells of such weight and size.

The chime bells of Yi are exquisitely cast and look very elegant. To help artists to perform music, there are instructions on each bell with 2 828 characters in all. There are also words about the hanging indication and musical temperament that are called the "valuable music theory work". The chime bells of Yi shows that, as early as the Warring States Period, China already had a very rich musical culture. The chime bells still could produce a pure and accurate note after unearthed. The tone is excellent and the timbre is pure.

After excavation of the chime,

Chinese musicians created a melody entitled *Bianzhong Yuewu* (music and dance accompanied by chime bells), to once again demonstrate the charm of ancient Chinese music.

▶ 注解 Note

① 战国时期一个小国——曾国的国君，名字叫乙。
Yi is the king of Zeng, one of the small countries during the Warring States Period.

1 | 2

1. 曾候乙编钟
   Bronze chimes unearthed from the Tomb of Marquis Yi of the Zeng State
2. 编钟乐舞
   Bianzhong Yuewu (music and dance accompanied by chime bells)

金 缕玉衣

Jade Suit Sewn with Gold Thread

衣服的质地一般都是棉麻丝绸，可是在中国的历史上，却出现过用黄金和玉石做成的衣服——金缕玉衣。

汉代的帝王贵族十分迷信玉能够保持尸骨不朽，更把玉作为一种高贵的礼器和身份的象征，于是便用玉衣作葬服，把许多四角穿有小孔的玉片，用金丝、银丝或铜丝编缀起来，分别称为"金缕玉衣"、"银缕玉衣"、"铜缕玉衣"。

1968年，从河北满城汉墓中出土的两套金缕玉衣，向世人展示了古代玉衣的真面目。

这两套玉衣的主人，是西汉中山靖王刘胜和他的妻子窦绾。

从外观上看，玉衣的形状几乎与人体一模一样，分为头部、上衣、裤管、手套和鞋五个部分。玉衣的各部分由玉片组成，玉片的大小、形状，是根据人体的不同部位设计的，绝大多数玉片是长方形和方形，少数是梯形、三角形和多边形。制作时，先在玉片的角上穿孔，再用黄金制成的丝缕把它们编结起来。刘胜的玉衣比较肥大，全长1.88米，由2 498块玉片组成，用了大约

1 100克金丝。窦绾的玉衣稍小，全长1.72米，由2 160块玉片和700克金丝组成。在2 000多年前的汉代，能制作出这样精美的玉衣，可见当时的工匠已具有了相当高的设计水平和精湛的制作工艺。

实际上，古代贵族试图"不朽"的愿望是不可能实现的，这种以玉衣作葬服的制度，到三国时被下令废止。

Jade Suit Sewn

with

Gold Thread

Ordinarily, the texture of clothes is cotton, flax or silk. However, there were suits made of gold and jade, that is "Jade Suit Sewn with Gold Thread".

The emperors of the Han Dynasty believed that jade could prevent their corpses from decaying, and they regarded jade as full of dignity and nobility. Therefore, they used jade suits as their grave clothes. Gold thread, silver thread or copper thread was used to link pieces of four-square jade separately that are called Jade Suit Sewn with Gold Thread, Jade Suit Sewn with Silver Thread and Jade Suit Sewn with Copper Thread.

The two sets of jade suits of the Han Dynasty tomb unearthed in Mancheng of Hebei Province in 1968 revealed to the world the real features of such grave clothes. Their owners were Liu Sheng,

Prince Jing of Zhongshan, and his wife, Dou Wan, of the Western Han Dynasty (206 BC—25 AD).

In appearance, a jade suit follows the shape of a human body. It consists of five parts, i.e., head mask, coat, trousers, gloves and shoes. Each part is made of pieces of jade. The size and shape of each jade piece was designed according to its position. Most jade pieces are shaped in square or rectangular form, but there are a few in trapezoid, triangle or multisided shapes. Each jade piece is perforated at its corners, through which a gold thread goes through to sew the pieces together. Liu Sheng's jade suit is rather large, 1.88 m long and made up of 2 498 pieces. The gold thread used for this suit is about 1 100 g in weight. Dou Wan's jade suit is smaller, 1.72 m long and made up of 2 160 pieces. The gold thread used for this suit is about 700 g in weight.

Such refined suits made some 2 000 years ago in the Han Dynasty indicate the high design level and excellent craftsmanship of that time.

In fact, of course, the rulers' dream of preventing their corpses from decaying could never be realized. The practice of wearing jade suits was banned during the Three Kingdoms Period (220—280).

1 | 2

1. 金缕玉衣
   The jade suit sewn with gold thread
2. 金缕玉衣局部
   Part of the jade suit sewn with gold thread

铜奔马

Bronze Galloping Horse

1969年，在中国西部甘肃省武威的一座东汉古墓中，出土了一件珍贵的文物——铜奔马。

这匹青铜骏马，浑身布满了斑驳的铜绿。虽然铜奔马只有34.5厘米高，但它强健饱满的身躯，显得十分雄浑矫健。那奔腾的四蹄、飞扬的长尾、微微张开的口鼻，逼真地表现了骏马疾驰的形象。更巧妙的是，它的右后蹄下踏着一只展翅疾飞的龙雀，形象地表现出骏马奔驰的速度超过了飞鸟，展现了快马飞奔蹄不沾土的雄姿，反映了古代人民对骏马的喜爱。

中国政府已将其作为中国旅游的标志。

Bronze Galloping Horse

In 1969, a galloping horse in bronze was unearthed in an Eastern Han Dynasty (206 BC—220 AD) tomb in Wuwei, Gansu Province in western China.

The 34.5 cm-high bronze horse, covered with spots of verdigris, has a full and robust body. The prancing legs, flying tail, slightly dilated nostrils portray a galloping horse. What is ingenious about it is that one of its hind feet is stepping on a flying swallow. That means the galloping horse is faster than a flying swallow. This also shows the ancient people's love for horses.

The Chinese Government has designated it as the symbol of tourism.

1 | 2

1、2. 铜奔马
Bronze galloping horse

永乐大钟

The Great Bell of Yongle

2000年，千年轮回，世纪之交，为了迎接这个历史性的时刻，在除夕之夜零点到来的瞬间，一件有580多年历史的巨钟，在北京上空轰然而鸣，108下钟声激越、磅礴。发出这辞旧迎新钟声的就是永乐大钟。

永乐大钟系明代永乐年间（1420年前后）铸造，享有"古代钟王"之誉。永乐大钟用铜、锡、铅合金铸成，构造合理，工艺精湛，高达6.75米，钟口直径3.3米，重46 500千克，悬挂在北京大钟寺内一座高约20米的钟楼里。

永乐大钟最为绝妙之处在于钟身内外都铸有佛经、咒语，总计230 000多字。

永乐大钟历经500多年，依然完好无损，声音圆润洪亮，穿透性极强，可传四五十千米以外，余音达3分钟之久。日本著名声学家北村音一教授在聆听了大钟的钟声后，由衷地赞叹："这是我听到的世界上最美妙的钟声。"

The Great Bell of Yongle

To welcome the historical moment, millennium, the year of a thousand year's palingenesis and the turn of the century, a huge bell with a history of more than 580 years rang in Beijing right at zero o'clock on New Year's Eve. The 108 strokes were exciting and majestic. The bell is the Great Bell of Yongle.

The Great Bell of Yongle, cast during the Yongle period of the Ming Dynasty (around 1420), has enjoyed the reputation of "King of Ancient Bell". It is made of an alloy of copper, tin and lead with sound structure and exquisite techniques. The bell, 6.75 m high, with a diameter of 3.30 m, weighing 46 500 kg, is hung in a tower about 20 m high in the Great Bell Temple in Beijng.

The most marvelous part of the Great Bell of Yongle lies in its more than 230 000 characters of Sutra and incantation which were cast inside and outside of the bell body.

After more than 500 years, the Great Bell of Yongle is still in mint condition. Its plumy and rotund sound with strong penetrating force can spread 40 to 50 km and its after sound can keep up to 3 minutes. A famous Japanese acoustician highly praised it after listened to the bell, "This is the most dulcet bell of the world I've ever heard."

```
      2
1  ┌─────
      3
```

1. 永乐大钟
   The Great Bell of Yongle
2. 永乐大钟钟纹
   The pattern on the Great Bell of Yongle
3. 北京大钟寺亭台
   The pavilion in the Great Bell Temple in Beijing

古代钱币

Ancient Coins

中国古代货币是世界上起源最早的货币之一。通行2 000余年的方孔圆钱，曾对亚洲的一些国家和地区产生了深远的影响，从而形成了具有东方特色的货币体系。

在钱币出现之前，人们只能用实物交换东西，比如，用一只羊换一袋米。三四千年前，中国人的祖先开始把珍贵的贝壳当作钱，叫贝币。随着商品交换的发展，天然的贝壳不够用了，于是人们又用铜来制造钱币。

2 000多年前，在中国的春秋战国时期，出现了刀形、铲形和圆形的铜钱。

公元前221年，秦始皇统一中国后，把秦国使用过的圆形有方孔的铜钱作为全国统一的货币，这种钱可以用绳子穿起来带在身上。钱上面的文字，具有很高的考古价值。

到了公元前118年，汉武帝改用"五铢"钱币作为全国统一的货币。这种五铢钱一直沿用了700年，是中国历史上使用时间较长的古货币。西汉末年，王莽也铸造了几种货币，多是仿刀形、铲形的钱币，看起来古朴美观，但使用寿命很短。

公元621年，唐高祖废除了五铢钱，改用通宝、元宝等名称，铸造了"开元通宝"钱币。

从这以后，钱币多用国号①、年号②命名，并在背面铸上文字，说明铸造的时间、地点或铜钱的价值。这种通宝形的钱币，唐以后各个朝代都沿用，到清末民初，经历了1 000多年的时间。

中国还是世界上最早使用纸币的国家。北宋末期，四川成都有16家富商共同印制发行了一种纸币——交子，上面印有房屋、树木、人物等图案。这是中国最早的纸币。

中国古代钱币是收藏家珍贵的收藏品。

1. 春秋时代钱币
   Coins of the Spring and Autumn Period
2. 开元通宝
   Kaiyuan tongbao (one kind of coin during the Tang Dynasty)
3. 交子
   Jiaozi (paper currency)

Ancient Coins

China is one of the earliest countries to adopt coins. The round coin with a square hole, which had been circulating for more than 2 000 years, had a far-reaching impact upon some countries and regions of Asia. It led to a monetary system with oriental characteristics.

Before the appearance of coins, people resorted to barter trade. For instance, a sheep was traded for a bag of rice. About 3 000 to 4 000 years ago, ancient Chinese used precious shells as money. As commerce developed, people began to use copper to mint coins.

During the Spring and Autumn Period more than 2 000 years ago, there appeared copper coins in the shape of a knife, spade and circle.

In the year of 221 BC, Emperor Qinshihuang unified the whole country and adopted a round coin with a square hole in the middle as a unified currency. Such coins could be held together by a string and carried about. Characters cast on the sides of the coin are of high value for archaeology today.

In 118 BC, Emperor Wu of the Han Dynasty used the *wuzhu* coin as the national currency. *Wuzhu* lasted for 700 years. In the late Western Han Dynasty (206 BC— 25 AD), Wang Mang also minted some coins, mostly in the shape of a knife or spade. They looked rather antique and pretty, but their life was short.

In 621, Emperor Gaozu of the Tang Dynasty abolished the *wuzhu* coin and adopted coins named *tongbao*, *yuanbao*, etc. He founded the *kaiyuan tongbao* coin. Since then, coins were named after the dynasty code or the year code. The coining time and place, and the value were also cast on the coins. This system continued until the late Qing Dynasty (1644—1911) and the early Republic of China (1911—1949), namely, more than 1 000 years.

China is also the earliest country to use paper currency. In the late Northern Song Dynasty (960—1127), 16 wealthy merchants of Chengdu of Si-chuan Province jointly issued, the earliest paper currency in China.

Today, ancient Chinese currency has become a precious item for collection.

▶ 注解 Notes

① 国家的称号，如汉、唐、宋、元、明等。
The title of the reigning dynasty, like Han, Tang, Song, Yuan, Ming and so on.
② 一般指古代帝王用来纪年的名称。
The title of an emperor's reign in ancient China.

敦 煌 莫高窟

Dunhuang Mogao Grottoes

敦煌莫高窟在甘肃省敦煌市东南，创建于前秦，到唐时就已经达到了1 000余窟，至清代1 000余年中不断修建。现存洞窟492个，保存着历代彩塑2 400多尊，壁画50 000余平方米。如果将它们连接起来，可以组成一个长达25千米的瑰丽画廊。

敦煌佛像均为泥制彩塑，分为单身像和群像，造型生动、神态各异，最大者高33米，最小者仅 0.1 米。

敦煌莫高窟是世界上壁画最多的石窟群，敦煌壁画是敦煌艺术的主要组成部分，规模宏大，内容丰富。敦煌壁画主要可以分为佛像画、经变画、民族传统神话题材壁画、供养人画像四类。佛像画是壁画的

1 2 1. 敦煌莫高窟
     Dunhuang Mogao Grottoes
  3   2. 敦煌驼队
     Camel team of Dunhuang
     3. 敦煌佛像
     The Buddha's statue in Dunhuang

主体，内容包括各种佛像、菩萨等。其中体态俏丽、翩翩起舞的敦煌飞天形象更是让人难忘。

在敦煌莫高窟492个洞窟中，几乎每一窟都画有飞天。早期石窟中，飞天身材粗短，大嘴大耳，很明显受印度飞天和西域飞天的影响。但到唐朝时，敦煌飞天的艺术形象就完全中国化了，她没有翅膀，没有羽毛，衣裙飘逸，彩带飞舞。

敦煌壁画的设色富丽堂皇，艳而不俗，以石绿、石青、朱砂等矿物染料为主色，层次分明，因为矿物染料稳定性很强，历经千年依然艳丽如初。

敦煌莫高窟是当今世界上规模最宏伟、保存最完好的佛教艺术宝库，被联合国教科文组织列入世界文化遗产名录。

2000年，以敦煌石窟壁画为基础创作的大型舞剧《大梦敦煌》在中国北京上演。

Dunhuang Mogao Grottoes

The Dunhuang Mogao Grottoes, located at southeast of Dunhuang city, were first constructed in the Former Qin Dynasty. It reached more than 1 000 caves till the Tang Dynasty and was constantly built up the following 1 000 years till the Qing Dynasty. Now more than 2 400 painted sculptures and more than 50 000 square meters frescos of past dynasties are saved in the 492 existing caves. If they are connected together, that will form a magnificent gallery of 25 km.

Dunhuang joss, all painted sculptures made of mud, are divided into single and group ones, and have vivid shapes and different presences with the tallest to 33 m and shortest to 0.1 m only.

The Dunhuang Mogao Grottoes are the caves that have the most frescos in the world, and the Dunhuang frescos are the main part of the Dunhuang art. With a grand scale and rich contents, the Dunhuang frescos can be mainly grouped under four heads which are Joss Paintings, By the Change Paintings (refer to huge paintings which organize the central matter of Sutra to a complete story with clear arrangements), Paintings of Folk, Tradition and Myth, and Dependents Portraits Paintings (refer to the portraits of dependents who were Buddhist believers and financed construction of caves, and the portraits of their families and servants). Joss Paintings, the main body of frescos, include different kinds of joss and Bodhisattva, among which the image of the flying god with a pretty and

dancing posture is even more memorable.

In Dunhuang's 492 grottoes, almost every one of them has flying gods. Flying gods in early caves are stocky with a big mouth and big ears, which is evidently influenced by the flying gods in the Indic and Western Region. However, the artistic image since the Tang Dynasty has completely had the Chinese style, which is without wings and feathers but with flyaway dress and colored ribbons.

The tint of the Dunhuang frescos is magnificent and colorful but not vulgar. With stone green,

azurite and vermilion, etc. As its main colors, it still keeps its original flamboyant and clear beauty after thousands of years because of mineral colors' strong stability.

The Dunhuang Mogao Grottoes are the most majestic and well preserved mine of Buddhism art in the world till now and was included into the World Heritage List by UNESCO.

In 2000, the large-scale dance drama *Dream of Dunhuang*, created on the base of the Dunhaung Frescos, was shown in Beijing.

| 1 | 2 |
| | 3 |

1. 敦煌佛像
   The Buddha's statues in Dunhuang
2、3. 敦煌壁画
   The wall-paintings in Dunhuang

中国古代建筑

Ancient Chinese Architecture

概 述

Introduction

建筑，是人类文明的一个重要标志。在这方面，中国人具有非凡的智慧和创造力。

从金碧辉煌的宫殿，到多姿多彩的民居；从诗情画意的亭台楼阁，到奇巧别致的宝塔古桥，千百年来，中国人继往开来，博采众长，创造出一个又一个奇迹。

Introduction

Architecture is an important symbol of human civilization. In this field, the Chinese people have extraordinary wisdom and creativity.

From resplendent imperial palaces to diverse civilian residences, from picturesque pavilions and kiosks to unique pagodas and bridges, the Chinese people have for centuries created one architectural wonder after another.

1. 北京颐和园
   The Summer Palace in Beijing
2. 北京天坛祈年殿
   The Imperial Sacrificial Altar of the Temple of Heaven in Beijing
3. 山西应县木塔
   The Wooden Pagoda in Yingxian county, Shanxi Province
4. 江苏苏州拙政园
   Humble Administrator's Garden in Suzhou, Jiangsu Province

1	3	4
2		

宫廷

The Imperial Palace

宫廷，简单说，就是皇帝的家。

为显示皇家至高无上的地位和统领天下的威严，中国古代宫廷的设计、建筑都特别追求雄伟壮观和富丽华贵。

古代宫廷的设计，一般分为前后两部分：前面是皇帝处理朝政的地方，后面是帝王、后妃们居住的地方。宫殿建筑采取严格的中轴对称的布局方式，两侧的建筑整齐而对称。重重院落，层层殿堂，展示了皇宫的齐整、庄严和浩大。

宫廷建筑大都采用大屋顶。这种大屋顶不但华美壮丽，而且对建筑物起到了很好的保护作用。大屋顶层层飞翘的屋檐和屋角，使屋面形成了巧妙的曲线，这样，雨水从屋顶流下，会被排得更远，从而保护了木造的宫殿不受雨淋。大屋顶上装饰的鸟兽，不但给庄严的宫殿罩上了一层神秘的色彩，也对古建筑起到了固定和防止雨水腐蚀的作用。宫廷建筑的屋顶上，一般都铺设金黄色的琉璃瓦，因为金黄色象征皇权，所以只有皇室才能使用这种颜色。

用木材建造房屋，是中国古代建筑的

1. 乾清宫
   Palace of Heavenly Purity
2. 守护太和殿的铜狮
   Copper lion guarding the Hall of Supreme Harmony
3. 太和殿全貌
   A panorama of the Hall of Supreme Harmony

1	
2	3

基本特点。宫廷建筑的梁柱、门窗等，都是用木材建造的，而且被漆成了象征喜庆、富贵的朱红色。有的地方，还描绘龙凤、云海、花草等彩画。鲜艳的颜色，不但体现了帝王殿宇的华贵，也对木制的建筑起到了防潮、防蛀的保护作用。

几千年来，中国历代帝王都不惜人力、物力和财力，建造规模巨大的宫廷。可惜的是，这些辉煌的建筑大都在战火中被毁坏了。目前保存最完整的古代宫廷建筑，就是位于北京市中心的故宫博物院。故宫又名紫禁城，这座明清两朝的皇宫，是目前世界上最大的木结构建筑群，先后住过24位皇帝。

北京故宫内的太和殿，是中国最大的木结构大殿，建在三层汉白玉台基上。台基四周的石柱和台阶上，雕刻有精美的石龙和各种花纹。用整块巨石铺成的石阶御道，雕刻着海浪、流云和翻腾的巨龙，十分壮观。

故宫是一处豪华壮丽的殿宇之海，更是一座建筑艺术的博物馆。

The Imperial
Palace

The imperial palace was the residence of the emperor and his family.

In order to show the supremacy of the imperial family and their authority to rule the country, palace architects in ancient China unanimously pursued grandeur and magnificence in their design and construction.

The imperial palace complex in ancient China was usually divided into two parts. The front part was for the emperor to meet his ministers and talk about state affairs, while the rear was used for residential purposes only. The main buildings were all built along a central south-north axis, while auxiliary buildings stood symmetrically on each side. Row upon row of courtyards and lines after lines of palatial halls

demonstrated regal uniformity, solemnity and dignity.

Most of the palace buildings adopted large sloping roofs. The roof was not only decorative, but also protective, as the overhang with upturned corners ensured that rain water would flow along the roof grooves and fall into places far from the wooden structures of the building. Zoomorphic ornaments on the upturned roof corners were intended to add a sense of mystery to the place, and moreover, served a practical purpose in fastening the roof and keeping water out. The roofs were made of glazed golden tiles. Since this color was a symbol of imperial power, it could only be used by the imperial family.

Wooden buildings were a basic feature of ancient Chinese architecture. Beams, pillars, windows, gates were all made of wood and were painted red symbolizing happiness and riches and honor. Pictures of dragons, phoenixes, clouds, flowers and grass were sometimes painted on the surface, which not only made the buildings look more magnificent but had the practical purpose of protecting the wood from damp and infestation.

For thousands of years, emperors in Chinese history spared no manpower, materials and resources in building gigantic palaces and imperial gardens. Unfortunately, most were destroyed in war. The best-preserved palace building today is the Palace Museum, known as the Forbidden City, in Beijing. It is the largest wooden structural complex in the world today and had been used by 24 emperors of both the Ming (1368—1644) and Qing (1644—1911) dynasties.

The Hall of Great Harmony in the Palace Museum in Beijing is the largest wooden structure in China today. It was seated upon 3 layers of white marble stone foundations, surrounded by stone columns and stone steps inscribed with patterns of dragons

and flowers, all of which were exquisitely carved. At the back of the Hall is the steps and pathway, paved with monolithic stones. All the stones were sculpted with waves, clouds, and giant flying dragons, symbolizing the imperial magnificence.

The Palace Museum is a palace of luxury and extravagance, moreover, it's a museum of architecture arts.

1. 屋顶的琉璃瓦
   Glazed golden tiles on the roof
2. 故宫全貌
   A panorama of the Imperial Palace
3. 屋顶上装饰的小兽
   Little beast decoration on the roof
4. 角楼
   The watch tower

1	3
2	4

寺庙

Temples

1 | 2
　| 3

1. 四川峨眉山万年寺
   The Wannian Temple in Mt. Emei, Sichuan Province
2. 山西五台山牌坊
   The memorial arch in Mt. Wutai, Shanxi Province
3. 山西五台山佛塔
   The tope in Mt. Wutai, Shanxi Province

　　中国是个多宗教的国家，既有土生土长的道教，又有从外国传入的佛教、伊斯兰教和基督教等。道教的建筑称"宫"或"观"，伊斯兰教有清真寺，基督教有教堂，寺庙与佛塔、石窟则被称为佛教的三大建筑。

　　佛教是从印度传入中国的，但中国的佛教建筑已经明显地被中国化了。中国古代寺院的布局大都是正中路前为山门，山门内左右为钟鼓楼，正面为天王殿，后面是大雄宝殿，再后便是藏经楼，正中路左右布置有僧房、斋堂等建筑。整个寺庙的布局、殿堂的结构、屋顶的建造等，都仿照皇帝的宫殿，金碧辉煌，气势庄严，显示出了中国佛教建筑的特色。

　　佛教的寺庙大都建在远离

闹市的山中。尤其是四大佛教
名山五台山、峨眉山、九华
山、普陀山，更是集中了中国
历代著名的寺庙建筑，如五台
山的佛光寺、南禅寺等。

南禅寺和佛光寺均建于唐
代，南禅寺是中国现存最早的
一座木结构寺院建筑；佛光寺
内的塑像、壁画、墨迹和建筑
被称为"四绝"。

佛教在中国流传很广，不
计其数的佛教寺庙遍布中国各
地，是中国佛教文化的突出体
现，记载了古代社会文化的发
展和宗教的兴衰，具有重要的
历史价值和艺术价值。

Temples

China is a country with diversified religions. Apart from the indigenous Taoism, there are Buddhism, Islam and Christianity which were introduced into China from foreign lands. Taoist structures are called *gong* (palace) or *guan* (temple); mosque is the term for Moslem structure and church for a Christian structure; temple, tope and grotto are called the "Three Great Structures of Buddhism".

Although Buddhism was first introduced into China from ancient India, Buddhist buildings have obviously been localized since then. Most of the ancient temples were designed in a way that the entrance gate would face the central main road. Inside the gate, to the left and right were the Bell and Drum Towers. Confronted was the Hall of God, followed by the Hall of Great Wisdom. Further back was the Tower of Scriptures. Other structures such as monk's residences, kitchens and dining rooms, were located at the sides along the center passage. The Chinese ancient temple was a vivid imitation of the imperial palace building, in terms of its layout, the structure of the main altar room, and the construction of the roof structure. While inheriting the palace building's grandeur and magnificence, the Chinese Bud-

dhist temple structure created its own unique style.

Most of Buddhist temples are built in remote mountainous areas far away from city centers. This is especially so with the Four Buddhist Holy Mountains, namely, Mt. Wutai, Mt. Emei, Mt. Jiuhua and Mt. Putuo, where renowned temple buildings over the past dynasties located, such as Foguang Temple and Nanchan Temple in Wutai Mountains.

Both Nanchan Temple and Foguang Temple were built in the Tang Dynasty. Among them, Nanchan Temple is the earliest timber structure temple surviving in China. Foguang Temple is famous for its statues, mural paintings, calligraphy and architecture. They are commonly known as the "Four Wonders".

Buddhism has been practiced extensively in China as numerous temples have been constructed throughout the country. These monastery establishments not only symbolize Buddhist culture, record the ancient social and cultural development, but also witness the rise and fall of Buddhism. They are of great historical and artistic value.

园林

Classical Gardens

```
1 | 2
  |---
  | 3
  |---
  | 4
```

1. 江苏苏州拙政园
   Humble Administrator's Garden in
   Suzhou, Jiangsu Province
2. 北京颐和园的桥亭
   The bridge pavilion in the Summer
   Palace in Beijing
3. 北京颐和园
   The Summer Palace in Beijing
4. 北京颐和园昆明湖上的玉带桥
   The Jade Belt Bridge in Kunming
   Lake in the Summer Palace in Beijing

中国各地的古典园林，风景优美，建筑奇特，是中外游人向往的游览胜地。

中国古典园林的最大特点是讲究自然天成。古代的园林设计家在建园时，巧妙地把大自然的美景融合在人造的园林中，使人能从中欣赏到大自然的奇峰、异石、流水、湖面、名花、芳草，感觉就像在画中游览。

中国古典园林在布局上还有含蓄、变化、曲折的特点，比如园路要"曲径通幽"，讲究景中有景，一步一景；园中的建筑要与自然景物交融在一起，形状式样变化多样；花草树木要高低相间，四季争艳……

中国古典园林的另一个特点，是巧妙地将诗画艺术和园林融于一体。如园林建筑上的匾额、楹联、画栋、雕梁等，形成了中国古典园林艺术的独

等。南方的私家园林大多建在苏州、南京、杭州和扬州一带，如苏州的拙政园、留园，无锡的寄畅园，扬州的个园等。私家园林一般面积不大，但经过建筑家的巧妙安排，园中有山有水，景物多变，自然而宁静。

特风格。

中国的古典园林大致可以分为北方皇家园林和南方私家园林两类。北方的皇家园林往往利用真山真水，并且集中了各地建筑中的精华。黄色的琉璃瓦，朱红的廊柱，洁白的玉石雕栏，精美的雕梁画栋，色彩华美，富丽堂皇。保存到现在的著名皇家园林有北京颐和园、北海公园、承德避暑山庄

Classical **Gardens**

Classical gardens throughout China, with their beautiful scenery and unique structures, attract many tourists.

The most prominent feature of classical Chinese gardens is the emphasis on the harmony between nature and human. Ancient garden architects success-fully integrated man-made scenes into the natural landscape, creating the impression of traveling in a picture of grotesque peaks, exotic rocks, flowing currents, tranquil lakes, fragrant flowers and rare plants.

Chinese classical gardens are often full of surprises in terms of scenes, variable in composition and complicated in design. Serpentine walkways, for instance, lead to places of tranquility. Much attention is paid to the creation of varied scenery; with each step, one can see a different scene. Buildings of different forms and different architectural styles are well integrated with

the garden scenery. Flowers, plants and trees are elaborately cultivated and planned with a definite eye on their heights and blooming seasons.

Another feature of classical Chinese gardens is that decorative art is ingeniously merged with the garden scenery. On buildings there are horizontal boards carved with calligraphy, antithetical couplets, and painted beams with carvings.

Classical Chinese gardens can be roughly divided into two categories, namely, the royal gardens in the north and private gardens in the south. Royal gardens tend to make use of natural elements in creating clusters of stylish architectural structures in imitation of the best in the country. With golden glazed titles, vermilion colonnades, white marble balustrades, refined ornamented beams, they are filled with a sense of magnificence and gran-

deur. The best-preserved royal gardens are the Summer Palace, the Beihai Park in Beijing and the Summer Resort in Chengde. Private gardens of the south are mostly seen in Suzhou, Nanjing, Hangzhou and Yangzhou, such as Zhuozheng Garden and Liuyuan Garden in Suzhou, Jichang Garden in Wuxi, Geyuan Garden in Yangzhou, etc. Small in size, those gardens are characteristic of ingenious designs; with miniature mountains and rivers and variable scenes, they are natural and tranquil.

1	2
	3
	4

1. 河北承德避暑山庄
   The Summer Resort in Chengde, Hebei Province
2. 北京北海公园
   Beijing Beihai Park
3. 北京颐和园建筑物上的装饰
   The decoration on architectures in the Summer Palace, Beijing
4. 河北承德避暑山庄金山
   Jinshan in the Summer Resort in Chengde, Hebei Province

塔

Pagodas

塔起源于印度，汉代随佛教传入中国。"塔"是印度梵语的译音，本意是坟墓，是古代印度高僧圆寂后，用来埋放骨灰的地方。

中国古代的塔，是中印建筑艺术相结合的产物。中国的古塔建筑多种多样，从外形上看，由最早的方形发展成了六角形、八角形、圆形等多种形状。从建塔的材料分，有木塔、砖塔、石塔、

铁塔、铜塔、琉璃塔。中国古塔的层数一般是单数，通常有5层到13层。

中国现存的著名古塔有：陕西西安的大雁塔、山西应县木塔、河南开封铁塔、河北定县开元寺砖塔、杭州的六和塔、北京香山的琉璃塔等等。这些古塔反映了中国悠久的历史和高超的建筑艺术。

应县木塔位于山西省境内，建于距今约1 000年前，共有9层，高近70米，是世界上现存最古老最高大的木结构塔式建筑。它前后曾经历7次大地震，仍然岿然不动。

1. 山西应县木塔
   The Wooden Pagoda in Yingxian county, Shanxi Province
2. 山西应县木塔檐廊
   The eave of the Wooden Pagoda in Yingxian county, Shanxi Province
3. 陕西西安大雁塔
   The Great Dayan Pagoda in Xi'an, Shaanxi Province

Pagodas

The pagoda originated from India, and was introduced to China along with Buddhism in the Han Dynasty. The pagoda, a transliteration from Indic Sanskrit, originally meant the grave where the remains of Indian monks of high rank were kept after they passed away.

The ancient pagodas we see today are a combination of both Indian and Chinese architectural art, and they come in various shapes and forms. As far as appearance is concerned, there are circular, hexagonal and octagonal pagodas. If classified by building materials, there are pagodas built with wood, bricks, rocks, iron, bronze, glazed tiles or even gold, silver or pearls. Normally, the number of stories varies from five to 13, but it is always an odd number.

The existing famous ancient pagodas include the Great Dayan Pagoda in Xi'an, the Wooden Pagoda in Yingxian County of Shanxi Province, the Iron Pagoda in Kaifeng of Henan Province, the Kaiyuansi Brick Pagoda in Dingxian county of Hebei Province, the Liuhe Pagoda in Hangzhou, the Liuli Pagoda at the Fragrant Hills in Beijing. Those ancient pagodas reflect the long history of China as well as the high level of architectural craftsmanship.

The Wooden Pagoda in Yingxian county, Shanxi Province, was built 1 000 years ago. It has 9 stories, and is up to 70 m high. It is the oldest and highest still existing timber pagoda building in the world. Through seven earthquakes, it has remained absolutely still.

桥梁

Bridges

在中国古代建筑中，桥梁是一个重要的组成部分。几千年来，勤劳智慧的中国人修建了数以万计奇巧壮丽的桥梁，这些桥梁横跨在山水之间，便利了交通，装点了河山，成为中国古代文明的标志之一。

西安灞桥是中国最古老的石柱墩桥，建于汉代。灞桥全长386米，有64个桥洞，自古就是连接古都长安以东广大地区的交通要道，为中国已知时代最早、规模最宏伟、桥面跨度最长的一座大型多孔石拱桥。古时候，长安人送别亲友，一般都要送到灞桥，并折下桥头柳枝相赠。久而久之，"灞桥折柳赠别"便成了一种特有的习俗。如今，经过整修的古灞桥已焕然一新，周围的风景也更加动人。

位于河北省赵县的赵州桥，建于1 400多年前的隋代，是世界上第一座用石头建造的单孔拱桥，它的设计者李春是一位著名的工匠。赵州桥的设计有许多独到之处：50多米长的赵州桥，桥面坡度非常平缓，便于车马、行人上下；桥拱两肩上的4个小拱洞，不但节省了石材，减轻了桥的重量，还加大了洪水的流量。这些精心的设计和高超的技术，使古老的赵州桥至今仍十分坚固。

北京城外永定河上的卢沟桥，已经有900多年的历史，是一座中外闻名的桥梁。卢沟桥全长260多米，桥两侧200多根护栏石柱上，雕刻有形态各异的石狮子，是卢沟桥上最有趣的景致。游人到此游玩，总忍不住要数一数上面究竟有多少石狮子。

中国古代著名的桥梁还有很多，如福建晋江的五里长桥平安桥、泉州洛阳桥、杭州西湖九曲桥、苏州宝带桥及北京颐和园的玉带桥等。

Bridges

The bridge is one of the most important components of ancient Chinese architecture. For thousands of years, the Chinese have built tens of thousands of ingeniously designed and magnificent bridges. Crossing over mountains, spanning rivers, they have facilitated transportation, beautified landscapes and have become one of the marks of ancient Chinese civilization.

Baqiao Bridge in Xi'an, built in the Han Dynasty, is the earliest bridge with stone piers in China. It is 386 m long with 64 arches. It served as the key passage linking the vast areas to the east of the capital city Chang'an. It is by far the oldest in age, longest in span, and most grandiose in scale, multi-span stone arch bridge known today. In ancient days, when local residents of Chang'an bade farewell to a rela- tive or a friend, they would usu- ally see him off at Baqiao Bridge. Besides, they would break a twig of a nearby willow tree and give it to the traveler as a token of good wishes. Gradually, this practice became a local custom. Today, the bridge has been reno- vated and its surroundings have become more intriguing.

Zhaozhou Bridge in Zhaoxian County of Hebei Province dates back 1 400 years ago to the Sui Dynasty. It is the first single arch stone bridge in the world. Its designer, Li Chun, was a famous mason. There are many unique features about this bridge. Some 50 m long, it has mild slopes that make it easy for horse-pulled carts and pedestrians to cross. On its shoulders there are four arch-shaped holes, which not only save building materials and lessen the weight of the bridge but also help ease the flow of wa- ter in time of flood.

Lugou Bridge over the Yongding River in the suburbs of Beijing has a history of more than 900 years. It is 260 m long with more than 200 stone columns on both sides. The most interesting scene is that each column is crowned with a carved lion which has its individual posture. Visitors would usually count the stone lions to know the exact number.

There are many other ancient bridges in China. The famous ones include Ping'an Bridge in Jinjiang and Luoyang Bridge in Quanzhou of Fujian Province, Jiuqu Bridge in the West Lake of Hangzhou, Baodai Bridge in Suzhou and the Yudai Bridge in the Summer Palace of Beijing.

	2
1	3

1、3. 北京卢沟桥
Lugou Bridge in Beijing
2. 河北赵州桥
Zhaozhou Bridge in Hebei Province

中国工艺美术

Chinese Arts and Crafts

概 述

Introduction

中国的工艺美术有着悠久的历史。原始社会新石器时期的陶器，可以说是最早的工艺美术品。此后，商周的青铜器，战国的漆器，汉唐的丝织品，宋朝的刺绣，明清的景泰蓝和瓷器等，都以其精美、名贵闻名于世。

中国传统的工艺美术，制作精美，技艺高超，不但具有鲜明的民族风格和地方特色，而且种类繁多。很早以前它们就已走向世界，向世人展示了自己的风采。

Introduction

Chinese arts and crafts have a long history. Earthenware of the primitive society of the Neolithic Age is the earliest artistic work. The bronze ware of the Shang (16th century BC—11th century BC) and Zhou (11th century BC—221 BC) dynasties, lacquer ware of the Warring States Period (475 BC—221 BC), silk fabrics of the Han (206 BC—220 AD) and Tang (618—907) dynasties, embroidery of the Song Dynasty (960—1279), *cloisonné* and porcelain of the Ming (1368—1644) and Qing (1644—1911) dynasties, all enjoy worldwide reputation for their exquisiteness and refinement.

Made with high craftsmanship, traditional Chinese arts and crafts are of striking nationalistic features and rich varieties. They have long been shipped around the world.

```
1 | 3
  |   4
2 |
  | 5
```

1. 瓷器:弥勒佛
   Porcelain: Laughing Buddha
2. 景泰蓝象形瓶
   Cloisonné elephant-shaped vase
3. 缠枝牡丹瓷瓶
   Porcelain vase with peony pattern
4. 瓷枕
   The pillow
5. 唐三彩女陶俑
   Women figurines of Tang tricolor pottery

唐三彩

Tang Tricolor Pottery

唐三彩，是流行于唐代的一种带有多种釉色的彩色陶器的通称。它的釉色有绿、蓝、黄、白、赭、褐等多种，而一般以黄、绿、赭为主，所以称为唐三彩。

唐三彩种类很多，主要分为人物、动物和器物三种。人物有文臣、武将、贵妇、男僮、女仆、艺人、胡人等。动物有马、骆驼、牛、羊、狮、虎等。器物有盛器、文房用具、室内用具等。古时，唐三彩很少用作日用品和陈设品，大部分用作随葬品，主要出产、流行于中国的中原地区，供这一带的大小官僚们使用。

唐三彩经过艺人们的精心制作，呈现出了各种深浅不同的黄、赭、绿、翠蓝、茄皮紫等色彩，产生了一种斑斓富丽的艺术效果。由于在制作过程中釉质的自然下流，烧制好的唐三彩会产生许多复杂奇妙的变化，因此，没有任何两件唐三彩作品是完全一样的。

唐三彩的艺术造型，反映了当时社会的风貌和时代特征。强壮有力、神态潇洒的武士俑、天王俑和肥壮丰满的马、骆驼等，充分表现了唐初国力的强盛，从脸部稍胖、体态丰满的女俑，可以看出唐朝人是以胖为美的……

千姿百态、色彩绚丽的唐三彩制品，是中国独特的艺术瑰宝。

1 | 2

1. 唐三彩仕女
   Beauty of Tang tricolor pottery
2. 唐三彩骑马胡人
   A Hu people on horse: Tang tricolor pottery

Tang Tricolor Pottery

Tang tricolor pottery, referring to the tri-colored glazed pottery of the Tang Dynasty, is the general designation of the colorful pottery with multi-glaze color which flourished in the Tang Dynasty. Glazes are normally green, blue, yellow, white, ochre, brown, etc. It is called "Tang tricolor pottery" because the basic pigments are yellow, green and ochre.

There are various types of Tang tricolor pottery, which be classified as types of human figurines, animals and objects. Human figurines include images of ministers, generals, ladies, boy servants, maids, artisans and Hun people, etc. Animals include models of horses, camels, cattle, sheep, lions and tigers, etc. Objects include containers, stationery and tools for daily use.

In ancient days, Tang tricolor pottery was rarely used for display or as tools, but mostly by the aristocrats as funerary objects. It was produced in the Central Plain of China and wide used by the local officials.

When making a Tang tricolor pottery, deliberate care is taken in presenting different shades of yellow, ochre, green, blue and dark purple to produce a gorgeously colorful effect. In the process of firing, glazes would drip down the surface of a piece of Tang tricolor pottery and get mingled so as to cause a myriad of changes. Due to the delicacy in making, no two pieces are identical.

The artistic modeling of Tang tricolor pottery well reflects the life of the society at that time. Robust and elegant warriors, Heavenly King, strong and rampant horses, and camels all indicate the prosperity of the early Tang Dynasty. Female figurines of the Tang Dynasty all look plump, showing that plumpness was regarded as a kind of beauty at that time.

Tang tricolor pottery is of such great variety in terms of shapes, postures and colors that it is regarded as uniquely Chinese.

瓷器

Porcelain

英语中的"china"一词有两个意义，一个是中国，一个是瓷器。西方人很早就把中国与瓷器联系在一起，这是因为制瓷技术是中国人发明的。瓷器是从陶器发展来的，如果从生产原始瓷器的商代算起，中国的瓷器大约有3 000多年的历史了。

中国的制瓷技术从东汉以后发展很快，各个历史时期都出现了别具特色的制作瓷器的名窑和陶瓷新品种。唐代浙江越窑的青瓷和河北邢窑的白瓷是非常名贵的瓷器。宋代河北定窑的白瓷，河南钧窑的钧瓷以及浙江龙泉窑的青瓷，都是瓷器中的无价珍宝。从宋代起，龙泉的青瓷开始远销到世界上许多国家。现在土耳其伊斯坦布尔博物馆里就收藏有宋、元、明初的

龙泉青瓷1 000多件。

元代以后，制瓷业迅速发展起来的江西景德镇，被称为中国的"瓷都"。景德镇瓷器轻巧精美，其中的青花瓷①、粉彩瓷②、青花玲珑瓷③、薄胎瓷④被视为珍宝。中国明代著名的航海家郑和，七次率船队远涉重洋，到达东南亚各国和非洲等地，随船带去的物品中，就有大批青花瓷器。

后来发展起来的湖南醴陵、河北唐山、广东石湾、山

东淄博等地的陶瓷，也都以它们各自的特色闻名于世界。

中国瓷器不仅是精美的日用品，也是珍贵的艺术品。自汉唐以来，中国瓷器就大量销往国外，中国的制瓷技术也逐渐传遍世界各地。

▶ **注解 Notes**

① 一种白底蓝花的瓷器。
Porcelains with blue patterns on the white base.

② 是在吸收中国绘画技法后发展起来的，先在烧成的白瓷上画出图案，再填上颜色，经过高温烧成，瓷面颜色绚丽多彩。
Absorbing traditional Chinese painting techniques, it is done by first making a design on a piece of white porcelain, and then filling in the colors before firing. It has splendid colors.

③ 先在瓷胎的主要部位一刀刀雕出米粒形状的洞，再在其他部位画上青花图案，然后上釉烧成。
It is produced firstly by carving small holes in the main part of the base, then drawing the blue pattern on the other parts of the base before glazing and firing.

④ 这种瓷器薄得像蛋壳，在薄而透明的瓷胎上画有各种花纹。
It is as thin as an egg shell, with patterns painted on its transparent walls.

Porcelain

"China" in English has two meanings, China as a country and china as porcelain. Westerners have linked the country of China with porcelain since a long time ago, because the technique of manufacturing porcelain was originally invented in China. Porcelain was developed on the basis of pottery. If calculated from the appearance of the primitive porcelain in the Shang Dynasty, it has a history of about 3 000 years.

The techniques of manufacturing porcelain have developed rapidly since the Eastern Han Dynasty (25—220). Famous kilns producing porcelain products with unique features and new pottery and porcelain varieties constantly came forth in subsequent dynasties. Celadon manufactured in the Yue Kiln of Zhejiang Province and white porcelain produced in the Xing Kiln of Hebei Province in the Tang Dynasty are very precious. White porcelain of the Ding Kiln in Hebei Province, Jun porcelain of the Jun Kiln in Henan Province, and celadon of the Longquan Kiln in Zhejiang Province in the Song Dynasty are all priceless treasures. After the Song Dynasty, celadon wares produced by the Longquan Kiln in Zhejiang began to be exported abroad. The Istanbul Museum in Turkey alone has a collection of more than 1 000 pieces of celadon wares made in the Longquan Kiln in the Song, Yuan and early Ming dynasties.

After the Yuan Dynasty, the porcelain industry rose swiftly in Jingdezhen of Jiangxi Province, which became known as the Capital of Porcelain. The porcelain ware of Jingdezhen is light and artful in weight, refined and exquisite in design. The most precious items include Blue and White Porcelain, Colored Porcelain, Exquisite Blue and White Porcelain and Eggshell Porcelain. A famous navigator named Zheng He of the Ming Dynasty sailed seven times across the oceans to many countries in Southeast Asia and Africa. Most of the commodities he took with him were Blue and White Porcelain wares.

The later developed ceramics in Liling of Hunan Province, Tangshan of Hebei Province, Shiwan of Guangdong Province, Zibo of Shandong Province, are also well-known for their respective features.

Chinese porcelain wares are not only daily handy necessities, but also precious arts and crafts. From the Han and Tang dynasties, Chinese porcelain wares and their manufacturing techniques gradually spread all over the world. Today, China continues to create new varieties of precious porcelain wares.

1 | 2

1. 人物纹青花瓷坛
   Blue-and-white porcelain vase with figure patterns
2. 蔓草纹青花瓷瓶
   Blue-and-white porcelain vase with weeds patterns

景泰蓝

Cloisonné

在中国的北京，有一种驰名中外的特种工艺品——景泰蓝。

景泰蓝也叫珐琅，是在明朝景泰年间发展起来的，因为当时使用的釉色多是宝石一样的蓝色，所以，人们把这种工艺品称为"景泰蓝"。

制作一件精美的景泰蓝产品，一般需要经过30多道工序。工人们首先要把铜料打成瓶、罐、盒、盘等器物，然后用头发那么细的铜丝，在铜胎上镶出美丽的花纹图案，再填上各种颜色的釉料，放在炉子里烧四五次，最后还要打磨光亮，镀上黄金，一件美丽多彩的艺术品才算最后完成。

独具民族特色的北京景泰蓝，从它问世以后，一直是明清两代皇宫中贵重的陈设品。在1904年美国芝加哥世界博览会上，北京景泰蓝还获得过一等奖。目前，中国保留下来最早的景泰蓝制品，是明朝宣德年间的产品。

景泰蓝可以制成瓶、罐、盒等珍贵的陈设装饰品，也可以制成很多种实用工艺品，如花瓶、台灯、烟具、酒具、茶具等。目前，中国的景泰蓝产品已经远销到世界各地。

Cloisonné

Cloisonné, also known as *jingtailan* is a unique art form originated in Beijing.

Cloisonné is also enamel, which flourished and reached it's peak of development during the reign of the Ming emperor Jingtai (1450—1457). As the objects were mostly in blue color, *cloisonné* came to be called *jingtailan* (Jingtai Blue) in Chinese.

One needs to go through more than 30 procedures to *make a cloisonné*. Copper is first used to make the base, after which the pattern is stuck on the bronze body by oblate brass wires as thin as hairs; the inlay pattern is then filled in by enamel glaze material in different colors kept apart by the wire strips. After being fired four or five times in a kiln, the work piece is polished and gilded into a colorful and lustrous work of art.

Since the Beijing *cloisonné* with unique national character was invented, it was mainly used as elegant ornaments in the imperial palaces of the Ming and Qing dynasties. At the World Expo of 1904 held in Chicago, Beijing *cloisonné* won the first prize. The earliest *cloisonné* articles reserved till now are products in the period of Xuande during the Ming Dynasty.

Some *cloisonné* articles are made in forms of vases, jars and boxes; others are designed for ornamental purposes, adding extra beauty to things that are useful, such as vases, lamps, cigarette cases, wine jars, tea sets, etc. Nowadays, *cloisonné* articles have been exported around the world.

	2
1	3

1. 景泰蓝花瓶
   Cloisonné vase
2. 景泰蓝象形瓶
   Cloisonné elephant-shaped vase
3. 景泰蓝佛像
   Cloisonné Buddha image

扇子

Fan

1、3. 字画折扇
Folding fan with Chinese calligraphy
and painting

2. 浙江杭州有名的"王星记"扇子
The famous brand *Wang Xingji* fans
produced in Hangzhou, Zhejiang
Province

1	2
	3

扇子是人们消暑纳凉的工具。在炎热的夏季，它能给人带来阵阵清凉。自古以来，中国的扇子就带着艺术品的风韵，具有独特的民族风格。

大约在3 000多年前的商周时期，中国就有扇子了。中国扇子的种类非常多，有纸扇、绢扇、葵扇、羽毛扇、竹编扇等。扇子的形状也有方有圆，还有梅花、海棠、葵花等形状。

在扇面上题诗作画，是中国扇子的一大特色。从古到今，中国许多著名的书法家、画家都喜欢"题扇"、"画扇"，留下了不少精美的佳作。

在中国最常见的是折扇，拿在手里既方便又潇洒。中国生产折扇最有名的地方是杭州。杭州折扇往往采用名贵的材料做扇骨。著名的黑纸扇、檀香扇、象牙扇，不但是中国扇子中的佳品，在世界上也很有名。

Fan

In summer, the fan can drive away summer heat and help bring cooling breeze. Since old ages, the Chinese fan has been carrying artistic and unique national style.

The fan first appeared in China, about 3 000 years ago, in the Shang and Zhou dynasties. There are many kinds of Chinese fan, such as paper f an, silk fan, palm fan, feather fan, bamboo-knitted fan, etc. Regarding the shapes of the fan, there are rectangular, round, pentagonal, hexagonal and sunflower-shaped fans.

Writing poems and drawing pictures on the cover of a fan is another characteristic of the Chinese fan. From ancient times till now, many famous Chinese calligraphers and painters enjoyed themselves in doing so, which has left us a lot of excellent works.

The folding fan is the most common in China. It is convenient to carry and handsome to look at. Hangzhou is the most famous place for producing fans in China. The frame of the Hangzhou folding fan is usually made of precious materials. The famous black paper fan, sandalwood fan and ivory fan are not only the notable products among Chinese fans but also famous around the world.

风筝

Kite

风筝，古时候也叫纸鸢、鹞子，是中国人发明的。相传2 000多年前，中国著名的能工巧匠鲁班用竹木削制成了会飞的木鹊。五代时，李邺用纸扎糊成纸鸢，用线放飞到天空。后来，古人又在纸鸢头上安了丝弦，风吹丝弦，发出了好像古筝一样的声音，从此，人们把纸鸢称为风筝。风筝出现以后，曾经被用来为军事和通信服务。

北京、天津、山东潍坊、江苏南通和广东阳江等地，是中国风筝的著名产地。制作风筝，要先用竹条捆扎风筝的骨架，再把纸或绢糊在骨架上，然后画上色彩均匀的图案。制作风筝需要十分精巧的技艺，放飞风筝也要有独到的技术，这样，才能使风筝在空中自由平稳地飞翔。

中国的风筝品种式样很多，有禽、兽、虫、鱼等动物形风筝，最常见的是燕子、蝴蝶和鹰形风筝；也有以"孙悟空"等神话人物为题材的风筝；还有一种蜈蚣或龙形的长串风筝，升上天空后，就像巨龙凌空飞舞，十分壮观。

放风筝是一项有益于身体健康的体育活动。所以，世界上许多国家十分流行放风筝。中国人不仅把放风筝当作有趣的游戏和有益于身体健康的体育活动，也常常把精美艳丽的风筝挂在墙壁上欣赏。目前，中国的风筝已经远销到日本以及东南亚和欧美的许多国家，受到了世界各国人民的欢迎。

近年来，中国山东的潍坊每年都要举行盛大的国际风筝大会，因为，中国是风筝的故乡。

Kite

Kite, also called *zhiyuan* or *yaozi* (paper kite in the shape of an eagle, swallow,etc.) in ancient China, was invented by the Chinese people. It is said that Lu Ban, a well-known ingenious carpenter, made a bamboo magpie that could fly. During the Five Dynasty Period (907—960), a man named Li Ye invented a paper kite in the shape of an eagle and flew it in the sky. Later on, people began to fix on kites some strings, which, when high in the air, would vibrate and ring in the breeze like a *guzheng* (a stringed instrument). Since then, the popular Chinese name for the kite had become *fengzheng* (wind *zheng*). It was once used for military purposes as well as for delivering messages.

The renowned places producing kites in China are Beijing, Tianjin, Weifang of Shandong Province, Nantong of Jiangsu Province and Yangjiang of Guangdong Province. To make a kite, one need first make a frame and then cover it with paper or thin tough silk, which can then be painted with pictures. It requires high craftsmanship to make a good kite and particular skills to fly a kite steadily in the sky.

There are various designs of Chinese kites, including birds, beasts, insects and fishes, of which the most popular are swallow, butterfly and eagle. There are also kites made in the shape of characters of mythical stories such as the Monkey King. And when the centipede-or-dragon-shaped kite composed of many sections is flown up high, it thrashes and dances about like a huge dragon in the air.

Because flying kites is beneficial to one's health, it is gaining popularity in many countries. The Chinese regard it as a game as well as a sport. Some people hang kites on the wall for decoration. Chinese kites are now available for sale in Japan, Southeast Asia and many countries in Europe and America.

In recent years, an international kite festival has been held annually in Weifang of Shandong Province since China is the birthplace of kite.

1 | 2
  | 3

1. 放风筝
   Flying kites
2. 纸鸢
   Zhiyuan (paper kite)
3. 金鱼风筝
   Goldfish kite

灯彩

Fancy Lantern

灯彩，民间也叫"花灯"。每逢春节、元宵节等喜庆的日子，中国的城市和乡村，家家户户都要挂灯笼。

中国的灯彩是用竹、木或金属做框架，再裱糊上纸或绫绢做成的。有的灯笼上还画着彩色的古今故事，或者贴上剪纸。

中国花灯的品种非常多，比如逢年过节时悬挂的大红宫灯；能够转动的走马灯；孩子们喜爱的公鸡灯、狮子灯、金鱼灯、莲花灯、白菜灯、花篮灯等动物花卉灯……据说，广东佛山还有一种奇特的芝麻灯，灯上的图案是用一粒粒的芝麻粘贴成的，人们说它是"能吃的灯"。

现在，每逢年节，中国各地仍然举行各种大型的灯会，灯会上除了展览各种传统的灯彩，还展出许多运用现代科学技术制作的彩灯。此外，在哈尔滨等北方城市，每年冬季还要举行冰灯灯会。人们用冰块雕刻成高大的建筑、可爱的动物和神话传说中的仙女，在灯光的照耀下，晶莹剔透的冰灯，仿佛把人们带到了奇妙的世界。

1　2
　3

1. 龙灯头部
   The head of a dragon lantern
2. 灯会上各种各样的花灯
   Various lanterns at the lantern fair
3. 冰灯
   Ice lanterns

Fancy Lantern

Fancy lantern, also called Huadeng, are widely used for decorations in both rural and urban areas in China on New Year's Day and other festivals and holidays.

On the whole, it mainly consists of a frame made of bamboo strips or metal wire covered with paper or thin gauze. Some lanterns are painted with characters in ancient or current stories, or pasted with paper-cuts.

Many types of traditional lanterns fit the description of "fancy"; those that are commonly seen include large palace lanterns, lanterns with revolving figures, and lanterns in the shape of animals or plants such as a rooster, lion, goldfish, lotus, Chinese cabbage, flower basket, etc. In Foshan of Guangdong Province, there is a kind of lantern whose pictures are made of sesames, which people call an edible lantern.

Large lantern fairs are held everywhere in China during festivals. Apart from traditional lanterns, there are many lanterns made with modern technology. In winter, cities in North China, like Beijing and Harbin, hold Ice Lantern festival. Huge sculptures of buildings, animals and fairies are illuminated by colorful lights to give the transparent look of a magical wonderland.

刺绣

Embroidery

刺绣，是中国著名的传统手工艺品，已经有3 000多年的历史。人们用丝、绒或棉线，在绸缎和布帛上穿针引线，绣出各式各样美丽的花纹和图案。中国刺绣的品种很多，江苏的苏绣、湖南的湘绣、广东的粤绣和四川的蜀绣，被人们称为中国"四大名绣"。

苏州出产的苏绣，已经有2 000多年的历史。苏绣艺人能用40多种针法，1 000多种花线绣出各种花鸟、动物和苏州园林的图案。苏绣绣工精细，图案秀丽，特别是苏绣小猫，明亮的眼睛，蓬松的毛丝，就像真的一样，称得上是苏绣的精品。

湖南省的别称是湘，湖南出产的刺绣被称为湘绣。湘绣至少也有2 000多年的历史了。由于一些画家参加了湘绣的设计工作，所以湘绣作品带有中国画的特色和意境。俗话说"苏绣猫，湘绣虎"，湘绣狮虎，生动地表现出了狮、虎的凶猛，是湘绣的传统产品。

广东省的别称是粤，出产在广东的刺绣就被称为粤绣。粤绣至少有1 000多年的历史。粤绣色彩艳丽，图案整齐，其中最多的是龙、凤。"百鸟朝凤"、"九龙屏风"是粤绣中的优秀作品。

四川省的别称是蜀，出产在四川的蜀绣，早在1 000多年前就已经十分有名了。蜀绣的针法有1 000多种，既能刺绣花鸟鱼虫，又能创作山水人物。蜀绣的传统作品有"芙蓉鲤鱼"和"公鸡鸡冠花"等。

除了"四大名绣"之外，北京的京绣、温州的瓯(ōu)绣、上海的顾绣、苗族的苗绣也都很有特色。

刺绣可以用来装饰，可以做服装、被面、枕套、床罩等生活用品，也可以成为华贵的艺术品和陈设品，深受人们喜爱。

1

2

1. 蜀绣
   Sichuan embroidery
2. 穿着绣花衣服的彝族妇女
   The Yi Nationality women in embroidered dress

Embroidery

Embroidery is a renowned traditional Chinese handicraft with a history of more than 3 000 years. On a piece of silk or cloth, people embroider all kinds of beautiful pictures and patterns with threads of silk, wool or cotton. Among various kinds of embroidery, the best products come from four provinces: Jiangsu (notably Suzhou), Hunan, Guangdong and Sichuan.

Suzhou Embroidery, or Su Xiu, has a history of 2 000 years. Suzhou artists are able to use more than 40 ways of needling and 1 000 different types of threads to make flowers, birds, animals and even gardens on a piece of cloth. Suzhou Embroidery is refined and exquisite. The best-known work is an embroidered cat with bright eyes and fluffy hair, looking vivid and lifelike.

Hunan Embroidery, or Xiang Xiu, has a history of at least 2 000 years as well. Since artists of traditional Chinese painting are involved in designing pictures and patterns, the embroidery in Hunan has an air of traditional Chinese painting. Typical embroidery shows images of lions and tigers that are so vivid that one can feel their ferocity.

Guangdong Embroidery, or Yue Xiu, dates back to at least 1 000 years. It is usually colorful and bright with neat patterns, with a dragon and phoenix predominating among the images. Prominent works are "Hundred Birds Pay Homage to the Phoenix" and "Screen of Nine Dragons".

Sichuan Embroidery, or Shu Xiu, became known as early as 1 000 years ago. With over a thousand ways of needlework, artists are able to create flowers, birds, fishes and insects, as well as landscapes and human figurines. Its exemplary works are "Hibiscus and Carps" and "Roosters and Coxcombs".

Apart from the above four types, fine embroidery is also made in Beijing, Wenzhou, Shanghai and by the Miao ethnic communities.

Embroidery can be used in many ways. It is often adopted in clothing, quilt covers, pillowcases and bed sheets. It can also be displayed as a work of art or used for decorative purpose.

丝绸

Silk

Silk

中国是最早生产丝绸的国家。传说是黄帝的妻子嫘（sāo）祖发明了养蚕、缲丝和织绸的技术。考古学家们认为，中国的桑蚕丝织技术，至少有4 000多年的历史。丝绸很早就成了古代宫廷贵族的主要衣料和对外贸易的重要商品。

中国古代丝绸品种丰富多彩。自从2 000多年以前，汉代著名的外交家张骞打通了通往欧洲、西亚许多地区的"丝绸之路"，华美的中国丝绸就开始源源不断地输往欧洲和西亚各国。西方人十分喜爱中国丝绸，据说，公元1世纪，一位古罗马皇帝曾穿着中国的丝绸袍去看戏，顿时轰动了整个剧场。从此，人们都希望能穿上中国的丝绸衣服，中国也因此被称为"丝国"。

丝绸美化了人们的生活，也促进了中国和世界各国的友好往来。

Silk

China is the earliest country to have produced silk. Legend has it that Lei Zu, wife of Emperor Huangdi, invented sericulture, silk reeling and weaving. Chinese archaeologists believe the technology of silk weaving has at least a history of 4 000 years. Silk fabrics had been the main materials to make clothes for the noblemen and their families as well as an important commodity for export since long ago.

There were various kinds of ancient Chinese silk. As early as the Han Dynasty of 2 000 years ago, Zhang Qian, a famous diplomat of the time, opened up the "Silk Road" leading to West Asia and Europe. It was along this road that silk was continuously transported to those countries. Westerners were very fond of Chinese silk. It is said that during the first century AD, a Roman emperor went to a theater wearing silk, which made a great stir in the audience. Since then, people wished to wear clothes made of Chinese silk. China, therefore, was called the "Silk Country".

Silk has made people's life beautiful and promoted friendly exchanges between China and other countries.

```
1
—————
2 | 3
```

1. 中式丝绸衣服
   Chinese style silk dress
2. 丝绸
   Silk
3. 宋代丝绸服饰
   Silk dress of the Song Dynasty

蜡染 和蓝印花布

Batik and Blue Calico

　　蜡染和蓝印花布是中国民间的传统印染工艺品。

　　蜡染的主要方法是：先在白布上画好几何图案或花、鸟、鱼、虫的轮廓，然后用蜡刀把溶化了的蜡液填在画好的花纹上，再把布浸入靛蓝液中浸染。颜色达到一定的深度后，把布取出晾干，再用水煮脱蜡，就印成了蓝底白花的蜡染布。由于蜡性较脆，容易产生裂纹，染料渗入裂缝后，印成的花纹中往往产生一丝丝很细的冰裂纹，产生了一种意想不到的装饰效果。蜡染有单色染和复色染两种，有的民族还用四五种颜色套色印染，色彩自然而丰富。许多民族喜欢用蜡染布做衣裙、被面、头巾、背带等。

　　蓝印花布也是一种蓝白两色的花布，在中国的南北各省都有生产。蓝印花布的制作方法是：先把纸刻成花板，蒙在白布上，然后用石灰、豆粉和水调成防染粉浆进行刮印，再放入靛蓝染液中浸染，晾干以后，刮去防染浆，就成了蓝白两色的花布。蓝印花布有白底蓝花的，也有蓝底白花的，花样一般有花卉、人物及传说故事，大多用来做衣料、被面、门帘、帐子、围腰等。

　　现代都市生活中，别具民族风格的蜡染和蓝印花布，赢得了越来越多人的喜爱。

```
1 | 2
--+--
  | 3
```

1. 苗族蜡染花布
   Batik cloth of the Miao Nationality
2. 蜡染花包
   A batik bag
3. 身着蜡染服饰的苗族妇女
   The Miao Nationality women wearing batik dress

Batik and Blue Calico

Both batik and blue calico are traditional printing and dyeing arts and crafts popular among Chinese.

The process of batik making is delicate: first draw some designs or contours of images of a flower, bird, fish or insect on a piece of white cloth, then use a special brass knife to scoop melted wax to fill in those designs or contours as it hardens on the cotton cloth. The cloth is immersed completely in a jar of indigo dye bath so that the unwaxed parts take on color. The dyed cloth is boiled to melt off the wax and to leave clear patterns in white on a blue ground. Since wax is easy to crack, the dye penetrates fine cracks naturally formed in the solidified wax, leaving hair-thin blue lines on the undyed white designs and enhancing the charm of the final product. Batik can be dyed with a single or multiple colors, while some ethnic peoples adopt four or five colors to make the cloth motley and look even more gorgeous. In the ethnic areas, batik is used extensively to make clothes art quilt covers, headscarves, belts, etc.

Blue calico is also white-and-blue cloth which is produced in many provinces of China. The method of making blue calico is to cover a piece of white cloth with a paper cut, then spread a layer of a mixture of lime, bean powder and water over it and dip it in an indigo dye bath. After being dried in the shade, the layer of the mixture is scraped off and there is a finished blue print with two colors, either white background with blue designs or blue background with white designs. Pictures on such cloth are usually flowers, human figurines or legends. Blue calico is used for making clothes, quilt covers, door curtains, canopies and belts.

Batik and blue calico with strong nationalistic features has become more and more popular in modern urban life.

剪纸

Paper-Cuts

很多外国人都喜欢中国的剪纸，因为它美丽精巧，带着独特的东方神韵，能使人感到浓浓的生活气息和欢乐喜庆的气氛。

剪纸，就是用剪子、刻刀在大红纸或其他有色纸上剪刻出各种装饰性的花样和图案。中国的剪纸艺术大约有2 000多年的历史，是中国民间十分常见的工艺品。

中国的剪纸大多出自农村妇女之手，她们剪刻出的各种花样，大都是农民最关心、最喜爱和最向往的事物，有家禽、家畜、农作物、花鸟、娃娃、戏曲故事、吉祥图案等，常常在过年过节和喜庆吉日时使用。贴在窗子上的叫窗花，贴在门楣上的叫挂签，还有墙花、顶棚花、喜花、灯花和刺绣的花样，品种特别多。鲜艳美丽的剪纸给中国普通百姓的生活带来了欢乐和喜气。

中国剪纸分单色和彩色两种，单色的朴素大方，彩色的绚丽多彩。由于各地人民的生活习惯不同，各地民间剪纸的风格也不同。中国比较有名的剪纸有陕西的窗花、河北蔚县的戏曲人物以及南方少数民族的绣花底样等。内容丰富、花样繁多的民间剪纸，已经成为美化人们生活的艺术品。

目前，中国剪纸已被联合国教科文组织列入世界文化遗产。

1	3
2	4

1. 剪纸十二生肖：猪
   One of the paper-cut of twelve symbolic animals: pig
2. 剪纸十二生肖：龙
   One of the paper-cut of twelve symbolic animals: dragon
3. 剪纸：四喜娃娃
   Paper-cut: four-happiness dolls
4. 剪纸："寿"
   Paper-cut: *shou* (longevity)

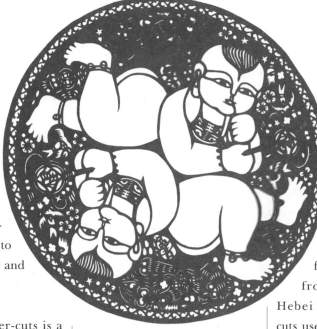

Paper -Cuts

Many Western-ers are fond of Chinese paper-cuts, because they are pretty and exquisite with a unique oriental style. Indeed, Chinese pa-per-cuts help viewers to feel the real daily life and a festive atmosphere.

The making of paper-cuts is a popular folk art with a history of more than 2 000 years in China. In the hands of an artisan, a piece of red or other colored pa-per can be turned into any of a wide variety of patterns with the help of a knife or a pair of scis-sors.

Chinese paper-cuts are mostly created by women in rural areas. The designs are familiar ones close to peasants' life, such as fowls, domestic animals, crops, flowers, birds, babies, episodes from local operas, auspicious symbols, etc. They are used on the Chinese Lunar New Year or other festivals, usually pasted on windowpanes, door lintels, walls, ceilings, lamps, etc. Some are used as copies for embroidery. Their elegant lines and pleasing images add delight and festivity to the life of the ordinary Chi-nese people.

Paper-cuts fall into two catego-ries: the simple and natural single-colored ones, and the gorgeous and colorful ones. As custom varies from place to place, pa-per-cuts of different regions are differ-ent in style. Well-known paper-cuts in China are those for windowpanes from Shaanxi Province, figurines of local operas from Weixian County of Hebei Province, and paper-cuts used as embroidery copies among the ethnic minorities in southern China. Rich in content, great in variety, paper-cuts serve to make people's life more beautiful.

Chinese paper-cut has been list-ed as one of the world's cultural heritages by UNESCO.

玉雕

Jade Carving

玉雕是中国最古老的雕刻品种之一。早在新石器时代晚期，中华民族就有了玉制工具。商周时期，制玉成为一种专业，玉器成了礼仪用具和装饰佩件。玉石历来被人们当作珍宝，在中国古代，玉被当作为美好品质的标志和君子风范的象征。

玉，实际是优质的石。玉石的种类非常多，有白玉、黄玉、碧玉、翡翠及玛瑙、绿松石、芙蓉石等。

玉石加工雕琢成为精美的工艺品，称为玉雕。工艺师在制作过程中，根据不同玉料的天然颜色和自然形状，经过精心设计、反复琢磨，才能把玉石雕制成精美的工艺品。

玉雕的品种很多，主要有人物、器具、鸟兽、花卉等大件作品，也有别针、戒指、印章、饰物等小件作品。北京的故宫博物院中收藏的大型玉雕"大禹治水"，高224厘米，宽96厘米，重约5 300多千克，充分显示了中国玉雕的高超技艺。

中国玉器的主要产地有北京、上海、广州、辽宁、江苏、新疆等地。中国的玉雕作品在世界上享有很高的声誉。

1. 赏月仙子
   Fairies admiring the moon
2. 玉雕跪人
   Jade caving kneeler
3. 玉兽
   Jade beast
4. 凤纹玉佩
   Jade ornament with the phoenix patterns
5. 勇士骑马
   The jade warrior riding on a horse

1	3	4
2		5

Jade Carving

Jade carving is one of the oldest carving arts in China. Crude jade tools appeared in China as early as in the late Neolithic Age. Jade carving became an industry in the Shang (16th century BC—11th century BC) and Zhou (11th BC—221 BC) dynasties, and jade wares were used in rituals or as decorative pendants. In ancient China, jade was also regarded as a symbol of refinement and moral ethics.

Jade is a high-quality stone and has a good many variants. There are white jade, yellow jade, jasper, jadeite, agate, turquoise, etc.

Jade carving refers to the process to carve a piece of jade into a fine article of art. A carving artist has to thoroughly examine a piece of jade, cudgel his brains to make a design according to its natural colors and shape, and turn it into an artistic work.

Jade can be carved into human figurines, containers, images of birds, animals, flowers as well as small things like a brooch, ring, seal or decorative object. What is worth mentioning is the huge jade carving in the Palace Museum in Beijing. It is called "Da Yu Harnesses Flood", which is 224 cm in height, 96 cm in width, and about 5 300 kg in weight.

It demonstrates the high skill of Chinese carving artists.

Jade wares are mainly produced in Beijing, Shanghai, Guangzhou, Liaoning, Jiangsu, Xinjiang, etc. Chinese jade carving works enjoy a high reputation in the world.

石狮

Stone Lion

狮子是中国人心目中的"灵兽",被誉为"百兽之王"。在中国,随处都可以见到石雕的狮子。

由于中国人把狮子视为吉祥、勇敢、威武的象征,所以人们在修建宫殿、府第、房屋及陵墓时,总喜欢用石头雕成各种各样的狮子,安放在门口,用来"驱魔避邪",把守大门。在古代,设置石狮子是有一定规矩的,一般门左边的是雄狮,雄狮的右脚踩着一只绣球象征威力。门右边的是雌狮,雌狮用左脚抚慰小狮子,象征子孙昌盛。

在中国历史上,北京曾是五个封建王朝的都城,因此,在北京城内外,遗存下许许多多各式各样的石狮。其中,天安门前的那对最大,中山公园社稷坛门外的那对最古老。人们常说"卢沟桥的石狮子——数不清",可见卢沟桥的石狮之多。现在人们在北京看到的石狮,大多是明清时代的工匠们雕刻的,显得比较温顺。如果要看汉唐时期强健威猛的石狮,只能到中国的另一个古都西安去观赏了。

如今,石狮作为威武和吉祥的象征,又出现在繁华的街市和银行、商厦、公园的门前。据说,狮子爱玩"夜明珠",所以,石狮的口中多半都含着一颗能活动的圆球。

1. 晋祠石狮
   Stone lion in Jinci
2. 卢沟桥石狮
   Stone lion on the Lugou Bridge
3. 乾陵石狮
   Stone lion at the Qian Mausoleum

1
—
2 | 3

Stone Lion

In the minds of the Chinese, the lion is the Magical Beast King of all animals. Wherever one goes, one can see lions made of stone.

As the Chinese regard lion as a symbol of auspiciousness, bravery and power, stone lions of all kinds are often placed in front of palaces, mansions, houses and tombs to guard against evil. But there were rules about it in ancient days. Normally, a male lion was placed on the left side of the gate with its right paw on a ball, which is a symbol of power. A female lion was placed on the right side of the gate with its left paw fondling a small cub, which is a symbol of a prosperous lineage.

In Chinese history, Beijing served as the capital for five dynasties. So, there exists numerous stone lions of various types in and outside the city. The largest pair stands in front of the Tian'anmen Gate, while the oldest pair guards the en-trance to the Altar of Land and Grain in Zhongshan Park. The balustrades of Lugou Bridge in the western suburbs of Beijing are carved with numerous lions, hence the saying, "as many as the lions of Lugou Bridge, too numerous to count". The stone lions we see today in Beijing were mostly carved during the Ming (1368—1644) and Qing (1644—1911) dynasties. They look rather mild. Powerful and fierce-looking stone lions carved in the heyday of the Han (206 BC—220 AD) and Tang dynasties (618—907) can be found only in Xi'an, another ancient capital.

Today, stone lions also appear at the entrance to banks, office buildings, parks or even in the street. The lion is said to be fond of the legendary luminous pearl. So, most stone lions have a movable stone pearl held in the mouth.

文房四宝

Four Treasures of the Study

自古以来，人们写字作画离不开纸、墨、笔、砚。这四种文具被称为"文房四宝"。

中国文房四宝的品种十分丰富。其中最著名的是宣纸、徽墨、湖笔和端砚。

纸 宣纸是一种名贵的纸张，早在唐代，就已经作为贡品献给皇帝。由于这种纸的产地在安徽省的宣城附近，所以被人们称为"宣纸"。宣纸洁白、细密、均匀、柔软，拉力大，吸水力强，墨色一落到纸上，就能很快渗透，最能表现出中国书法和绘画的特点。由于宣纸存放很长时间都不会破碎、变色，也不易被虫蛀，所以，很多中国古代的宣纸字画保存了几百年、上千年，仍然完好无损。

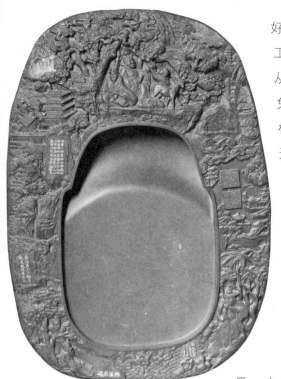

好的毛笔要经过70多道工序，制笔工人们要从千千万万根羊毛、兔毛、黄鼠狼毛中一根一根地挑选，然后进行搭配组合，才能制成优质的毛笔。中国最有名的毛笔是浙江湖州生产的湖笔。湖笔有200多种，是中国文房四宝中的珍品。

砚　砚是研墨的工具，在中国已有3 000多年的历史。端砚、歙砚、洮河砚、澄泥砚并称中国四大名砚。其中最著名的是端砚，由广东省肇庆市端溪出产的端石制成。端砚出墨快，墨汁不易干燥结冰。端砚不但是名贵的工艺品，还是献给皇帝的贡品。

1 | 2 3 / 4

1. 中国孩子在写毛笔字
Chinese children are doing handwriting with a Chinese brush.
2. 端砚
Famous ink stone produced in Duanxi
3. 中国人在做宣纸
Chinese people are making Xuan paper.
4. 徽墨
Ink stick produced in Huizhou, Anhui Province

墨　历代的中国书画家对用墨都十分讲究。安徽徽州生产的徽墨是中国最好的墨。徽墨从唐朝开始生产，到现在已经有1 000多年的历史。由于制作徽墨的原料中加入了名贵的中药和香料，有的还加入了黄金，所以，这种墨不但色泽黑润，而且香气浓郁，保存几十年后仍然可以使用。

笔　文房四宝中的笔指毛笔。毛笔的生产和使用可以追溯到几千年以前。毛笔的原料主要是兽毛和竹管。制作一支

纸、墨、笔、砚对中国文化和传统书画艺术的发展起到了非常重要的作用，一直到今天，人们仍称它们为"文房四宝"。

Four Treasures

of the Study

In the old days, one needs paper, ink stick, Chinese brush and ink stone to write or paint. They are called "four treasures of the study".

There are a great number of varieties of them, and the best-known ones are the paper of Xuancheng, the ink stick of Huizhou, the Chinese brush of Huzhou and the ink stone of Duanxi.

Paper

The best paper used for writing or painting with a Chinese brush is called Xuan paper since it was produced in a place near Xuancheng in Anhui Province. Being high quality paper, it was used as a tribute to the emperor early in the Tang Dynasty (618—907). Xuan paper is white, smooth, refined, even, soft, resilient and absorbent. As soon as the ink touches the paper it quickly seeps in, which can best present the characteristics of Chinese calligraphy and paint-

ing. As Xuan paper can be preserved for a long time without decay or change of color, and is insect proof, many ancient calligraphic works and traditional Chinese paintings have been preserved intact for several hundred years or even a thousand years.

Ink Stick

Chinese calligraphers and artists paid particular attention to the quality of the ink stick. The best ink stick is produced in Huizhou, Anhui Province. It was first produced in the Tang Dynasty more than a thousand years ago. Some Chinese medicine and perfume or even gold flakes are mixed into the materials in order to make better ink stick. Ink made by such a stick is particularly black with some fragrance. Ink sticks made in Huizhou can still be used after scores of years.

Chinese Brush

The production and use of the Chinese brush can be dated back several thousand years. A Chinese brush is made primarily of hairs from a beast and a small bamboo pipe. It takes 70 processing methods to make a good Chinese brush. Tens of thousands of hairs of a sheep, rabbit or weasel have to be chosen one by one and bound together to make the

brush. The best-known Chinese brush is manufactured in Huzhou, Zhejiang Province, which produces more than 200 types.

Ink Stone

The ink stone is used for grinding the ink stick in order to make ink. The ink stone has a history of 3 000 years in China. Ink stones produced in Duanxi, Shexian County, Taohe River and Henan, Hebei and Shanxi provinces (Chengni ink stone) are the best-known types. Ink produced on an ink stone of Duanxi takes less time to prepare and will not easily dry up. In ancient times, the ink stone of Duanxi was not only a precious artistic object but also a tribute to the emperor.

Paper, ink stick, Chinese brush and ink stone have played very important roles in the development of traditional Chinese calligraphy and painting.

1. 文房四宝
   Four treasures of the study
2. 毛笔
   Chinese brushes
3. 砚
   Ink stone

1	2
	3

中国民俗
Chinese Folk Customs

概　述

Introduction

中国人的生活多姿多彩，有许多很有意思的民俗。最有意思的可能要数中式婚礼了。中国人结婚与西方人不大一样，西方人要进教堂，而中国人要大摆宴席；西方人要上帝赐福，而中国人要拜天地，拜父母；西方人穿着洁白的婚纱举行婚礼，而中国传统的婚礼需要新郎新娘穿红衣服，因为红色在中国象征着吉利、喜庆。从结婚这件事上就可以很明显地看出中国有着不同于外国的民俗文化。其实，不仅是婚礼，包括小孩儿满月、春节、十二生肖属相等等，中国都有着独特的文化，这其中展现了中国人对幸福安康、吉祥如意的美好生活的向往。

Introduction

The Chinese life is colorful with many interesting folkways. The Chinese wedding may be a focus of interest. There are many differences between the Chinese and the West in weddings, as the people in the West go to church while the Chinese celebrate with a feast. Westerners hope that God will bless them while the Chinese thank heaven and their parents. Westerners wear white wedding dresses while the bride and groom wear red according to Chinese tradition, because red symbolizes good luck. In this way we know that China's folk culture is obviously different from that of the west. In fact, this can be seen not only in marriage but also with a baby's completion of its first month of life and the Spring Festival, etc. China has its unique culture, which shows the Chinese's wish for a happy and lucky life.

1	4
2 3	5

1. 龙的剪纸
   Dragon paper-cut
2. 彩陶泥偶
   Painted earthen dolls
3. 春节对联
   Spring Festival couplets
4. 风筝
   Kite
5. 舞狮
   Lion dance performance

中国人的姓名

Names of the Chinese People

中国人的姓，产生在母系氏族社会，那时候，人们以母亲为中心组成一个个的氏族，为了相互区别，就把姓作为氏族的称号。姓的来源，大概有以下几种情况：一、母系社会，以母亲的名为姓。二、以远古时代人们崇拜的动物为姓，如马、牛、羊、龙等。三、以封地封国为姓，如赵、宋、秦、吴等。四、以祖先的官职为姓，如司马、司徒等古代官职，就成了后代子孙的姓。五、以祖先的爵位或谥号为姓。六、以住地的方位和景物为姓。七、以职业为姓，如做陶器的人姓陶。八、以祖先的名号为姓，如中国人的祖先黄帝名叫轩辕，后来，轩辕就成了一个姓。

中国人的姓有一个字的单姓，也有两个字和两个字以上的复姓。中国有史以来到底有过多少个姓，到现在也没有准确的统计数字。当代中国人正在使用的汉姓约有3 500个左右。在其中100个常见姓氏中，最大的三个姓氏是李、王、张。

中国人的名也具有自己的传统和特点。中国人的姓名都是姓在前，名在后。名有一个字的，也有两个字的。同一家族中的人，名字要按辈分排列，同辈人的名字里，往往要有一个相同的字。古人的姓名比现代人的复杂，有文化、有地位的人除了姓、名以外，还

1. 百家姓墙
   Hundred surnames wall
2. 诸葛亮和诸葛村
   Zhuge Liang and the Zhuge Village
3. 吴氏族谱
   The genealogy of the surname Wu

有字和号。如：宋代文学家苏轼，姓苏，名轼，字子瞻，号东坡居士。唐代诗人李白幼年时居住在四川的青莲乡，他就给自己取号"青莲居士"。

中国人的名字往往有一定的含义，表示某种愿望。有的名字中包含出生时的地点、时间或自然现象，如"京"、"晨"、"冬"、"雪"等。有的名字表示希望具有某种美德，如"忠"、"义"、"礼"、"信"等。有的名字中有表示希望健康、长寿、幸福的意思，如"健"、"寿"、"松"、"福"等。男人的名字和女人的名字也不一样，男人的名字多用表示威武勇猛的字，如"虎"、"龙"、"雄"、"伟"、"刚"、"强"等。女人的名字常用表示温柔美丽的字，如"凤"、"花"、"玉"、"彩"、"娟"、"静"等。

现在，中国人起名已经没有古人那么多的讲究了。一般只有小名、大名，名字也不一定按辈分排列。然而，给孩子取一个好听、有意义而且与众不同的名字，仍然是许多中国人所希望的。

Names
of the Chinese People

陈家祠

Chen's family ancestral temple

The surnames of the Chinese people appeared during the matriarchal society, when clans were constituted with mothers at the center. And clans distinguished themselves from each other by using the name. The surname has roughly several origins as follows: 1. With the first name of the mother as the surname of the clan in the matriarchal society. 2. With the creatures worshipped in remote antiquity as the surname, such as 马 (horse), 牛 (cattle), 羊 (sheep), 龙 (dragon), etc. 3. With ancient states' names as the surname, such as 赵 (Zhao), 宋 (Song), 秦 (Qin), 吴, (Wu), etc. 4. With ancient official titles eventually adopted as the surname, such as 司马 (Sima) and 司徒 (Situ). 5. With the rank or title of nobility as the surname. 6. With the location and scene in residential places as the surname. 7. With the profession as the surname. For instance the person who makes pottery has the surname of 陶 (pottery). 8. With ancestors' official and courtesy names as the surname.

For example, the Chinese nation's ancestor was named 轩辕 (Xuanyuan), which later became a surname.

Some are one-character surnames, while others are compound surnames made up of two or more characters. Up to now, there is no exact statistic on how many surnames there are in China. Contemporary Chinese use about 3 500 Chinese surnames. Among the 100 commonly used surnames, the three most common are Li, Wang and Zhang; Zhuge, Ouyang, Situ and Sima are the common compound surnames.

In China, the surname comes first, and is followed by the given name, and the latter has its own traditions and features. It can have one or two characters. In the same clan, the given name is arranged in the order of seniority in the family hierarchy. And the given names of the peers usually have one Chinese character in common if there are more than one character in their given names. The names of the ancient men were more complicated than those of the modern people. People of literacy and status have both a style name and an alternative name, along with the surname and given name. For example, a man of letters Su Shi in the Song Dynasty had the style name Zizhan and the alternative name Dongpo. The poet Li Bai in the Tang Dynasty lived in the Qinglian Village in Sichuan Province in his childhood, and thus he styled himself Qinglian Jushi (retired scholar).

Chinese names usually have a certain meaning, expressing some kind of wish. Some names embody the location, time or natural phenomenon when the person was born, such as Jing (Beijing), Chen (morning), Dong (winter), and Xue (snow). Some names indicate the expectation of possessing some virtues, such as Zhong (loyalty), Yi (justice), Li (etiquette), and Xin (faith). Some names have the meaning of health, longevity and happiness, such as Jian (health), Shou (longevity), Song (pine, representing longevity), and Fu (happiness). Male names are different from female ones: men's names usually have the character meaning power and vigor, such as Hu (tiger), Long (dragon), Xiong (grandeur), Wei (magnificence), Gang (hardness), and Qiang (strength). And the names of females usually use characters representing gentleness and beauty, such as Feng (phoenix), Hua (flower), Yu (jade), Cai (colors), Juan (graceful), and Jing (quiet).

Today, the Chinese do not pay as much attention to naming, as did ancient folk. Generally a person has an infant name and an official one, and the given names are not necessarily arranged in the order of the seniority in the family hierarchy. However, it's still the Chinese people's wish to give their children a name which sounds good and meaningful.

十二属相

Twelve Symbolic Animals

十二生肖玩具
Twelve symbolic animals toys

中国民间有一个传统习俗，人一出生，就有一种动物作他的属相。属相，也叫"生肖"，是中国民间传统的纪年和计算年龄的方法。

中国古代的纪年法是帝王年号与"干支"并用，其中"干支纪年法"从史书上有明文记载的公元前841年（庚申年），一直沿用到现在。"干"是"天干"，由10个字组成，这10个字是：甲、乙、丙、丁、戊、己、庚、辛、壬、癸。"支"是"地支"，由12个字组成，这12个字是：子、丑、寅、卯、辰、巳、午、未、申、酉、戌、亥。把天干的10个字和地支的12个字按顺序配合起来，可以得到60种排列，如：甲子、乙丑、丙寅……这60种排列周而复始，循环使用，每60年叫做"一个甲子"。如公历的2001年，是农历的辛巳年，公历的2002年，是农历的壬午年；而60年后，2061年又是辛巳年，2062年又是壬午年。从东汉（25—220）时开始，人们又用鼠、牛、虎、兔、龙、蛇、马、羊、猴、鸡、狗、猪12种动物来配十二地支，组成了十二生肖，也叫十二属相。这就是：子鼠、丑牛、寅虎、卯兔、辰龙、巳蛇、午马、未羊、申猴、酉鸡、戌狗、亥猪。这样，子年是鼠年，丑年是牛年，寅年是虎年……于是，每个人一出生，就有一种动物作他的属相。子年出生的属鼠，丑年出生的属牛，寅年出生的属虎，以此类推。

现在，中国人在用公历纪年和计算年龄的同时，仍然习惯用属相纪年和推算年龄。

Twelve Symbolic Animals

It is traditional in China, when a person is born, one animal (*shuxiang*) is used to symbolize this year. *Shuxiang*, also called *shengxiao* (any of the 12 animals representing the Earthly Branches), is a traditional way in China to number the years and to record a person's age.

The ancient Chinese people invented the method to designate the years by the Heavenly Stems and Earthly Branches. The Heavenly Stems consist of ten characters: *jia* (Heavenly Stem One), *yi* (Heavenly Stem Two), *bing* (Heavenly Stem Three), *ding* (Heavenly Stem Four), *wu* (Heavenly Stem Five), *ji* (Heavenly Stem Six), *geng* (Heavenly Stem Seven), *xin* (Heavenly Stem Eight), *ren* (Heavenly Stem Nine), and *gui* (Heavenly Stem Ten). And the Earthly Branches are composed of 12 characters: *zi* (Earthly Branch One), *chou* (Earthly Branch Two), *yin* (Earthly Branch Three), *mao* (Earthly Branch Four), *chen* (Earthly Branch Five), *si* (Earthly Branch Six), *wu* (Earthly Branch Seven), *wei* (Earthly Branch Eight), *shen* (Earthly Branch Nine), *you* (Earthly Branch Ten), *xu* (Earthly Branch Eleven), and *hai* (Earthly Branch Twelve). Combining each of the 10 Heavenly Stems with one of the 12 Earthly Branches in sequence creates 60 chronological symbols. For example, *jiazi* (Heavenly Stem One Earthly Branch One), *yichou* (Heavenly Stem Two Earthly Branch Two), *bingyin* (Heavenly Stem Three Earthly Branch Three), etc. These 60 symbols are used in circles and thus each year has a chronological symbol. For example, 2001 corresponds to *xinsi*, 2002 to *renwu* in the lunar calendar; after 60 years, 2061, once again, corresponds to *xinsi*, and 2062, to *renwu*. Later, people used 12 animals (rat, ox, tiger, rabbit, dragon, snake, horse, sheep, monkey, rooster, dog and pig) to correspond to the 12 Earthly Branches, forming the 12 Symbolic Animals, namely, Earthly Branch One Rat, Earthly Branch Two Ox, Earthly Branch Three Tiger, Earthly Branch Four Rabbit, Earthly Branch Five Dragon, Earthly Branch Six Snake, Earthly Branch Seven Horse, Earthly Branch Eight Sheep, Earthly Branch Nine Monkey, Earthly Branch Ten Rooster, Earthly Branch Eleven Dog, and Earthly Branch Twelve Pig. Thus the *zi* Year is the Year of the Rat, and the *chou* Year is the Year of the Ox, and the *yin* Year is the Year of the Tiger, etc. Therefore, when a person is born, he has an animal as his symbolic animal. The year 2002 was a *renwu* year under lunar calendar, also the Year of Horse, and so children born in this year are all Horse babies.

Even though the Chinese people now number the years and their age under the Gregorian calendar, they still continue to use the symbolic animals. As long as people know a person's probable age and his symbolic animal, people can infer his exact age and year of birth.

小孩儿满月与抓周

One-Month-Old Feast and One-Year-Old Catch (*Zhuazhou*) of Babies

在中国，小孩儿的满月酒和抓周仪式独具特色。在孩子的成长过程中，这两个仪式有里程碑式的纪念意义。

小孩儿出生满一个月的那天，孩子的家人一般要招呼亲朋挚友，邀请他们一起来庆祝孩子满月。按照中国的传统，这一天，家里会充满了喜庆和节日的氛围，满月酒要办得热热闹闹才行。不过最近这些年，这个习俗在城市尤其是年轻夫妇中有逐渐被淡化的趋势。但是，小孩儿满月对于每个家庭来说，仍然都是一个非常值得纪念的高兴的日子。

"抓周儿"中的"周"是小孩儿满一周岁的意思。关于"抓周儿"，最早记载于北齐。"抓周儿"也就是在小孩儿满周岁那天，吃中午的长寿面之前，摆上经书、笔、墨、纸、砚、算盘、钱币、账册、首饰、花朵、胭脂、吃食、玩具等，如果是女孩儿则要加摆铲子、勺子（炊具）、剪子、尺子（缝纫用具）、绣线、花样子（刺绣用具），再由大人将小孩抱来，令其端坐，父母及他人不给予任何的引导或暗示，任孩子随意挑选，看他先抓什么，后抓什么，并以此为依据来预测孩子可能存在的志趣和将从事的职业以及前途。

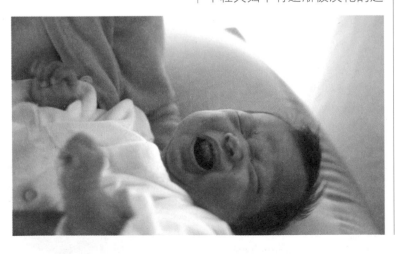

One-Month-Old Feast and One-Year-Old Catch (*Zhuazhou*) of Babies

In China, the one-month-old feast and one-year-old catch of a baby are of unique Chinese characteristics. These two ceremonies are of milestone-like significance in the growing process of a baby.

On the day when a baby is a month old, the family of the baby will invite their friends and relatives to a ceremony to celebrate the occasion. In a traditional one-month-old ceremony, there will be a rejoicing and festive atmosphere in the family and the feast is supposed to be lively and joyful. However, in recent years this custom has been gradually abandoned among city dwellers, especially among young couples. Nevertheless, the one-month-old ceremony of a baby still remains a memorable and happy moment for every family.

Zhou in the word *zhuazhou* means

"a baby is one year old". The earliest historical record about *zhuazhou* appeared during the Dynasty of Northern Qi. On the day when a baby is a year old, the family of the baby will lay out sutras, brush pens, ink sticks, paper, ink slabs, abacus, copper coins, account books, jewelries, flowers, rouge, foods, toys, etc. For girls, scoops, scissors, rulers, thread, scissor-cut (articles for embroidery) will be added. The parents then put the baby in front of these articles and make

it sit up. Nobody will give any instruction or cue to the baby so that it is left free to choose by itself. Watching the baby catch the articles it likes, the family can then make predictions about its potential interests, future career and development.

1. 满月
   One-month-old child
2. 抓周
   One-year-old catch
3. 拨浪鼓
   Rattle-drum

婚礼

Wedding

结婚是人生中的一件大事。传统的中式婚礼古朴而又热闹，隆重、喜庆并且礼节周全，场面的铺陈颇具特色，不过在现代，尤其是在城市里，已经很少见了。

花轿是传统婚礼的核心内容之一。结婚时，新娘要坐在花轿里从娘家被抬到男方家中。花轿一般分四人抬，八人抬两种，又有"龙轿"、"凤轿"之分。除去轿夫之外，还有持笙锣、伞、扇等的随行人员，一般的轿队少则十几人，多则几十人，很是壮观。传统

的中式婚礼中，新娘要蒙着红盖头，在伴娘的伴随下，由新郎手持的大红绸牵着，慢慢地登上花轿。在新娘乘花轿去往男方家里的途中，颠花轿是必不可少的热闹场面。轿夫一起左摇右摆使花轿不稳，新娘坐在里面也是左右摇晃。有的时候，新郎甚至不得不代替新娘或者和新娘一起向众人抱拳施礼求饶，而这个时候，众人欢笑不止，实际上是为了增添新人成婚之日的喜庆气氛。

中式传统婚礼的最重要的部分便是拜堂成亲。新人走到天地桌前，上面摆放有装满粮食的斗，斗的四周写上"金玉满斗"四个大字，以红纸封口，斗内四角放若干硬币，以供拜完天地后看热闹的亲朋好友掏出来求取吉利之意。斗中要插一柏枝，枝上缀有铜钱，这个柏枝便被称作"摇

钱树"。斗旁放一杆秤、一面镜、织布机杼、一灯或一蜡烛。新郎在右，新娘在左，并肩站在天地桌前，执事人高声喊道："一拜天地，二拜高堂，夫妻对拜"。民间的说法认为，男女只有拜过天地后才能算作是正式夫妻，因此对这个拜堂的仪式非常重视。还有民间习俗有这样有趣的讲究，即如果新郎在结婚的当天因故不能拜天地，就让他的姐妹抱只公鸡来代替。

坐完花轿、拜完天地，接下来新人要入洞房了。洞房是一直延续下来的叫法，新人入了洞房以后，按照习俗，新郎新娘的同辈亲友聚集在洞房里，对新郎新娘开一些充满性暗示的玩笑。这时即便过头一点，新郎新娘也不会生气，而是想办法巧妙化解，因为亲朋好友闹洞房图的是高兴和热闹。

Wedding

Marriage is the most important thing in the life. In China, a traditional wedding is simple and lively, ceremonious, and joyful. There are some unique features in this ceremony, but in modern society, especially in the city, it is hardly seen any more.

The bridal sedan is the core of the traditional wedding. In wedding, the bride should sit in the sedan, then be lifted from her mother's home to her husband's home. Generally, there are two kinds of sedan, that is, four-lifter and eight-lifter, also divided into "dragon sedan" and "phoenix sedan". There are so many suites who hold gongs, umbrellas, fans and so on, besides lifters. In group, there are more than ten people at least, and the occasion is very magnificent. In a traditional wedding, accompanied with a bridesmaid, the bride wearing a red veil and led along by the bridesgroom who holds a red silk in his hand, enters the bridal sedan. On the way to the husband's home, lifters jolt the sedan as it is necessary in a joyful wedding. Lifters swing the sedan from left to right, causing the bride to sit unsteadily inside. Sometimes the bridegroom has to substitute for his bride or beg to everyone else, while, all laugh to adding to the jubilance.

The wedding ceremony is the most important part of a traditional Chinese wedding. The newlyweds go to the table for heaven and earth where there is a *dou* (a kind of basket) full of grain. The *dou* is written with "gold and jade fill the *dou*" on the brim and is sealed with red paper. There are many coins placed in the four corners of the *dou* to provide the "luck" meaning to the guests. There is a cypress branch, called "ready source of money", decorated with copper coins. Besides, one steelyard, a mirror, a loom, a lamp or a candle are also placed near the *dou*. Afterwards, the groom stands on the left side, the bride right by his side, while the director prompts, "First bow to the heaven and earth; second bow to the parents; third bow to each other". According to the folk saying, they will not be the formal couple until bowing to the heaven and earth. As a result, people pay a great attention to this ceremony. An interesting custom is that if the groom cannot come to this ceremony, he should ask his sister to hold a cock instead.

After taking the bridal sedan, bowing to the heaven, it's time for the newlyweds to go to the bridal chamber. According to custom, their relatives and friends get together in the bridal chamber to banter the newlyweds. At this time, the newlyweds will never get angry even if the teasing games are a bit outrageous, but will try to skillfully dissolve since the relatives and friends intend to delight them.

	2	1. 花轿
1		Bridal sedan
		2. 拜天地
		Bow to the Heaven and Earth

四灵——古代吉祥的象征

Four Deities—Symbol of Auspice in Ancient Times

中国古代认为麒麟、凤凰、龟和龙是有灵性的动物，因此，把它们称为"四灵"，作为祥瑞的标志。其实，除了龟以外，其他三种都是传说中的动物，是人们自己想象和创造出来的。

传说中的麒麟，身体像鹿，遍体披着鳞甲，头上长独角，角上生有肉球，脚像马蹄，尾像牛尾。麒麟被认为是有德性的仁兽，历代帝王都把它看作是太平盛世的象征。在北京的故宫和颐和园等皇帝的住处和花园里，都能见到麒麟，有铜铸的，也有石雕的。在民间，麒麟也很受重视。春节期间，中国江南各地的人们常抬着纸扎的麒麟，到各家门前表演，表达美好的祝愿。另外，在中国还有"麒麟送子"的传说，人们一方面用麒麟象征有出息的子孙；另一方面也表示了祈望早生贵子、家道繁荣的意思。

凤凰头顶美丽的羽冠，身披五彩翎毛，它是综合了许多鸟兽的特点想象出来的瑞鸟形象。凤凰是中国传说中的"百鸟之王"，标志着吉祥、太平和政治的清明。凤和龙一样，被历代帝王当作是权力和尊严的象征。凤冠、凤车等与凤有关的东西，只有皇家和仙人才能使用。不过，后来凤凰也成了民间百姓的吉祥物。尤其在中国传统的婚礼上，凤成了新娘礼服和头饰上的装饰，代表着吉祥和喜庆。在民间的传统图案纹样中，凤凰也被广泛应用，寓意吉祥和太平。凤凰还常和其他吉祥物配合成纹图，如"龙凤呈祥"、"凤麒呈祥"等，也是吉祥如意的象征。

龟在四灵中是唯一存在的动物，也是动物中寿命最长的。人们不仅把龟当成健康长寿的象征，还认为它具有预知未来的灵性。在古代，每当举行重大活动之前，巫师都要烧烤龟甲，然后根据龟甲上爆裂的纹路来占卜吉凶。所以，人们称龟为"神龟"、"灵龟"。神龟在中国曾经受到过极大的尊敬，在古代帝王的皇宫、宅院里，都有石雕或铜铸的神龟，用来象征国运的久远。

龙被人们认为是中国最大的神物，也是最大的吉祥物。人们都很熟悉龙的形象，但是谁也没见过真的龙。龙和凤、麒麟一样，是人们想象出来的动物，它长着牛头、鹿角、虾眼、鹰爪、蛇身、狮尾，通身还长满了鳞甲，是由多种动物复合而成的。在人们的想象

中，龙能在地上行走，能在水中游弋，能在云中飞翔，充满了无穷的神力。几千年来，封建帝王把它当作权力和尊严的象征，普通老百姓也认为它是美德和力量的化身，是吉祥之物。因此，在中国到处都可以见到龙的形象。宫殿、寺庙的屋脊上，皇家的用具上，处处刻着龙、画着龙；老百姓在喜庆的日子里，也要张贴龙的图案，还要舞龙灯、划龙船；给孩子起名字也愿意用上"龙"字。龙作为"四灵"中最大的吉祥物，已成为中华民族的象征。全

世界各地的中国人都认为自己是"龙的传人"。

1	2
	3

1. 麒麟
   The kylin
2. 灵龟
   The miraculous tortoise
3. 凤凰
   The phoenix

Four Deities—Symbol of

Auspice in Ancient Times

In ancient China, there were four kinds of animals which are the symbol of luck and peace. The Chinese think that the kylin, the phoenix, the tortoise and the dragon are miraculous, calling them as "Four Lucky Animals". In fact, except for the tortoise, the other three are all legendary animals which were created from the imaginations of the Chinese.

The kylin in legend has a body like a deer in scutum. There is a single nubby horn on its head. The feet are just like the hooves of horses, and the tail is just like the oxtail. The kylin is regarded as a very kind animal with a moral character. All of the emperors in the past dynasties regarded it as the symbol of peace. In the Forbidden City and the Summer Palace of Beijing, there are many statues of kylin. Some are copper-casting, some are stone-carving. Among people, the kylin is also highly respected. During the Spring Festival, people in southern China make the paper kylin in the festival opera to express their best wishes to each other. Moreover, there is another legend called "Kylin Brings the Son", in which it both symbolizes the success of a new generation and represents the wish for the birth of a son and continuation of the family tree.

The phoenix has a beautiful crista on its head and colorful feathers on the body. It is an imaginary lucky bird that is combined from characters of many other birds and animals. The phoenix is the King of the Birds in Chinese legend, meaning luck, peace and rightness. The phoenix, with the dragon, were regarded by the emperors as the symbol of their power and dignity. The phoenix coronet, the phoenix carriage and all other things that are related to the phoenix were specially reserved for royalty and the divine. However, the phoenix became a mascot among the people. Especially in the traditional Chinese wedding, the phoenix is the most important decoration on the bridal dress and headwear, signifying luck and happiness. In Chinese traditional designs and drawings, the phoenix image is quite popular and it brings luck and peace to the people. The phoenix is also designed together with other mascots, like the "Dragon and Phoenix", the "Phoenix and Kylin", etc. They all have the meaning of luck.

The tortoise is an exception in the "Four Lucky Animals", as it really exists and has the longest life span among animals. The Chinese not only regard it as the symbol of longevity, but also think it has the ability to foresee the life. In old China, before significant activities, the fortuneteller will always bake the shell of tortoise, and then read the future according to the cracks in the shell. Therefore, the tortoise was called "Saint Tortoise". The Saint Tortoise was highly respected in China. In the emperor's palaces and houses

there were statuaries of tortoises which were made of copper or stone, giving a blessing for the long life of the dynasties.

The dragon is regarded as the number one animal of the Chinese totem, and it is the most important mascot. The people are quite familiar with the image of the dragon, but nobody has ever seen a real one. The dragon was born from the imagination of the people just like the phoenix and kylin. It has a bull's head, a deer's horn, a lobster's eyes, an eagle's claws, a snake's body, a lion's tail and is covered with scutum. It is a combination of different kinds of animals. In the imagination, the dragon can walk on land, swim under water, and fly in the sky. It has incredible powers. Over thousands of years in China, the emperors treated it as the symbol of power and dignity, and in the mind of the common people, it also had virtue and power. It is definitely a lucky totem. One could find the image of the dragon every-

```
1 |     2
  |_____
  |  3
```

1. 龙凤石路
   A stone pathway with the dragon and phoenix patterns
2. 灵龟
   The miraculous tortoise
3. 龙凤瓷瓶
   Porcelain vase with the dragon and phoenix patterns

where in China. On the roof of the palaces and temples, on the devices of royalty, the dragon is painted and sculptured. During festivals, people will post the picture of the dragon, and play the dragon light and dragon boat. Even when they name their children, they like to use the word dragon. Being the most important one among the "Four Lucky Animals", the dragon now has become the symbol of the whole Chinese nation. The Chinese all over the world call themselves the Dragon's descendants.

吉祥 图案

Images of Blessing

中国民间，流传着许多含有吉祥意义的图案。每到年节或喜庆的日子，人们都喜欢用这些吉祥图案装饰自己的房间和物品，以表示对幸福生活的向往，对良辰佳节的庆贺。

中国的吉祥图案始于距今3 000多年前的周代，后来在民间流传开来。今天，吉祥图案仍然是中国人生活中不可缺少的内容。

中国的吉祥图案内容极其广泛，这里介绍最常见的几种："双喜"字，是双喜临门、大吉大利的意思，民间常在办喜事时采用。

"寿"字，字头经过加工美化，变成对称的图案，是长寿的意思。

"福寿双全"，是由蝙蝠和寿字组成的图案。"蝠"与"福"同音，表示幸福长寿。

两个"有"字组成的对称图案，意思是顺也有，倒也有。在中国农村常用来贴在收藏谷物的器具上，表示丰收富裕。"百吉"，也叫"盘长"。它无头无尾，无始无终，可以想象为许多个"结"，谐"百吉"之音，作为百事吉祥如意的象征，也有福寿延绵、永无休止的意思。"五福捧寿"，图案中5个蝙蝠环绕一个寿字。五福是长寿、富贵、康宁、道德、善终。

"四合如意"，4个如意从四面围拢勾连起来，象征诸事如意。

Images of Blessing

There are many images which are meant to give good blessings in China. In the festivals or celebrations, people like decorating their houses and devices, for the blessing of a happy life and to celebrate the festivals.

The images of blessing in China started in the Zhou Dynasty around 3 000 years ago. Until today, the images of blessing are still an important content of the Chinese life.

The content of the images of blessing are quite broad, but here we introduce several kinds that are more popular:

Shuangxi—double happiness. It means happiness and luck. It is normally used in weddings.

Shou—longevity. It has been designed and prettified to be symmetrical, which means health and long life.

Fushou shuangquan—luck and health. It has the image of a bat and the word *shou*. In Chinese, the pronunciation of the bat is similar to that of luck, therefore it has the meaning of luck and long life.

A symmetrical image with two *you*. The *you* means having and wealthy in Chinese. In the counties of China, people post the image on the utensils for storing food, meaning a good and fruitful harvest.

Baiji is also called *panchang*. It can be imagined as the endless ties, which have the similar pronunciation as *jie* in Chinese. The meaning of *baiji* is endless luck in life.

Wufu pengshou—Five bats bring long life. There are five bats surrounding the word *shou*. Taking the pronunciation of the word bat, it means five different kinds of good aspects: long life, wealth, health, virtue, and happy end.

Sihe ruyi — Four s-shaped wands are enclosed and connected with each other on four sides, symbolizing everything goes as one wishes.

民间 庙会

Folk Temple Fair

庙会是中国民间的一种社会活动，据说起源于古代的祭祀土地神，以后逐渐变成了一种民间物品交流的集市和文化表演的场所。

庙会一般设在寺庙里和寺庙附近的空地上，在节日或规定的日子举办，有的只在每年春节期间举办。虽然各地举办庙会的时间不同，但基本内容都差不多。庙会期间，农户、商贩带着自己生产的农产品、土特产和从各处收集来的古玩玉器、花鸟鱼虫，到庙会上进行交易；各路手艺人设摊展卖民间工艺品和特色小吃；民间艺人搭台表演歌舞曲艺……人们喜气洋洋地赶来买卖物品，观看表演，品尝小吃，热闹非凡。

现在，北京市每年春节都举办庙会。比较有名的有白云观庙会、地坛庙会、龙潭湖庙会、隆福寺庙会等。北京的庙会保留了许多传统习俗，像白云观庙会的骑驴逛庙会、打金钱眼等。庙会上出售的物品也很有北方特色，像空竹、风车、刀枪剑戟等玩具；冰糖葫芦、茶汤等小吃，都深受老百姓欢迎。

Folk Temple Fair

The temple fair is a kind of social activity in China. Legend has it that it originated in ancient times when people offered sacrifices to the village god, which later gradually evolved into a marketplace for people to exchange products and a place for cultural performances.

The temple fair, usually on the open ground in or near a temple, is held on festive or specified days. Some are held only during the Spring Festival. Although different places hold their temple fairs at various dates, the contents are similar. Farmers and merchants sell their farm produce, local specialties, and antiques, jade articles, flowers, birds and fish; craftsmen set up their stalls to show and sell their handicrafts and specialty snacks; folk artists establish a stage for singing, dancing, and *quyi* (Chinese folk art forms, including ballad singing, story telling, comic dialogues, clapper talk, cross talk, etc.) performance. Ordinary people come to the temple fair to buy and sell goods, watch performances, and sample snacks, giving the temple fair a bustling atmosphere.

Now, Beijing holds many temple fairs every Spring Festival. Relatively famous temple fairs are those of the White Cloud Temple, the Altar of Earth, the Dragon Pool and the Temple of Intense Happiness. Temple fairs in Beijing have preserved many traditional customs, such as riding a donkey to stroll around the temple fair and throwing coins through the hole in the center of a copper coin in the White Cloud Temple. Many goods sold in the temple fair have typical northern features, such as toys like diabolo, pinwheel, knife, spear, sword and halberd; big sugarcoated haws on a stick and gruel of millet flour and sugar are widely popular among common people.

2
1　3

1. 庙会
   The temple fair
2. 庙会表演
   The temple fair performance
3. 庙会风车
   The temple fair pinwheels

舞狮

Lion Dance

舞狮大约起源于南北朝时期，到了唐朝，狮子舞已发展为上百人集体表演的大型歌舞。

舞狮在中国是一项传统体育项目，也是一种传统文化艺术，从北方到南方，从城市到乡村，逢年过节及庆典盛事，都可以看到欢快的舞狮。民间认为舞狮可以很好地把百姓的欢喜心情表达出来，也最能烘托热闹气氛。舞狮尤以广东地区一带最为盛行。用来舞动的狮子外形威武,动作刚劲,神态多变,广东人称它为"醒狮"。

中国百姓对狮子有图腾般的崇敬感，狮子在民间有很多传说，其位置仅次于龙,因此舞狮也就带有了不少神秘色彩。人们相信狮子是吉祥瑞兽，而舞狮能够带来好运，所以每逢节日和喜庆活动，都会舞狮助兴，祈求吉利和如意。专用于节庆场合纳福迎祥的舞狮，代代相传，从古代民间传统的娱乐活动，发展成为具有健身功能的体育运动。舞龙和舞狮的热闹场面在中国的电影中也是很常见的。

Lion Dance

The lion dance originated in the Northern and Southern Dynasties, developing into large-scale singing and dancing performed by hundreds of people collectively in the Tang Dynasty.

The lion dance is a traditional sport in China, as well as a kind of traditional culture and art. From the North to the South, from cities to countries, people can see cheerful lion dances on New Year's Day and on other festivals and celebrations. Folk people believe that the lion dance can express people's feelings of joy, and it can also set off the lively atmosphere. The lion dance is more popular in Guangdong area. The lion which is used to perform has mighty appearances, vigorous movements, and variable bearings. People in Guangdong call it the "awaking lion".

The Chinese people have a totemistic worship of the lion and have a lot of legends about lions. The lion's position is only next to the dragon so that it brings a mystery to the lion dance. People believe that the lion is a lucky beast that expresses joy and happiness. Therefore, the lion dance plays an important role at official celebrations and happy events to summon luck and fortune. This feat is passed on from generation to generation, from an ancient traditional entertainment activity to an athletic sport. The lion dance and dragon dance often appear in Chinese films.

1 | 2
| 3

1、2. 舞狮
Lion dance performance
3. 可爱的小狮子
A lovely lionet

春节

The Spring Festival

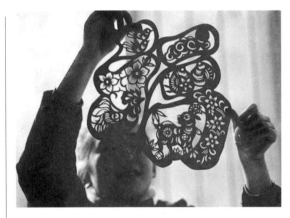

春节是农历的正（zhēng）月初一，是中国的农历新年。在中国的传统节日中，这是一个最重要、最热闹的节日。因为过农历新年的时候，正是冬末春初，所以人们把这个节日叫"春节"。

中国人过春节有很多传统习俗。从腊月二十三起，人们就开始准备过年了。在这段时间里，家家户户要大扫除，买年货，贴窗花，挂年画，写春联，蒸年糕，做好各种食品，准备辞旧迎新。

春节的前夜叫"除夕"。除夕之夜，是家人团聚的时候。一家人围坐在一起，吃一顿丰盛的年夜饭，说说笑笑，直到天亮，这叫守岁。除夕零点的钟声一响，人们还要吃饺子。古时候称23点到凌晨1点为"子时"，24点也就是零点叫"子正"，除夕的"子正"是新旧年交替的时候，人们在这时吃饺子，是取"更岁交子"的意思。这也是"饺子"名称的由来。

过了除夕就是大年初一。从初一开始，人们要走亲戚、看朋友，互相拜年。拜年，是春节的重要习俗。拜年时，大家都要说一些祝愿幸福、健康的吉祥话。

放爆竹是春节期间孩子们最喜欢的活动。传说燃放爆竹可以驱妖除魔，所以每年从除夕之夜起，到处就响起了接连不断的爆竹声。阵阵烟花，声声爆竹，给节日增添了喜庆的气氛。

春节期间，很多地方还要举办庙会。庙会上精彩的舞龙舞狮表演，各式各样的工艺品和地方小吃，吸引千千万万欢度佳节的人们。

尽管近几十年来的习俗有了很大变化，但是在中国和世界各地华夏子孙的心中，春节永远是最重要的节日，而鞭炮和饺子则是这个节日中最重要的两个元素。

The Spring Festival

The first day of the first lunar month is the New Year in the Chinese lunar calendar. Among the traditional Chinese festivals, this is the most important and the most bustling. Since it occurs at the end of winter and the beginning of spring, people also call it the Spring Festival.

Chinese have many traditional customs relating to the Spring Festival. From the 23rd day of the 12th lunar month, people start to prepare for the event. Every family will undertake a thorough cleaning, do their Spring Festival shopping, create paper-cuts for window decoration, put up New Year pictures, write Spring Festival couplets, make New Year cakes, and also prepare all kinds of food to bid farewell to the old and usher in the new.

New Year's Eve is the time for a happy reunion of all the family members, when they sit around the table to have a sumptuous New Year's Eve dinner, talking and laughing, until daybreak, which is called "staying up to see the year out". When the bell tolls midnight on New Year's Eve, people eat dumplings. In ancient times, midnight was called *zishi* (a period of the day from 11 pm to 1 am) and 12 pm was called *zizheng* when the old year ended and the New Year began. Dumplings (*jiaozi*) are eaten because it sounds the same as "change of the year and the day" in Chinese.

From the first day of the lunar year, people visit relatives and friends, to greet each other, which is an important custom for the Spring Festival.

Setting off firecrackers is the favorite activity of children in the Spring Festival. According to legend, this could drive off evil spirits. The continuous sound of firecrackers can be heard everywhere, adding to the atmosphere of rejoicing and festivity.

Many places hold temple fairs during the Spring Festival. The wonderful dragon lantern dance and lion dance performances, along with various handicraft articles and local snacks attract thousands of people.

These customs have been changed a lot over the years, but for the Chinese all over the world, the Spring Festival is the most important day, and firecrackers and dumplings are the two most important things of this day.

1 | 2

1. 贴窗花
   Pasting window paper-cuts
2. 包饺子
   Making dumplings

元宵节

The Lantern Festival

农历正月十五，是中国民间传统的元宵节。因为正月又叫元月，正月十五的晚上是一年里的第一个月圆之夜，"宵"是"夜晚"的意思，所以，正月十五这个节日就叫元宵节。元宵节，中国人有赏灯和吃元宵的习俗。俗话说"正月十五闹花灯"，因此，元宵节也叫灯节。

元宵节赏灯的习俗是从汉朝开始的，到现在已经有2 000多年的历史。元宵节这天，到处张灯结彩，热闹非常。夜晚一到，人们就成群结队地去观赏花灯。五光十色的宫灯、壁灯、人物灯、花卉灯、走马灯、动物灯、玩具灯……汇成一片灯海。有的花灯上还写有谜语，引得观灯人争先恐后地去竞猜。

元宵节吃元宵是中国人的传统习俗。早在宋朝（960—1276），就有这种食品了。元宵是一种用糯米粉做成的小圆球，里面包着用糖和各种果仁做成的馅，煮熟后，吃起来香甜可口。因为这种食品是在元宵节这天吃，后来人们就把它叫做元宵了。中国人希望诸事圆满，在一年开始的第一个月圆之夜吃元宵，就是希望家人团圆、和睦、幸福、圆圆满满。

The Lantern Festival

The 15th day of the first lunar month is the traditional Lantern Festival (Yuanxiao Festival in Chinese). *Yuanxiao* comes from the fact that the first lunar month is also called the Yuan Month and *xiao* means night. The night of the 15th day of the first lunar month marks the appearance of the first full moon. On the Lantern Festival, the Chinese people have the custom of enjoying lanterns and eating glutinous rice dumplings. There is a common saying that "Playing on the Lantern Festival".

The custom of enjoying lanterns on the festival started during the Han Dynasty, and has a history of more than 2 000 years. On that night, every place is decorated with lanterns and colorful streamers and there is a bustling atmosphere. As night falls, people go in crowds to enjoy colorful lanterns: palace lanterns, wall lamps, figure lanterns, flower lanterns, revolving horse lanterns, animal lanterns, and toy lanterns, of all hues and colors, forming a sea of flickering light and color. Some lanterns have riddles on them, which encourage people to strive to be the first to find the answer.

It is also a traditional custom to eat glutinous rice dumplings at this time. As early as the Song Dynasty (960—1279), there was such a kind of food. It is a round ball made of glutinous rice flour with a filling of sugar and kernels. When it is boiled, it is very savory, and tasty. Since it is eaten on the Lantern Festival, people call it *yuanxiao*. The Chinese people hope that everything is satisfactory (*yuanman* in Chinese), and to eat glutinous rice dumplings on the first night with a full moon in a year is to wish that family members will remain united, harmonious, happy and satisfied.

1	2
	3

1. 灯会
   Lantern fair
2. 龙灯
   Dragon lantern
3. 元宵
   Glutinous rice dumplings

清明节

The Pure Brightness Day

清明，是中国的二十四节气之一，也是中国一个古老的传统节日。清明节在农历三月（公历4月5日左右），此时正是春光明媚、空气洁净的季节，因此，这个节日叫做"清明节"。

清明节人们有扫墓祭祖和踏青插柳的习俗。中国人有敬老的传统，对去世的先人更是缅怀和崇敬。因此，每到清明节这天，家家户户都要到郊外去祭扫祖先的坟墓。人们为坟墓除去杂草，添加新土，在坟前点上香，摆上食物和纸钱，表示对祖先的思念和敬意。这叫上坟，也叫扫墓。

清明时节，山野小草发芽，河边柳树长叶，到处一片新绿，正是户外游玩的好时候。古人有到郊外散步的习俗，这叫"踏青"；还要折根柳枝戴在头上，叫"插柳"。据说插柳可以驱除鬼怪和灾难，所以，人们纷纷插戴柳枝，祈求平安幸福。

现在，殡葬方式有了很大改变。实行火葬、废止土葬后，田野里的坟墓越来越少了。但是，清明节祭祖、踏青是中国人的传统习俗，每到这一天，人们还是会用各种各样的方式来怀念自己的祖先，也会到郊外呼吸新鲜空气，观赏蓝天、绿树、小草和鲜花。

The Pure Brightness Day

The Pure Brightness Day, one of the 24 Seasonal Division Points, is also an ancient traditional festival in China. It falls in the third lunar month or around April 5th in the solar calendar, when the spring scene is radiant and enchanting and the air is refreshing, hence, its name.

On this day, people have the custom of sweeping the graves for their ancestors, take an outing in the countryside and wear a willow twig on the head. The Chinese have the tradition to respect the aged, and cherish the memory of their forefathers and respect them. Thus, when the day comes, every family will go to the countryside to hold a memorial ceremony at their ancestors' tombs. People get rid of any weeds growing around the tomb, add new earth, burn incense and offer food and paper coins to show their remembrance and respect for their ancestors. This is called "visiting a grave" or "sweeping a grave".

At this time, the grass of the countryside is burgeoning, willows along rivers have put forth new buds; it is fresh green everywhere, a good time for an outing. In ancient times, people used to wear a willow twig in their hair at this time because it was supposed to be able to drive away ghosts and disasters. Thus, people wear willow twigs to pray for safety and happiness.

Today, great changes have taken place in regard to funerals and interment. Since cremation began to be carried out and burials were abolished, there are less and less graves in the fields. But it remains a custom for the Chinese to offer sacrifices to their ancestors and go for a walk in the countryside, remembering their forefathers, breathing the fresh air and appreciating the blue sky, green trees, grass and flowers.

1 | 2

1. 清明节扫墓
   Sweeping grave for ancestor cult on the Pure Brightness Day
2. 鲜花纪念亲友
   Commemorating relatives and friends with flowers

端午节

The Dragon Boat Festival

农历五月初五，是中国民间传统的端午节，也叫"五月节"。过端午节时，人们要吃粽子、赛龙舟。据说，举行这些活动，是为了纪念中国古代伟大的爱国诗人屈原。

屈原是战国时期楚国人。战国时的齐、楚、燕、韩、赵、魏、秦七国中，秦国最强，总想吞并其他六国，称霸天下。屈原是楚国的大（dà）夫①，很有才能。他主张改革楚国政治，联合各国，共同抵抗秦国。但是，屈原的主张却遭到了奸佞的反对。楚王听信谗言，不但不采纳屈原的主张，还把他赶出了楚国的

国都。屈原离开国都后，仍然关心国家的命运。后来，他听到楚国被秦国打败的消息，非常悲痛，感到自己已经没有力量拯救祖国，就跳进汨罗江自杀了。这一天正是公元前278年，农历的五月初五。

人们听到屈原跳江的消息后，都划船赶来打捞他的尸体，但始终没有找到。为了不让鱼虾吃掉屈原的身体，百姓们就把食物扔进江中喂鱼。以后，每年五月初五人们都要这样做。后来，人们又改为用芦苇的叶子把糯米包成粽子扔进江里。于是，就形成了端午节吃粽子、赛龙舟的习俗。

时至今日，赛龙舟不仅仅限于端午节，龙舟文化活动也已经扩展至世界很多地方，甚至演变为重要的赛事。在中国农村，赛龙舟作为一项体育活动也已经深深扎根，赛龙舟夺锦标为人们所看重，民间甚至有"宁愿荒废一年田，不愿输掉一年船"的说法。

▶ **注解 Note**

① 古代官职。
An ancient official title.

1. 赛龙舟
Dragon boat race
2. 粽子
Zongzi
3. 屈原祠与屈原像
The Qu Yuan Temple and
the Qu Yuan Statue

The Dragon Boat Festival

The fifth day of the fifth lunar month is a traditional Chinese folk festival—the Dragon Boat Festival, also known as the "Festival of the Fifth Month". On that day, people eat *zongzi* (pyramid-shaped dumpling made of glutinous rice wrapped in bamboo or reed leaves) and hold dragon-boat races. It is said, these activities commemorate the great patriotic poet Qu Yuan in ancient China.

Qu Yuan lived in the State of Chu in the Warring States Period (475 BC—221 BC). Among the states of Qi, Chu, Yan, Han, Zhao, Wei and Qin, the State of Qin was the strongest, and it wished to annex the others to become even more powerful. Qu Yuan was a Dafu. He maintained that Chu's politics should be reformed and that it should unite with the other states to resist Qin. But his stand was opposed by crafty sycophants, who used malicious accusations to persuade the king of Chu not to adopt the idea and to drive Qu Yuan from the

capital. Despite being exiled, Qu Yuan was still concerned about the fate of the state. Later, when he heard the news that Qin had defeated the State of Chu, he was full of grief and felt that he had no power to save his motherland, so he drowned himself in the Miluo River. It was the fifth day of the fifth lunar month in 278 BC.

When people heard the news, they rowed their boats to try to find his corpse, but failed. In order to keep the fish and shrimps from eating his corpse, people threw food into the river to feed them. Thereafter, on each fifth day of the fifth lunar month, people would throw food into the river. Later, people used reed leaves to wrap *zongzi* for this purpose. Thus the custom of eating *zongzi* and staging the dragon boat race was formed.

Up to the present, the dragon boat race is not only limited to the Dragon Boat Festival, but has also spread to many places around the world, and even became an important match. In the rural areas of China, the dragon boat race has taken root as a physical activity. People say "We would waste one year's farming rather than lose one year's dragon boat race."

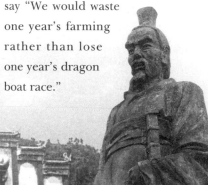

中秋节

The Mid-Autumn Festival

　　农历八月十五，是中国的传统节日中秋节。按照中国的历法，农历七八九3个月是秋季。八月是秋季中间的一个月，八月十五又是八月中间的一天，所以这个节日叫"中秋节"。中秋节这天，中国人有赏月和吃月饼的习俗。

　　秋季，天气晴朗、凉爽，天上很少出现浮云，夜空中的月亮也显得特别明亮。八月十五的晚上，是月圆之夜，成了人们赏月的最好时光。人们把圆月看作团圆美满的象征，所以中秋节又叫"团圆节"。

　　按照传统习惯，中国人在赏月时，还要摆出瓜果和月饼等食品，一边赏月一边品尝。因为月饼是圆的，象征着团圆，所以有的地方也叫它"团圆饼"。中国月饼的品种很多，各地的制法也不相同。月饼馅有甜的、咸的、荤的、素的，月饼上面还印着各种花纹和字样，真是又好看、又好吃。

　　秋天，人们一年的劳动有了收获。中秋节的晚上，全家人坐在一起赏月、吃月饼，心里充满了丰收的喜悦和团聚的欢乐。这时，远离家乡的人也会仰望明月，思念故乡和亲人。

The Mid-Autumn Festival

The 15th day of the eighth lunar month is China's traditional Mid-Autumn Festival. According to the Chinese lunar calendar, the lunar eighth, ninth and tenth months make up autumn. The eighth month falls in mid-autumn, and the 15th day is in the middle of the month, hence the name Mid-Autumn Festival. On that day, the Chinese have the custom of admiring the moon and eating moon cakes.

In autumn, it is fine and cool, with few floating clouds in the sky and the moon at night seems particularly bright. This is especially true on the 15th day of the eighth lunar month. Since people consider the full moon as the symbol of reunion and satisfaction, the festival is also called the Festival for Reunion.

According to traditional custom, the Chinese people enjoy fruits and moon cakes while admiring the moon. As the moon cake is round, symbolizing reunion, it is sometimes called "reunion cake". The Chinese moon cake has many varieties and production methods differ from place to place. There are sweet, salty, meat and vegetable fillings. It is carved with various decorative patterns and words.

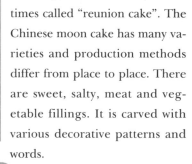

In autumn, people reap the harvests of their year's labor. On the night of the Mid-Autumn Festival, the whole family will sit together to admire the moon and eat moon cakes, filled with happiness for the bumper harvest and a family reunion. At that time, people far away from hometown will also look up at the moon and miss their hometown and family.

1　2 / 3

1、3. 月饼
Moon cakes
2. 工地的工人领月饼
Workers grabbing moon cakes

二十四节气

The 24 Seasonal Division Points

按照中国农历的纪年法，每个月都有两个节气，一年共有24个节气。

节气是中国农历特有的。中国古人在长期的生产劳动中，逐渐认识到地球绕太阳运行一周的时间是固定不变的365又1/4天，他们把它叫做"一年"；又根据太阳和地球的相互关系，把一年的天数分成24等份，用来表示季节和气候的变化。这样，每15天就有一个节气，每个月就有两个节气了。二十四节气在公历中的日期几乎是固定的，上半年（1—6月）的节气都在每个月的6日和21日前后；下半年（7—12月）的节气都在每个月的8日和23日前后。

二十四节气的名称和意义分别是：

立春、立夏、立秋、立冬，表示四季的开始。

春分、秋分，是一年中昼夜一样长的两天。

夏至，是一年中白天最长、黑夜最短的一天。

冬至，是一年中白天最短、黑夜最长的一天。

雨水，是开始下雨的意思。

惊蛰，表示春雷响过以后，冬眠的昆虫被惊醒了。

清明，是说春天到了以后，明净的春色代替了冬季寒冷枯黄的景色。

谷雨，表示从此雨水增多，对五谷的生长很有好处。

小满，表示在夏季成熟的农作物籽粒开始饱满了。

芒种，告诉人们小麦已经成熟了。

小暑、大暑，表示天气炎热的程度，大暑是一年中最热的时候。

处暑，表示炎热的天气快要过去了。

白露，告诉人们开始下露水，天气就要冷了。

寒露，表明露水已重，天寒加剧。

霜降，是开始下霜的意思。

小雪、大雪，表示到了下雪的时节和雪量大小的差别。

小寒、大寒，表示冬天寒冷的程度，大寒是一年中最冷的时候。

二十四节气对中国的农业生产起很大的作用，人们为了方便记忆，还编出了"二十四节气歌"：春雨惊春清谷天，夏满芒夏暑相连，秋处露秋寒霜降，冬雪雪冬小大寒……

The 24 Seasonal Division Points

According to the way of numbering the years in Chinese lunar calendar, there are two seasonal division points in each month, making 24 in a year.

The seasonal division points are peculiar to China. In the long period of labor, ancient men gradually realized the rule of climate change. According to the relationship between the sun and the earth, they divided all the days in a year into 24 parts to indicate the change of seasons and climate. Thus, there is a seasonal divisional point about every 15 days; those in the first half of the year (from January to June) all fall around the sixth or 21st day of the month, and those in the latter half of the year (from July to December), on about the eighth or 23rd day of the month.

The names and meanings of the 24 seasonal division points are:

The Beginning of Spring, the

春
Spring

Beginning of Summer, the Beginning of Autumn and the Beginning of Winter mark the start of four seasons. The Vernal Equinox and the Autumnal Equinox are the two points where the day and night are equal. The Summer Solstice has the longest day and shortest night in a year, while the opposite is true for the Winter Solstice. The Rain Water means the start of the spring

rains. The Waking of Insects indicates that the spring thunder awakens hibernating insects. The Pure Brightness means the onset of spring when a bright and clean spring scene replaces the cold, withered and yellow scene of winter. The Grain Rain indicates that from that day, there will be more rainfall, which is beneficial to the growth of crops. The Grain Budding shows that crops that will ripen in summer start to show plump seeds. The Grain in Ear tells people that the wheat has ripened. The Slight Heat and Great Heat indicate the full onset of summer, with the Great Heat being the hottest day of the year. The Limit of Heat shows that scorching summer days will soon be gone. The White Dew tells people that dew appears in the morning to show that the weather is turning cold, and, as this intensifies, we move on to the Cold Dew. The Frost's Descent means the appearance of the first frost of the season. The Slight Snow and Great Snow mean the arrival of the snowy season. The Slight Cold and Great Cold indicate the degree of coldness in winter, with the Great Cold being the coldest day of the season.

The 24 seasonal division points have great influence on the farming of China. For the convenience of memory, people compiled the *Song for the 24 Seasonal Division Points*:

Following the Beginning of Spring and Rain Water, the Waking of Insects awakens the Vernal Equinox. After the Beginning of Summer, Grain Budding, Grain in Ear, and Summer Solstice, the Slight Heat is connected with Great Heat. The Beginning of Autumn and Limit of Heat is followed by the White Dew, Autumnal Equinox, Cold Dew and then the Frost's Descent. And the

Beginning of Winter leads to the Slight Snow, Great Snow, Winter Solstice, Slight Cold and Great Cold...

1. 夏
   Summer
2. 秋
   Autumn
3. 冬
   Winter

中国人的生活

Life of the Chinese People

概　述

Introduction

　　中国人热爱生活，在生活中表现出独有的特点。美味的中国菜，现在基本在世界的各个地方都能品尝到；有着浓郁中国风情的旗袍、唐装也越来越受到各国时装界人士的喜爱。

　　中国人生活的艺术表现在生活中的方方面面。

1		3
2		4
		5

1. 茶壶
   Teapot
2. 京剧
   Beijing Opera
3. 年画
   New Year pictures
4. 绣花鞋
   Embroidered shoes
5. 民居
   Civilian residence

Introduction

The Chinese people love life, showing their unique characteristics in
life. Nowadays, delicious Chinese food
can be enjoyed everywhere in the world.
Traditional Chinese costumes with distinct oriental style, such as the cheong-
sam and Tang costume are also more
and more favored in the circles of international fashion.

In every aspect of their life, the Chinese
people show their artistic way of life.

旗袍与中国传统服饰

Cheong-Sam and Traditional Chinese Costumes

　　旗袍源自清代满族女性服饰，被誉为中国传统服饰文化的典范。它不仅在整体造型的风格方面符合中国文化和谐的特点，而且它的装饰手法也展现着浓厚的东方特质。另外，穿旗袍可以增加形体的修长感，配上中高跟鞋，更可以抬升人体的重心，将东方女性的端庄、典雅和含蓄的美展露出来。因此旗袍在中国民族服装中独领风骚，久盛而不衰。

　　中国男子的传统服饰比较有代表性的为长袍、马褂，长袍和马褂是满族男子的服装，盘领、窄袖，马褂是对襟，大都有马蹄袖，长袍为大襟。也有马褂、长袍相连的两部形式，这种形式的长袍只有下半

截，连扣在马褂的内下摆。长袍马褂给人的感觉是既不乏庄重，又显得洒脱和舒适。

2001年APEC会议各国元首穿着"唐装"集体亮相，掀起了一股以穿"唐装"为时尚的风潮。将"唐装"作为中式服装的通称，主要是因为国外都称华人居住的地方为"唐人街"，所以"唐人"穿的衣服自然就叫做"唐装"了。当今的"唐装"是由清代的马褂演变而来的，它的款式结构有四大特点：一是立领，上衣前中心开口，立式领型；二是连袖，即袖子和衣服整体没有接缝，以平面裁剪为主；三是对襟，也可以是斜襟；四是直角扣，也就是盘扣；另外从面料来说，则主要使用织锦缎面料等。

另外，中国不同地域和不同民族的服饰也各有特色。比如，肚兜就是关中和陕北的传统的贴身服饰，肚兜的形状像背心的前襟，上面用布带系在脖颈上，下面两边各有一条带子系在腰间，它可以避免肚子受凉，夏天时儿童穿在外面也显得天真烂漫。在儿童穿的肚兜上常常绣有虎头像和"五毒"[①]图案，寄寓了大人希望孩子健康成长的美好祝愿。再比如，中国少数民族彝族的服饰也很有特点。彝族妇女的头饰大致有缠头、包帕、绣花帽三类，其中红河地区妇女的头饰更是琳琅满目，以银饰为贵为美。披风是彝族男女皆备的特色服装，以动物皮毛、毛麻织品和草编制品为原料，以青、蓝二色为主。

1	2
	3

1. 旗袍
   Cheong-sam
2. 清代马褂
   The mandarin jacket of the Qing Dynasty
3. 马褂铜像
   Bronze figure in the mandarin jacket

Cheong-Sam
and Traditional Chinese Costumes

The cheong-sam has its origin in in the Manchu female's costumes in the Qing Dynasty and has been regarded as the model of Chinese traditional habilatory culture. As for the reason, the cheong-sam not only accords with the characteristic of harmony within Chinese culture in terms of the style, but also shows rich oriental idiosyncracy with regard to ornamental techniques. In addition, the cheong-sam will give more prominence to a lady's slender figure, and also help to heighten the center of gravity of human bodies together with high-heel shoes, so that civility, elegance and dignity will be fully displayed. Therefore, the cheong-sam developed its own trend, which has been long lasting.

As for the traditional clothes of Chinese men, the long gown and mandarin jacket are typical. Both of them have round-necks and narrow sleeves. The mandarin jacket can be seen as a kind of Chinese-style jacket with buttons down the front, mostly with sleeves like a horse's hoof. However, the front of long gowns, with buttons on the right, is basically large. There is also a type of garment combining the long gown and the mandarin jacket, and they will only have the under-half part, buttoning in the under lap of the mandarin jacket. The long gown and mandarin jacket will give the impression of comfortableness and ease as well as sobriety.

In 2001, the presidents struck a pose on the stage in Chinese-style costumes at the APEC Forum, and thus a trend of wearing Chinese style costumes came into being. The very reason why clothing with Chinese style has been labeled as Chinese-style costumes is that the place where overseas Chinese reside in has been called "China Town" and consequently the costumes which the Chinese wear are called Chinese-style costumes. Current Chinese-style costumes were transformed from the mandarin jacket of the Qing Dynasty, and there are four major characteristics in terms of design. First, Chinese-style costumes have a stand-up collar and buttons in the very middle of the front of the jacket;

1. 唐装
   Tang suits
2. 彝族服饰
   Dress and adornments of the Yi
   Nationality
3. 肚兜
   Dudou (Chinese underclothes)

1	2
	3

second, there is no seam between sleeves and jacket; third, the costumes are jackets with buttons down the front or in diagonal way; last, they have right-angled buttons. In addition, with regard to the outside material, Chinese costumes are mostly made with silk.

Moreover, the feature of clothing varies with areas and nationalities. For instance, the bellyband is the traditional close-fitting costume in Central China and north of Shaanxi. The bellyband is just like the front of vest with a lace tying to the neck and two laces tying to the waist, and it can prevent children from catch-ing a cold. The children's wearing of bellyband will also show their naivety. Most bellybands will be embroidered with the pattern of a tiger head and the "Five Poisons", which contain a parents' nice expectation of wishing their children health. To take the costumes of the Yi Nationality as another example, they are rather distinctive with three types of women's head wears including decorating brocade round the head, a handkerchief round the head and a cap with an embroidered case. Especially in the area of Honghe, women's head wears are full of beautiful colors and styles. They prefer silver ornaments to show their riches and beauty. However, the manteau can be regarded as the distinctive costumes for all people of the Yi Nationality, which are mostly made of fur, delaine, hemp and straw and whose colors are mainly cyan and blue.

▶ 注解　Note

① 中国民间将蝎、蛇、蜈蚣、壁虎和蟾蜍视为 "五毒"，据说可以起到避邪的作用。
The "Five Poisons" refer to scorpion, snake, centipede, gecko and toad in terms of Chinese folklores. It can be said that "Five Poisons" can keep away the evil.

中国饮食

Chinese Cuisine

中国饮食博大精深。中国菜不但花样多，而且具有色、香、味、形俱佳的特点。

由于中国地域辽阔，各地的物产、气候和生活习惯不同，因此人们的口味也各不相同：南方人口味清淡，北方人口味较重，四川人喜欢吃辣，山西人喜欢吃酸……这样，在中国就形成了各具地方风味特色的菜系。其中，鲁菜、川菜、淮扬菜和粤菜被称为中国的"四大菜系"。

鲁菜，也称山东菜，擅长爆、烧、炸、炒等，很讲究菜汤和奶汤的调制。鲁菜中比较有名的有"德州扒鸡"、"糖醋黄河鲤鱼"等。

"粤菜"也叫广东菜，它的用料比较广泛、花色品种也很多，注重口感的鲜嫩和爽滑。粤菜著名的菜品有"油包鲜虾仁"、"烤乳猪"等。

川菜具有麻、辣、油重和味浓等特点，川菜的代表菜肴有"鱼香肉丝"、"宫保鸡丁"、"怪味鸡块"、"麻婆豆腐"等。

淮扬菜集淮河沿岸、长江下游的扬州、镇江、淮安等地菜肴的精华，特点是注重选材，讲究火工，并且注重菜品造型的美观。著名菜肴有"叫化（huā）鸡"、"盐水鸭"、"清炖蟹粉狮子头"等。

到北京的客人，一般都要尝尝有名的"北京烤鸭"。北京烤鸭是北京的名菜，它以色泽红艳、肉质细嫩、味道醇厚、肥而不腻的特色而驰名中外，最著名的烤鸭店是全聚德。

| 1 | 2 |

1、2. 北京烤鸭
Beijing roast duck

Chinese Cuisine

Chinese cuisine enjoys the reputation for its color, scent, taste, and design, as well as its variety.

Due to the vast territory, abundant resources, varied climate and different living habits in China, people from different places have quite different flavors of food, for instance, southerners like light food while northerners are on the opposite, Sichuan people like spicy food, but Shanxi people like sour food. As a result, many different cuisines unique to certain areas are formed, among which that of Lu, Chuan, Huaiyang and Yue are called the "Grand Four Categories of Chinese Cuisine".

Shandong cuisine, also known as Lu Cai for short, is characterized by quick-frying, stir-frying, braising and deep-fat frying. It focuses on the confection of vegetable soup and milk soup. Famous dishes include Dezhou stewed chicken, sweet and sour carp, etc.

Yuc Cai is short for Guangdong Cuisine, which is famous for its wide selection of materials, variety of designs and colors, and original forms. It features tender and refreshing taste.

Famous dishes are: saute shrimp, roast suckling pig, etc.

Chuan Cai, short for Sichuan Cuisine, is famous for being spicy, hot, oily and salty. Famous dishes include: fish-flavored pork threads, diced chicken with chili pepper, multi-flavor chicken, pockmarked woman's bean curd, etc.

Huai Yang Cuisine is represented by the dishes from the places along the Huaihe River and in the lower reaches of the Changjiang River like Yangzhou, Zhenjiang and Huai'an. It's characterized by the careful selection of materials, the timing of cooking and the controlling of the heat, and the beautiful appearance of the dishes. Famous dishes include: Hangzhou roast chicken (commonly known as beggar's

1 | 3
--- | 4
2 |

1. 冷盘
   Cold dishes
2. 广东菜
   Guangdong Cuisine
3. 烹制佳肴
   Cooking
4. 饺子宴
   The dumpling banquet

chicken), salty duck, braised pork balls with stewed crab, etc.

Visitors to Beijing will, definitely have a taste of the Beijing roast duck, which is the representative dish of Beijing. It enjoys an international reputation for its date-red, shining with oil, but with a crisp skin and tender meat. The place that offers very good Beijing roast duck is the Quanjude Restaurant.

中国茶

Chinese Tea

中国人喜欢喝茶，也常常用茶来招待朋友和客人。茶叶是中国人生活中的必需品。

茶树原产于中国。中国古人发现茶树后，起初是把茶叶作为药用，后来才当作饮料。中国茶叶按照制作方法分为绿茶、红茶、乌龙茶、花茶、沱茶、砖茶等几大类，各类茶中又包括许多品种。

绿茶嫩绿鲜艳，是不经过发酵的茶。著名的绿茶品种有杭州西湖龙井茶、江苏碧螺春茶、安徽黄山的毛峰茶和产于安徽六安县一带的六安瓜片茶。

红茶是经过发酵的茶，沏出的茶水颜色红艳。中国著名的红茶有安徽的祁红茶和云南的滇红茶。

乌龙茶是一种半发酵的茶，茶叶松散粗大，茶水颜色金黄。最好的乌龙茶是产在福建武夷山的武夷岩茶。

花茶是中国独有的一个茶类，是在茶叶中加入香花熏制而成的。最有名的花茶是福建产的茉莉花茶。

沱茶是产于云南、四川的一种茶，经过压制，像个圆圆的馒头。

砖茶，形状像砖头，是蒙古族、藏族等少数民族喜欢喝的茶。

喝茶不但可以止渴，还能消除疲劳，帮助消化，预防一些疾病。长期饮茶，对人的身体健康很有益处。

1 2
   3

1. 盖碗茶
   Teabowl with a cover
2. 茶艺
   A tea ceremony
3. 采茶
   Tea-picking

Chinese Tea

The Chinese people like to drink tea, and often entertain friends and guests with it. The tea-leaf is a necessity in the life of the Chinese people.

China is the homeland of tea. The ancient Chinese first used it for medicinal purposes before developing tea as a drink. As regards the method of making tea, the Chinese variety can be classified into green tea, black tea, oolong tea, scented tea, *tuo* tea (bowl-shaped compressed mass of tea leaves), and brick tea, each consisting of many types.

Green tea is not fermented. Famous green tea includes the Longjing tea from the region of the West Lake in Hangzhou, the Biluochun tea from Jiangsu, the Maofeng tea from Huangshan Mountain of Anhui Province, and the Liu'an Guapian tea from Liuan County of Anhui Province.

Black tea is fermented, and is brilliant red. Famous Chinese black tea is the keemun tea of Anhui Province, and the Dian black tea (Yunnan black tea) of Yunnan Province.

Oolong tea is half fermented, its leaves being loose and thick, and the tea is golden yellow. The best oolong tea is produced in Wuyi Mountain of Fujian Province.

Scented tea is peculiar to China, which is made by smoking tea leaves with fragrant flowers. The most famous one is jasmine tea produced in Fujian Province.

Tuo tea, produced in Yunnan and Sichuan provinces, is compressed like a round steamed bun.

Brick tea is shaped like a brick, and is a favorite of the Mongolian and Tibetan ethnic groups.

Drinking tea can quench one's thirst, dispel fatigue, help digestion and prevent some diseases. The constant drinking of tea is quite beneficial for people's health.

中国酒

Chinese Wine

中国考古人员曾经在距今4 000多年前的"二里头文化"中发现盛酒的陶器，可见，在那个时候，就有人开始饮酒了。

中国历史上有关酒的故事很多：晋代诗人陶渊明不能一日无酒；唐代大诗人李白"斗酒诗百篇"等等。

中国是个礼仪之邦，凡事注重规矩。就拿喝酒来说，也有很多有意思的事儿。比如在宴席上，如果想表示对长辈或者上级的尊重，晚辈就会主动举杯敬酒，在喝掉酒之前，两个人会碰一下酒杯表示亲近，捧杯的时候，晚辈举杯不能比长辈高，这表示尊重。主动敬酒的人会把一杯酒全部喝完，以此来表示自己的诚意。中国人喝酒一般比较热闹，大家说说笑笑，气氛融洽。有的时候为了增加热闹的气氛，喝酒的时候还要行酒令。其实行酒令就是在酒桌上的游戏，不同的酒令有着不同的规则，参与游戏的人，输了就要喝酒。古代的读书人行酒令一般是对诗或是对对联。

中国的名酒很多，如：茅台、五粮液、汾酒、竹叶青、泸州老窖、古井贡酒等，都是享誉世界的名酒。

1	2
	3

1. 古代酒壶与酒杯
   Flagon and goblet of ancient times
2. 酒窖
   Wine cellar
3. 酒厂
   Brewery

Chinese Wine

Chinese archaeologists have discovered pottery wine vessels at the ruins of Erlitou Culture which dates back to over 4 000 years ago. It proves that the Chinese people began to drink wine at that time.

There are many stories about wine in Chinese history. Tao Yuanming, a poet in the Jin Dynasty, could not live without wine for a day. The great poet Li Bai in the Tang Dynasty could write 100 poems after drinking wine—the more wine he drank, the better the poem would be.

China is a country of amenity, attaching the importance to rules to everything. Taking drinking for an example, there are so many interesting things. For example, at a banquet, if someone wants to express his / her respect to their elders or superiors, he / she will toast. Before drinking the wine, they will touch their cups to show their affection. When they begin to drink, the younger's cup will be lower than the superior's to show his / her respect. The person who toasts on his / her own will empty one cup of wine at one go

to show his / her sincerities. It's a jolly time when the Chinese drink wine. On this occasion, everyone will be in a friendly mood. Sometimes rules for drinking will be set in a game when people drink in order to increase the liveliness. There are various kinds of rules for drinking, one of which is unchangeable, that is, for the people participating in the games, the loser will drink. In ancient times, among the intellectuals, the rules for drinking were generally to supply the antithesis to a given poem or phrase.

China has many famous brands of wine such as Maotai, Five-Grain Liquor, Fen Liquor, Bamboo-Leaf Green Liquor, Luzhou Liquor, Gujing Tribute Wine and so on, which enjoy a worldwide reputation.

中国民居

Civilian Residence

由于中国疆域辽阔，民族众多，各地的气候条件和生活方式不同，因此，各地人们居住的房屋的样式和风格也不相同，形成了多姿多彩的民居风格。

在中国的民居中，最有特色的是北京四合院、西北黄土高原的窑洞、内蒙古草原的"蒙古包"和福建、广东等地的客家土楼等。

北京四合院　在北京城大大小小的胡同中，坐落着许多由东、南、西、北四面房屋围合起来的院落式住宅，这就是四合院。

四合院的大门一般开在东南角或西北角，院中的北房是正房，正房建在砖石砌成的台基上，比其他房屋的规模大，是院主人的住室。院子的两边建有东西厢房，是晚辈们居住的地方。南房则是仆人住处或杂物间等。在正房和厢房之间建有走廊，可以供人行走和休息。

北京有各种不同规模的四

1 | 2

1. 北京四合院
   Siheyuan in Beijing
2. 窑洞
   Cave-dwelling

合院，但不论大小，都是由一个个四面房屋围合的庭院组成的。最简单的四合院只有一个院子，比较复杂的有两三个院子，富贵人家居住的深宅大院，通常是由好几座四合院并列组成的。四合院的围墙和临街的房屋一般不对外开窗，院中的环境封闭而幽静，特别适合居住。

窑洞　中国黄河中上游一带是黄土高原。生活在黄土高原上的人们，利用那里又深又厚、立体性能极好的黄土层，建造了一种独特的住宅——窑洞。窑洞又分为土窑、石窑、砖窑等几种。土窑是靠着山坡挖成的黄土窑洞，这种窑洞冬暖夏凉，保温隔音效果最好。石窑和砖窑是先用石块或砖砌成拱形洞，然后在上面盖上厚厚的黄土，又坚固又美观。由于建造窑洞不需要钢材、水泥，所以造价比较低。随着社会的发展，人们对窑洞的建造不断改进，黄土高原上冬暖夏凉的窑洞越来越舒适美观了。

客家土楼　土楼是广东、福建等地的客家人的住宅。客家人的祖先是1 900多年前从黄河中下游地区迁移到南方的汉族人。为了防范骚扰，保护家族的安全，客家人创造了这种庞大的民居——土楼。一座土楼里可以住下整个家族的几十户人家，几百口人。土楼有圆形的，也有方形的，其中，最有特色的是圆形土楼。圆楼由两三圈组成，外圈十多米高，有一二百个房间，是生活居住区；第二圈两层，一般是客房；中间是祖堂，能容下几百人进行公共活动。土楼里有水井、浴室、厕所等，就像一座小城市。客家土楼高大、奇特，设计与建造融科学性、实用性、观赏性于一体，是一座宏伟壮观的"土宫殿"，受到了国内外许多建筑大师的称赞。

Civilian Residence

Due to the vast expanse of China, the presence of many ethnic groups, different climatic conditions and ways of life, the residences of people in different parts of the country differ in terms of design and style, forming colorful styles of civilian residence.

The most representative civilian residences of the Chinese people are the *siheyuan* of Beijing, cave-dwellings of the Loess Plateau in northwest China, and the earthen tower of Kejia (or Hakka) people in Fujian Province and Guangdong Province.

Siheyuan

There are a large number of quadrangles called *siheyuan*, which are compounds enclosed by inward-facing houses on four sides, in the alleyways (hutungs) of Beijing.

The entrance gate of a *siheyuan* is usually set at the southeast or northwest corner of the compound. The main south-facing house, the center of a *siheyuan*, stands on a terrace built with bricks and stones. Larger than other houses in the compound, it is used by the master of the family. On both sides of the compound are houses for the younger generations. Corridors connect all the houses, used for people's walking and having a rest. The north-facing houses are generally used for servants or for stacking sundries.

Beijing has *siheyuan* of all sizes, but, no matter what the size, there will be an enclosure wall with houses built on four sides. The simplest *siheyuan* has only one courtyard in the middle, but there are ones with three or four courtyards surrounded by houses. A large *siheyuan* formerly occupied by a wealthy family actually comprises several *siheyuan*. The enclosure walls and the houses on the side of the alley usually do not have windows. Therefore, the inside of the compound is tranquil and peaceful.

Cave-Dwellings

The middle and upper reaches of the Yellow River comprise the Loess Plateau. People living on the plateau make use of the solid and thick loess to build unique residences called cave-dwellings. These can be further divided into earthen, rock-walled and brick-walled types. Earthen cave-dwellings are hollowed out of mountain slopes; they are warm in winter and cool in summer, and are also soundproof. Stones or brick-walled cave-dwellings are usually built with stones or bricks first into an arch-shaped house and then covered with a thick layer of earth. Since there is no need for steel and cement, the building costs are low. As society progresses, construction of cave-dwellings keeps improving, and today, such houses are more comfortable inside and more pleasant in appearance.

Earthen Tower of Kejia People

Earthen towers, or *tulou*, are residences of the Kejia (Hakka) people in Guangdong and Fujian provinces. The forefathers of Kejia people were Han people who migrated to the south from the middle and lower reaches of the Yellow River over 1 900 years ago. For both privacy and security, they built large residences known as earthen towers. One such tower is able to hold a score of families of a whole clan with a total of several hundred people. The towers are round or square in shape, but the round-shaped tower is the most impressive. It is made up of two or three circles of houses. The outer circle could be as high as a dozen meters,

with one hundred to two hundred rooms. The ground floor is used as kitchens and dining rooms. The second floor is used for storage. The third and fourth floors are the living quarters and bedrooms. The second circle has two stories with 30 to 50 rooms. They are mostly used as rooms for guests. In the middle there is an ancestral hall with a holding capacity of several hundred people where public activities are carried out. Within an earthen tower, there are bathrooms, toilets and a well. It is like a small town indeed. The huge size and the unique design of the earthen tower are highly acclaimed in international architectural circles.

1

2

1. 四合院装饰
   Decorations within *siheyuan*
2. 客家土楼
   The earthen tower of Kejia people

马车、轿子与布鞋

Horse-Drawn Carriage, Sedan Chair and Cloth Shoes

中国古代最重要的交通工具就是马车。

最初的车辆，都是由人力来推动的，称为人力车。后来人们开始用牛、马拉车，称为畜力车。马车是供古代贵族出行和作战用的，而牛车则一般是用来运载货物的。在中国古代，马车或牛车是非常重要的交通工具。

轿子可以说是中国特有的交通工具了，主要由人来肩扛手抬。轿子在种类上有官轿、民轿和喜轿等；在用途上，有走山路和走平道的区别；在用材上，有竹、木、藤之分等等。

其实大多数古人坐不起马车，也很少坐轿子，平常时候都得穿着布鞋自己走路。布鞋的制作讲究精工细作，一双布鞋鞋底一般用布二十几层，均用手工纳底，纳制需消耗鞋线20余米，针脚1 000多针，耗时2至3天才能完成。布鞋穿上去柔软舒适，在人们日常走路、游历山川的时候会派上很大的用场。当然，现在在中国的城市里，已经很少有人穿布鞋了，大家都穿起了运动鞋、皮鞋，出行也不坐马车了，现在都坐汽车或者火车，甚至古人想也不敢想的飞机也已经成为普通的交通工具了。

1	2
	3

1. 马车
   Horse-drawn carriage
2. 布鞋
   Cloth shoes
3. 轿子
   Sedan chair

Horse-Drawn Carriage, Sedan Chair and Cloth Shoes

In ancient China, the most important vehicle was the horse-drawn carriage. The initial vehicles were driven by manpower, which were called jinricksha. Later, people began to use cattle and horses to pull the carriage. As for vehicles, they were used for ancient aristocrats to travel and battle. However, the oxcarts were generally used for loading goods. In ancient China, horse-drawn carriages and oxcarts were very essential vehicles.

The sedan chair can be regarded as the unique vehicle of China. It mainly has the virtue of lifting with shoulders and hands. As for its kind, the sedan chair can be classified into three types: sedan chair for officials, the civilian and weddings. According to purposes, the sedan chair has two types: one is for mountain roads, the other for flat roads. As far as the materials were concerned, there are three kinds, i.e. bamboo, wood and rattan.

Actually, most ancients couldn't afford to have a seat on horse-drawn carriages or in sedan chairs, therefore they usually walked by themselves in their cloth shoes. Cloth shoes were elaborately made. The soles of the shoes are made up of scores of layer of cloth and are completely handmade. During the course of making shoes, more than 20 meters of thread and one thousand stitches are used. What's more, craftsman spends two or three days to finish making cloth shoes. When wearing cloth shoes, one feels comfortable. When people are walking or traveling among mountains, cloth shoes will be a huge help. Certainly, in current China's cities, people seldom wear cloth shoes. Most people wear sneakers or leather shoes. People will take cars or trains, even the planes, rather than horse-drawn carriages, which were beyond the imagination of the ancients. These have already become common vehicles.

中医 中药

Traditional Chinese Medical
Science and Medicine

中国人很早就懂得用医药来治病疗伤，保障自己的健康。现在，中医中药已经传播到了世界许多地方。

相传上古时候的神农氏[①]，曾经亲自品尝百草，识别药用植物。现存最早的一部医书《黄帝内经》，比较系统地总结了春秋战国以前的医疗经验，为中医学奠定了理论基础。战国时期的著名医生扁鹊，最早用望、闻、问、切四种方法诊断病情。这四种方法一直沿用到今天，成为中医的传统诊断法。望，是观察病人的外表和精神状态；闻，是听病人喘息的声音；问，是询问病人的发病过程、自我感觉和饮食起居状况；切，是摸查病人脉搏跳动的情况。

中药的来源主要是植物，也有一些动物和矿物。这些东西经过特殊的炮制，被制成内服、外用的药剂。汉代著名的药物学著作《神农本草经》，记载了365种药物。南北朝时期的名医陶弘景，又添加了365种，写成《本草经集注》。明代名医李时珍编著的《本草纲目》，成书于公元1578年，全书共52卷，载药1 892种（李氏新增药物374种）。书中附有药物图1 109幅，方剂11 096首（其中8 000余首是李氏自己收集和拟定的）。这是中国医药学的代表性著作。

中国历史上的名医多不胜数，像扁鹊、华佗、张仲景、孙思邈、李时珍等，都以他们精湛的医术为病人解除了痛苦。现代中国也有很多中医名家，他们努力攻克医学难关，为人民造福。中国少数民族医学也有它的独到之处，像蒙医、藏医、维医、傣医等，都为各民族人民的健康幸福做出了自己的贡献。

中药店
The Chinese herbal medicine shop

Traditional Chinese Medical Science and Medicine

The Chinese people knew how to cure the sickness and protect their health by medical science and drugs long ago. Currently, traditional Chinese medical science and medicine has been spread to many places all over the world.

Legend has it that Shennongshi of ancient times once tasted 100 herbs in person to distinguish herbal plants. China's earliest existing medical book the *Canon of Medicine of the Yellow Emperor*, systematically summarized medical experience before the Spring and Autumn and the Warring States periods (770—221 BC), laying a theoretical foundation for traditional Chinese medical science. The famous doctor of the Warring States Period, Bian Que, was the first to use observation, auscultation and olfaction, interrogation, and palpation for diagnosis. Observation is to observe the patients' appearance and mental state; auscultation and olfaction are to listen to the patients' breathing; interroga-

tion is to inquire about the onset of the problem and the patients' own feelings, diet and daily life; and palpation is to feel the pulse of the patient.

Traditional Chinese medicine mainly comes from plants, and also some animals and minerals. These are made into oral or external medicines after being specially prepared. The famous medical book of the Han Dynasty (206 BC—220 AD) *Shennong's Materia Medica* recorded 365 herbs. The well-known doctor Tao Hongjing of the Northern and Southern Dynasties (420—589) added another 365 herbs and wrote *Variorum of Shennong's Materia Medica*. *The Compendium of Materia Medica*, written by the famous doctor Li Shizhen of the Ming Dynasty (1368—1644), was finished in 1578 AD. The book is composed of 52 volumes, including nearly 1 892 medicines (Li's newly-added medicine was 374), 1 109 pictures of medicine and 11 096 prescriptions (of which 8 000 ones were collected and set by Li). Such a masterpiece

can be considered as one of the representative works of Chinese medical science.

There are numerous famous doctors in Chinese history, such as Bian Que, Hua Tuo, Zhang Zhongjing, Sun Simiao, Li Shizhen, who relieved patients of pain with their consummate medical skills. In modern China, there are also many famous doctors who try hard to resolve serious difficulties and work for the well-being of the people. The medical sciences of China's ethnic minority groups, with distinctive features, have also contributed much, including that of the Mongolian, Tibetan, Uygur and Dai groups.

▶ 注解 Note

① 传说中农业和医药的发明者，也有一说认为神农氏就是炎帝。
The inventor of agriculture and herbal medicine was also said to be Yandi or the Red Emperor.

针灸术 与 麻醉术

Acupuncture and Moxibustion
Therapy and Narcotherapy

针灸术在中国已有几千年的历史。

中国古代有很多用针灸术为人治病的名医，像春秋战国时的扁鹊、东汉时的华佗等，他们治过不少疑难杂症，被誉为能使人起死回生的"神医"。公元1027年，宋代针灸医官王惟一，创造了针灸史上一大奇迹。他设计铸造了两具针灸铜人模型，在铜人体上精细地刻了十二经脉和354个穴位，供人学习针灸时使用。这是中国最早的医用铜人模型，也是中国针灸教育事业上的一个创举。

今天，古老的针灸术不但在中国广泛使用，为人们解除病痛，而且还漂洋过海，传到了全世界各个地方。

麻醉术就是用药物或针刺等方法使人的全身或某一部分暂时失去知觉，医疗上一般在实施外科手术时使用。世界上第一个发明麻醉手术的人是中国东汉时的"神医"华佗。

早在春秋战国时期，中国的民间医生就懂得并记载了某些药物所具有的麻醉作用。东汉名医华佗在认真研究古书的基础上，亲自去山野里采集具有麻醉作用的曼陀罗等药草，经过炮制加工，制成了麻醉药"麻沸散"。一天，人们抬来一个危重病人。华佗让病人喝下"麻沸散"，然后打开他的腹腔，清理了腐烂的肠子，在病人毫无痛苦的情况下完成了剖腹手术。这次手术是中国也是世界上有文字记载的最早的大型剖腹手术病例。

Acupuncture and Moxibustion Therapy and Narcotherapy

Acupuncture and moxibustion therapy has a history of thousands of years in China.

In ancient China, there were many well-known doctors using acupuncture and moxibustion therapy to treat patients, such as Bian Que of the Spring and Autumn Period (770 BC — 476 BC) and Hua Tuo of the Eastern Han Dynasty (25—220), who had treated some difficult and complicated cases, and thus were acclaimed as miracle-working doctors. In 1027 AD, Wang Weiyi, a medical official of acupuncture and moxibustion of the Song Dynasty (960—1279), designed and made two bronze human figures marked with acupuncture points, carefully carved 12 channels and vessels and 354 acupuncture points on the figures for people to use when learning the therapy. This was the earliest bronze human figure for medical use in China.

Nowadays, acupuncture and moxibustion therapy is not only widely used in China to relieve people of their diseases, it has also spread around the world.

Narcotherapy is to disable the body or one part temporarily by drugs or acupuncture, which is usually used in surgical operations.

As early as the Spring and Autumn and the Warring States periods (770 BC—221 BC), some Chinese doctors had known and recorded the anesthesia function of some drugs. The famous doctor Hua Tuo of the Eastern Han Dynasty, on the basis of carefully studying ancient books, went to the mountains and plains to collect herbs with an anesthesia function, such as jimsonweed, which were later made into narcotic drugs after being roasted and processed. One day, people carried a seriously ill patient to Hua Tuo. He let the patient drink the drug and then opened his abdominal cavity and cleared away his rotten intestines, completing the operation while the patient felt no pain. This operation was the earliest recorded large-scale laparotomy both in China and in the world.

1
2

1. 华佗
   Hua Tuo
2. 扁鹊
   Bian Que

汉语·普通话·方言

The Chinese Language & Mandarin & Dialects

汉语是中国汉民族使用的语言。汉语历史悠久，在3 000多年前就有了相当成熟的文字。

汉语是使用人数最多的语言之一，除了中国，新加坡、马来西亚等国也有相当一部分人使用汉语，分布在世界各地的几千万华侨、华裔，也以汉语的各种方言作为自己的母语。

汉语是中国人使用的主要语言，也是联合国的工作语言之一。

汉语的标准语是"普通

话"（在台湾省被称作"国语"），在新加坡、马来西亚等国被称作"华语"。普通话是现代汉民族共同语。它以北京语音为标准音，以北方话为基础方言，以典范的现代白话文①作为语法规范。普通话为中国不同地区、不同民族人们之间的交际提供了方便。

中国地域广阔，人口众多，即使都使用汉语言，各地区说的话也不一样，这就是方言。方言俗称地方话，是汉语在不同地域的分支，只通行于一定的地域。汉语目前有七大类方言：北方方言②、吴方言③、湘方言④、赣方言⑤、客家方言⑥、闽方言⑦、粤方言⑧。其中，北方方言是通行地域最广，使用人口最多的方言。客家话、闽语、粤语还在海外的华侨华人中使用。

汉语方言十分复杂。各方言之间的差异表现在语音、词汇、语法三个方面，其中语音方面的差异最明显。在中国东南沿海地区就有"十里不同音"的说法。如果各地人之间都用方言土语说话，就会造成交际上的困难。

中国人很早就认识到，社会交际应该使用一种共同语。与"十里不同音"的方言相比，各地人都能听得懂普通话。因为讲普通话有利于各民族、各地区人民之间的文化交流和信息传递，所以中国政府十分重视推广普通话的工作，鼓励大家都学普通话。

The Chinese Language and Mandarin and Dialects

The standard language of Chinese is Putonghua (Mandarin) (which is called *guoyu* (national language) in Taiwan Province). It is called *huayu* (Chinese language) in Singapore and Malaysia. Mandarin has the Beijing pronunciation as its standard pronunciation, the northern dialect as its basic dialect, and the typical modern vernacular Chinese as its grammatical standard. Mandarin offers convenience for communication between people in different areas or of different ethnic groups in China.

Used by the Han people in China, the Chinese language has a long history, having established a fairly mature written language more than 3 000 years ago.

The Chinese language has more than 1.2 billion users and can be regarded as the one spoken by the greatest number of persons. In addition to China, some people in Singapore and Malaysia also use Chinese, and millions of overseas Chinese and foreign citizens of Chinese origin distributed around the world use various Chinese dialects as native language.

The Chinese language is the main language used by Chinese, also one of the working languages of the United Nations.

China has a vast territory and a large population. Even though people all use the Chinese language, they speak in different ways in different areas, which are called dialects. Generally called local languages, dialects are branches of the Chinese language and are only used in certain areas. At present, the Chinese language has seven dialects: the northern dialect, the Wu dialect, the Xiang dialect, the Gan dialect, the Hakka, the Min dialect and the Yue or Guangdong dialect. Among them, the northern dialect is used most widely. The Hakka, the Fujian dialect and the Guangdong dialect are also used by overseas Chinese.

The dialects of the Chinese language are very complicated. Various dialects differ from each other in three aspects: pronunciation, vocabulary and grammar. And the difference in pronunciation is the most outstanding. There is a saying in the coastal areas of southeastern China: Pronunciations differ within 10-li (Chinese unit of measurement, 1 li=0.5 km) area. If all people in different areas speak in local dialects, it will lead to the trouble in communications.

The Chinese people had realized very early that a common language should be used in social intercourse. Compared with dialects differing within 10-li area, mandarin can be understood by all people. Since it is beneficial for cultural exchange and information transmission between ethnic groups and people in different places, the Chinese Government attaches great importance to popularizing mandarin and encourages people to learn it.

▶ 注解 Notes

① 白话文指现代汉民族共同语的书面语言。
Vernacular Chinese is the written language commonly used by modern Han people.
② 北方方言以北京话为代表，通行于中国的东北、华北、西北、西南、江淮地区。
The northern dialect, represented by the Beijing dialect, is commonly used in northeastern China, northern China, northwestern China, southwestern China and areas along the Yangtze and Huaihe rivers.
③ 吴方言以上海话为代表，通行于中国的江苏省、浙江省的部分地区。
The Wu dialect, represented by the Shanghai dialect, is commonly used in some areas in Jiangsu and Zhejiang provinces of China.
④ 湘方言以长沙话为代表，通行于中国的湖南省的大部分地区。
The Xiang or Hunan dialect, represented by the Changsha dialect, is commonly used in most areas of Hunan Province.
⑤ 赣方言以南昌话为代表，通行于中国的江西省和湖北省东南一带。
The Gan dialect, represented by the Nanchang dialect, is generally used in Jiangxi Province and southeastern Hubei Province.
⑥ 客家方言以广东的梅县话为代表，主要通行于中国的广东省东北部、福建省西部和北部、江西省南部。
The Hakka, represented by the Meixian dialect of Guangdong Province, is mainly used in northeastern Guangdong Province, western and northern Fujian Province, and southern Jiangxi Province.
⑦ 闽方言通行于中国的福建省、广东省潮汕地区、海南省、台湾省。
The Min dialect is generally used in Fujian Province, Chaoshan area of Guangdong Province, Hainan Province and Taiwan Province.
⑧ 粤方言俗称广东话。以广州话为代表，通行于中国的广东省中部和西南部、广西壮族自治区东部和南部、香港及澳门。
The Yue or Guangdong dialect, represented by the Guangzhou dialect, is generally used in central and southwestern Guangdong Province, eastern and southern Guangxi Province, Hong Kong and Macao.

《中国文化常识》

主　　编　任启亮
副主编　时　序
编写人员　任启亮　时　序　李　晨　李嘉郁　赵菁华　彭　俊
责任编辑　马耀俊
英文编辑　林美琪
美术编辑　阮永贤　刘玉瑜

《中国文化常识》（中英对照）

改编人员　张　轶　任会斌　毛丹丹　贾　宇
中文审稿　袁晓波　朱子仪
英文翻译　王国蕾
英文审稿　莘正坤　郭著章　Devon Williams

策　　划　刘　援　祝大鸣
项目负责　祝大鸣　梁　宇
项目编辑　梁　宇
责任编辑　艾　斌
版式设计　高等教育出版社美编室
美术编辑　张申申　赵　阳
封面设计　王凌波
插图选配　艾　斌
责任印制　朱学忠
图片来源　高等教育出版社　全景图片公司　ChinaFotoPress

图书在版编目（CIP）数据

中国文化常识 / 国务院侨务办公室，国家汉语国际推
广领导小组办公室 . —北京：高等教育出版社，
2007. 2
    ISBN 978-7-04-020714-9

    Ⅰ. 中 ...   Ⅱ. ①国 ... ②国 ...   Ⅲ. ①汉语－对外汉
语教学－语言读物②文化－基本知识－中国－汉、英
    Ⅳ. ① H195.5 ② G12

中国版本图书馆 CIP 数据核字(2006)第 128483 号

出版发行	高等教育出版社	
社　　址	北京市西城区德外大街 4 号	
邮政编码	100011	
总　　机	010 - 58581000	
经　　销	蓝色畅想图书发行有限公司	
印　　刷	北京佳信达艺术印刷有限公司	

购书热线　010 - 58581118
免费咨询　800 - 810 - 0598
网　　址　http://www.hep.edu.cn
　　　　　http://www.hep.com.cn
网上订购　http://www.landraco.com
　　　　　http://www.landraco.com.cn
畅想教育　http://www.widedu.com

开　本　787 × 1092　1/16
印　张　18.5
字　数　420 000

版　次　2007 年 2 月第 1 版
印　次　2007 年 8 月第 3 次印刷

本书如有印装等质量问题，请到所购图书销售部门调换。

ISBN 978-7-04-020714-9
06800